WOMEN
of the BIBLE

A One-Year Devotional Study
of Women in Scripture

Updated *&* Expanded

Ann Spangler
Jean E. Syswerda

ZONDERVAN®

ZONDERVAN.com/
AUTHORTRACKER
follow your favorite authors

Women of the Bible
Copyright © 2006 by Ann Spangler and Jean Syswerda

Requests for information should be addressed to:

Zondervan, *Grand Rapids, Michigan* 49530

ISBN-10: 0-310-60748-5
ISBN-13: 978-0-310-60748-9

Interior design by Pamela J. L. Eicher

Printed in the United States of America

08 09 10 11 12 13 • 25 24 23 22 21 20 19 18 17 16 15 14 13 12 11 10 9 8 7 6 5 4 3 2

WOMEN
of the BIBLE

To Judy Weaver
Your faith has strengthened mine.

—ANN SPANGLER

To my daughters,
Holly and Shelly
You have shown me the beauty of young women of God.

—JEAN E. SYSWERDA

Contents

Theme Index

Alphabetical Index
of Women

Index of
Background Topics

Introduction

$\mathscr{S}$hortly after we first published *Women of the Bible*, a publishing colleague confided how astonished he was by the book's immediate success. After encountering it in a local bookstore, he had confidently predicted it would never sell. He smiled as he told us this, glad for our sakes that his prediction had proved wrong. I think our colleague made an understandable mistake. He had underestimated the hunger women have for authentic stories about other women who reflect their own struggles to live with faith and hope.

The Bible is so much more than a dry compilation of genealogies, prophecies, and laws. It is the story of the most important relationship in the world, the one between God and his people. The setting of this story moves quickly from Paradise to a fallen world and then culminates, after much foolishness and suffering, in heaven itself. It reveals what was, what is, and what will be. As the story unfolds, it exposes the nature of our deepest problems and the roots of our worst sufferings. Through its various characters, we recognize the tug-of-war that takes place in our own souls as we struggle to respond to God.

Sometimes the most profitable and enjoyable way to understand any historical era is to learn the stories of its most famous men and women, people whose lives both reflect and influence the times in which they lived. The popular television series *Biography* does just this. The series promotes itself with an intriguing tagline, assuring us that "Every Life Has a Story." The same could certainly be said of the women of the Bible, whose lives reveal so much about God's character and his strategy for saving us.

Though we are familiar with Adam, Abraham, Noah, Moses, Samson, Saul, David, and Peter—a few of the Bible's most noteworthy men—many of us might fail to recognize Hagar, Miriam, Deborah, Naomi, and Esther, to say nothing of Jael, Rizpah, or Joanna. We know how the men fit into the story of salvation, but what of the women? What do their stories tell us about God's love and our own response to him?

STRUCTURE OF THE BOOK

Women of the Bible looks at the lives of fifty-two prominent — and not so prominent — women of Scripture, offering a fresh perspective on the story of salvation. The cast of characters is long and colorful, including a parade of prostitutes, evil queens, prophetesses, wealthy women, abused women, single and married women, and widows young and old. Far from being one-dimensional characters, these are real women who struggle with tragedy and sometimes create it, who risk their lives and their reputations for the sake of others, whose compassion and wisdom often save the day. Even though our culture is vastly different from theirs, we share many of their emotional responses and concerns. We agonize over infertility, worry about our children, long for a little affection, strive for wisdom, and sometimes harbor doubt about God's real intentions toward us. Their stories reveal so much about God's grace, his relentless love, and his creative ability to bring good out of the most desperate of circumstances.

This expanded and updated edition of *Women of the Bible* offers our readers several improvements and changes. Recognizing that many women have been using the Wednesday studies in a group setting, all fifty-two studies have been reviewed and streamlined, making them useful and relevant for groups as well as individuals. We have also added several appendices to the end of the book. These indexes and charts offer information and background on more of the women whose lives form such a vital part of Scripture.

In order to understand the significance of these women's stories, we have developed a devotional program that will help readers reflect on the life of one woman each week for an entire year. Each devotion combines five main elements: inspiration, background information, Bible study, Bible promises, and prayer. Here's how a week unfolds:

Monday: Her Story — an inspirational portrait of one woman's life.

Tuesday: Her Life and Times—background information about the culture of her day.

Wednesday: Her Legacy in Scripture—a short Bible study on her life with application to your own.

Thursday: Her Promise—Bible promises that apply to her life and yours.

Friday: Her Legacy of Prayer—praying in light of her story.

By focusing on each woman for five consecutive days, we hope to offer a unique devotional program, one that encourages reading, reflection, study, and prayer focused on the main female characters in the Bible. We've purposely left the readings for Thursday and Friday shorter than the others in order to give you ample time for reflection and prayer.

HOW TO USE THIS BOOK

We would suggest that you begin with Monday's portrait in order to understand the main elements of the woman's story. After that, you may want to read the specific Scriptures that pertain to her life, those mentioned as "Key Scriptures" in the introduction that immediately precedes her story. Though Monday's inspirational retelling at times relies on fictional techniques to bring out various dimensions of a story and the character's emotional responses, every effort has been made to remain close to the original text, drawing out reasonable implications from Scripture's account. Tuesday's reflection gives you an inside look at a particular aspect of the life and culture of the woman being studied. Wednesday's study is designed to balance Monday's inspirational account by sending you straight to the Bible so you can understand and apply the Scripture to your life. Thursday's promises take you a step further, offering Bible verses that can be meditated on, memorized, or copied onto cards that can be placed as reminders at work or at home. Friday's prayers are designed to build on everything you have already studied and reflected on during the week. By including a balance of praise, thanksgiving, confession, and petition as a basis for prayer, this section is designed to deepen your communion with God. Some of you may prefer to skip the study sections while others may want to linger there. There is no right or wrong way to use this book. We hope that you will give yourselves permission to read it in whatever way works best for you.

Ann has written the Monday and Friday pieces, and Jean has written those for Tuesday through Thursday. Together we hope they will prove a tool that can be used either in personal prayer and Bible study or within the context of a small group. However you approach *Women of the Bible*, each day's reading is designed to help you slow down and soak in the Scripture so that you can savor its riches, understanding anew how God acts in surprising and wonderful ways to draw you to himself.

We owe a special debt of gratitude to our editors, Sandy Vander Zicht, for her insight, encouragement, and advocacy; Rachel Boers, for her skilled and painstaking work on the original manuscript; and Verlyn Verbrugge, for his careful work on this updated edition. We are also grateful to our agent, Robert Wolgemuth, and to Sue Brower, Sherry Guzzy, and their creative marketing team for catching the vision for this book. We thank Leanne Van Dyk for her insightful theological review and comments. Few books can succeed without champions, and we are grateful that these are some of ours.

Of course, we alone are responsible for any deficiencies in the book. Whatever they might be, we hope they do not prevent you from gaining, as we have, a deeper appreciation for all the women of faith who have gone before us, living their lives in the light of God's presence.

ANN SPANGLER
JEAN SYSWERDA
2007

Eve

HER CHARACTER: She came into the world perfectly at peace with her God and with her husband, the only other person on the planet. She lived in Paradise, possessing every pleasure imaginable. She never knew the meaning of embarrassment, misunderstanding, hurt, estrangement, envy, bitterness, grief, or guilt until she listened to her enemy and began to doubt God.

HER SORROW: That she and her husband were banished from Paradise and the presence of God, and that her first son was a murderer and her second son his victim.

HER JOY: That she had once tasted Paradise, and that God had promised that her offspring would eventually destroy her enemy.

KEY SCRIPTURES: Genesis 1:26–31; 2–4

Monday

HER STORY

*T*he woman stirred and stretched, her skin soft and supple as a newborn's. One finger, then another moved in gentle exploration of the ground that cradled her. She could feel a warmth filling her, tickling her throat as it tried to escape, spilling out in the strong, glad noise of laughter. She felt surrounded, as though by a thousand joys, and then a touch calmed her without diminishing her joy.

Her eyes opened to a Brightness, her ears to a Voice. And then a smaller voice, echoing an elated response: "This is now bone of my bones and flesh of my flesh; she shall be called 'woman,' for she was taken out of man." Adam took hold of her, and their laughter met like streams converging.

The man and the woman walked naked and unashamed in Paradise. No shadows filled Eden—no disorder, discord, or fear.

Then one day a serpent spoke to the woman. "Did God really say, 'You must not eat from any tree in the garden'? ...You will not surely die. For God knows that when you eat of it your eyes will be opened, and you will be like God, knowing good and evil."

The woman listened. She remembered the Brightness, the Voice of God that had filled her with joy. Could she really be like God? Pressed hard by desire, she took the fruit and then shared it with her husband. Suddenly darkness spread across Eden. It came, not from the outside but from within, filling the man and the woman with shadows, cravings, and misery. Order gave way to disorder, harmony to discord, trust to fear.

Soon Adam and Eve heard the sound of their Creator walking in the garden, and they hid. "Where are you, Adam?" God called.

"I heard you in the garden," Adam replied, "and I was afraid because I was naked; so I hid."

Sin had driven its wedge inside their hearts, and God banished them from Eden, pronouncing judgment first on the wily serpent that had tempted the woman and then on her and on her husband. To the serpent's curse he added this promise: "I will put enmity between you and the woman, and between your offspring and hers; he will crush your head, and you will strike his heel." To the woman, God said: "I will greatly increase your pains in childbearing; with pain you will give birth to children. Your desire will be for your husband, and he will rule over you."

Then God warned Adam that after a lifetime of hard labor, his strength would decrease until his body would finally be wrapped in the dust from which God had formed him. The curse of death fell suddenly upon the new world.

So Adam and his wife were forced to flee Paradise, and Adam named her Eve, because she would be the mother of all the living. But her firstborn, Cain, became a murderer, and her second son, Abel, his victim.

As the years passed, sorrow chased sorrow in the heart of the first woman, and the last we see of her we imagine her not as a creature springing fresh from the hand of God, but as a woman in anguish, giving birth to another child. Her skin now stretches like worn canvas across her limbs, her hands claw the stony ground, grasping for something to hold on to, for anything to ease her pain. She can feel the child inside, filling her, his body pressing for a way of escape. The cries of mother and child meet like streams converging. And Seth is born.

Finally, with her child cradled against her breast, relief begins to spread across Eve's face. With rest her hope returns; a smile forms, and then, finally, laughter rushes from her lips. Try as she might, she cannot stifle her joy. For she remembers the Brightness and the Voice and the promise God gave: Sooner or later, despite many griefs, her seed would crush the serpent. In the end, the woman would win.

Tuesday

HER LIFE AND TIMES

CHILDBIRTH

*E*ve was the first woman to conceive a child, the first to harbor a fertilized egg in her womb. Did she understand the miracle taking place within her as her belly swelled and her child began to move? Did she know the wonder of love for a child yet unborn? The Bible doesn't give us those answers. But it does tell us that Eve recognized that life was in God's control. At Cain's birth she exclaimed, "*With the help of the LORD* I have brought forth a man" (Genesis 4:1).

God's judgment on Eve — "with pain you will give birth to children" — was no doubt exactly what Eve experienced in birthing this first child. It's the process we appropriately term *labor*. Eve likely bore the pain and went through the entire birth with only Adam's help.

Later, Hebrew women had the help of experienced midwives, who knew remedies for common delivery difficulties. Midwives' responsibilities after the birth included cutting the umbilical cord, washing the newborn, rubbing it with salt for cleansing, and then wrapping it in swaddling cloths.

The birth stool referred to in Exodus 1:16 was probably a low stool on which the mother-to-be squatted, allowing the force of gravity to aid in the birth process. The midwife and possibly other close relatives held the mother's hands to give comfort as well as stability as she bore down.

Women throughout the centuries have borne the results of Eve's sin. Their pain in childbearing unites them in a common bond of an experience shared. The experience is an unusual combination of the earthly and at the same time the unearthly. The pains, the panting, the mess and disorder connected with the birth of a child are of the earth, of Eve herself. But what is brought forth, and the bond experienced between the mother and the child, is unearthly, something only the Creator of life could forge.

Wednesday

HER LEGACY IN SCRIPTURE

Read Genesis 2:18–25.

1. What needs does Adam have that only a woman can fulfill?

2. What does being "one flesh" in a marriage mean, both physically and spiritually?

Read Genesis 3:1–24.

3. As the serpent tries to tempt Eve, what desires and fears in her does he appeal to?

4. What desires and fears make you vulnerable to temptation?

5. When caught after her sin, how does Eve experience each of the following?

   Shame

   Blame

   Pain

Thursday

HER PROMISE

*E*mbedded in the very curse put on Eve for her sin is a wonderful promise. God promises her, and succeeding generations: You "will give birth to children" (Genesis 3:16). God's grace and mercy are marvelously evident, even when he's pronouncing his judgment. He promises that the human race will continue even as he announces that death will now be inevitable.

Throughout Scripture, God's grace is often most beautifully evident within his judgments. When the world was so full of sin that he had to destroy it, God's grace saved Noah and his family. When the Israelites rebelled so thoroughly that captivity was inevitable, God's grace promised restoration. While judgment fell on David for his sin with Bathsheba, God's grace gave them Solomon as a son and successor.

When you are at your lowest, on your knees before God's judgment, never forget that his grace is still at work. And that is truly amazing.

Promises in Scripture

From the fullness of his grace we have all received one blessing after another.

—JOHN 1:16

But where sin increased, grace increased all the more, so that, just as sin reigned in death, so also grace might reign through righteousness to bring eternal life through Jesus Christ our Lord.

—ROMANS 5:20–21

Friday

HER LEGACY OF PRAYER

So God created human beings in his own image, in the image of God he created them; male and female he created them.

—GENESIS 1:27

REFLECT ON: Genesis 2:15–25: 3.

PRAISE GOD: Because he created you in his own image, making you a woman capable of reflecting his love, truth, strength, goodness, wisdom, and beauty.

OFFER THANKS: That imbedded in God's judgment of Adam and Eve is the promise of a Redeemer who will crush the head of our enemy, the devil.

CONFESS: Your own tendency to mar God's image in you by preferring your will to his.

ASK GOD: To help you surrender your life, so that he can fulfill his purpose for creating you.

Lift Your Heart

Find a peaceful setting, surrounded by the beauty of creation, to meditate on what life must have been like in the garden of Eden. Think about what your life would be like if you experienced peace in all your relationships, if you never suffered physical or emotional pain, if you were never confused or ashamed or guilty, if you always experienced God's love and friendship. Let your imagination run riot as it fills in the details of God's original intention for your life and for those you love.

Then consider this: You were made for paradise. The joys you taste now are infinitesimal compared to those that await you in heaven, for "no eye has seen, no ear has heard, no mind has conceived what God has prepared for those who love him" (1 Corinthians 2:9).

Father, give me a greater understanding of your original plan for our world. Help me to envision its beauty so I might live with a constant awareness that you intend to restore paradise to all who belong to you. May I surrender every sin and every sorrow to you, trusting that you will fulfill your purpose for my life. In Jesus' name I pray. Amen.

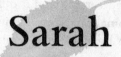

Sarah

HER NAME MEANS
"Chieftainness" or "Princess"

HER CHARACTER: Beautiful enough to attract rulers in the ancient world, she could be strong-willed and jealous. Yet Sarah was considered a loyal wife who did what was right and who didn't give in to fear.

HER SORROW: That she remained childless for most of her life.

HER JOY: That at the age of ninety, she gave birth to Isaac, child of the promise.

KEY SCRIPTURES: Genesis 12:1–20; 16:1–8; 17:1–22; 18:1–15; 21:1–13; Galatians 4:22–31

Monday

HER STORY

*S*arah was sixty-five, the age many of us retire, when she began a journey that would lead her into uncharted spiritual territory. Leaving behind their homeland, she and her husband, Abraham, moved hundreds of miles south to Canaan, a land fertile with the promises of God but barren of everything cherished and familiar. God had promised the land to Abraham and his offspring. From him would come not just a family, clan, or tribe, but an entire nation, a people who would belong to God as no other people had.

The promise spread like ripples from a stone pitched in water. If Abraham was to father a new nation, surely Sarah would be its mother. Yet she longed to give birth, not to a nation, but to one small child she could kiss and cradle.

At first Abraham and Sarah found it difficult to support themselves in their new homeland. Soon a famine made life so severe that they moved on to Egypt, where Abraham, fearful of Pharaoh, suggested a deceptive maneuver to save his skin: "I know what a beautiful woman you are. When the Egyptians see you, they will say, 'This is his wife.' Then they will kill me but will let you live. Say you are my sister [she was his half sister], so that I will be treated well for your sake and my life will be spared because of you."

So Sarah did as her husband asked, and Pharaoh soon added her to his harem of beautiful women. For the privilege, he paid Abraham in the currency of the day—a bevy of sheep, cattle, donkeys, camels, and servants. But though the two men seemed satisfied with their bargain, God was not. He proceeded to strike Pharaoh and his entire household with diseases. The Egyptian ruler soon summoned Abraham, demanding an explanation. As soon as he heard the truth, he allowed both Sarah and Abraham to leave, taking with them all the riches they had gained in Egypt.

So the couple moved home again. By now, several years had passed since Abraham and Sarah had heard the remarkable promise of God, but still there was no child. So Sarah took matters into her own hands. Following a practice common in the ancient world, she gave Abraham permission to sleep with her Egyptian maid, Hagar. Sarah's slave would become a surrogate mother for the promised child.

Before long, Ishmael was born. But the child brought only discord between the two women.

One day several years later, the Lord appeared to Abraham while he was sitting at the entrance to his tent.

"Where is your wife, Sarah?"

"There, in the tent," Abraham replied.

Then the Lord said, "I will surely return to you about this time next year, and Sarah your wife will have a son."

Now Sarah, who had been eavesdropping from inside the tent, laughed and said, "After I am worn out and my master is old, will I now have this pleasure?"

But the Lord said to Abraham, "Why did Sarah laugh and say, 'Will I really have a child, now that I am old?' Is anything too hard for the LORD? I will return to you at the appointed time next year and Sarah will have a son."

Because Sarah was afraid, she lied and said, "I did not laugh."

But he pressed her, saying, "Yes, you did laugh."

A year later, Sarah gave birth to Isaac, whose name means "Laughter." Of course the joke was not lost on the ninety-year-old mother, who exclaimed: "God has brought me laughter, and everyone who hears about this will laugh with me."

But Sarah's humor was short-lived. Fireworks flared once again between the two mothers until Sarah forced Hagar and Ishmael from Abraham's household, leaving them to wander in the harsh desert. And though God provided for the two outcasts, it was through Isaac that he would keep his promise of a new nation and a deliverer for his people.

Sarah died at the age of 127 and was buried in Hebron. Between Isaac's birth and her own death lay thirty-seven years, ample time to reflect on her life's adventure with God. Was she ashamed of her treatment of the ill-fated Hagar? Did she remember laughing when God told Abraham she would bear a child at the age of ninety? Did she appreciate the echoing irony in young Isaac's laughter? Did she have any idea she would one day be revered as the Mother of Israel—indeed, a symbol of the promise just as Hagar was to become a symbol of slavery under the law? Scripture does not say. But it is heartening to realize that God accomplishes his purposes despite our frailties, our little faith, our entrenched self-reliance.

True, Sarah's pragmatic attempts to help God keep his promise caused plenty of anguish. (Even in our own day, the struggle between Israel and her Arab neighbors stems from the ancient strife between two women and the children they bore.) Still, despite her jealousy, anxiety, and skepticism about God's ability to keep his promises, there's no denying that Sarah was a risk-taker of the first order, a woman who said good-bye to everything familiar to travel to a land she knew nothing about. A real flesh-and-blood kind of woman who lived an adventure more strenuous than any fairy-tale heroine, an adventure that began with a promise and ended with laughter.

Tuesday

HER LIFE AND TIMES

NAMES

*I*n Bible times names had a significance they often do not have today. The names that the mothers and fathers of these times gave to their children give us a glimpse into their personal experience, sometimes reflecting their emotional responses to a situation. When Sarah was ninety years old, God told her that she and Abraham would finally have the child for whom she had longed. She could hardly believe it! "After I am worn out and my master is old, will I now have this pleasure?" she exclaimed (Genesis 18:12). When her son was born, Sarah named him Isaac, which means "He Laughs," and she said, "God has brought me laughter, and everyone who hears about this will laugh with me" (Genesis 21:6).

Perhaps one of the Bible's most poignant scenes is played out when Rachel, in great pain and knowing she was dying, named her son Ben-Oni, meaning "Son of My Trouble." But Jacob, the child's father, loving this little one even in his sorrow, renamed him Benjamin, "Son of My Right Hand" (Genesis 35:16–20). When Hannah's son was born, she named him Samuel, which sounds like the Hebrew for "heard of God," because God had heard her cries for a child (1 Samuel 1:20). Many of the Old Testament prophets had names that spoke of their mission: Isaiah's name means "The LORD Saves," Obadiah's name means "Servant of the LORD," Nahum's name means "Comfort," and Malachi's name means "My Messenger."

Throughout Scripture, God gives to his people names that offer a picture of their significance and worth to him. We are his "treasured possessions" (Exodus 19:5; Malachi 3:17), the "people of his inheritance" (Deuteronomy 4:20), and "sons of the living God" (Hosea 1:10). We are his "friends" (John 15:15). No matter what your given name, God knows it. In love, he calls you to him by your name, and you belong to him (Isaiah 43:1).

Wednesday

HER LEGACY IN SCRIPTURE

Read Genesis 12:10–20.

1. Imagine yourself as Sarah in Egypt. What are you feeling at each point in this situation toward Abraham? Toward God? About yourself as a woman?

Read Genesis 16:1–6.

2. What impression do you get of Sarah in this episode? What does she want? What does she fear? How does she relate to people?

Read Genesis 18:10–15; 21:1–7.

3. What do these scenes tell you about Sarah?

4. God worked through Sarah's life in spite of her failings. How can God use you in spite of your imperfections?

5. Is your current situation more like Sarah's before or after God fulfilled his promises to her? Explain.

Thursday

HER PROMISE

*H*ow hard it was for Sarah (and is for us as well) to remember God's promises and to wait for him to fulfill them. God's promises are revealed and fulfilled in his own timing, which is often on a calendar far different from our own.

Waiting patiently for God to work may be one of the most difficult experiences of our Christian walk. We live in an age of the immediate. We think waiting, and doing so quietly, is somehow less worthy, perhaps even a bit lazy. We're great "do-it-yourselfers," but we often get in God's way when we take things into our own hands.

Do you have something you're waiting for God to do? Have you asked him for the salvation of your husband? Of a family member? Are you praying for a rebellious child to come home? Whatever the circumstances, God's timing is the best timing. When you're tempted to step in and make things happen on your own, think of Sarah. Her attempts to fulfill God's promise of a son through her servant Hagar had disastrous results. Remember that God has his own timetable, and rest in the assurance that he loves you and will fulfill his promises to you.

Promises in Scripture

Wait for the LORD;
  be strong and take heart
  and wait for the LORD.

—PSALM 27:14

I wait for the LORD, *my soul waits,*
  and in his word I put my hope.

—PSALM 130:5

Yet the LORD *longs to be gracious to you;*
  he rises to show you compassion.
For the LORD *is a God of justice.*
  Blessed are all who wait for him!

—ISAIAH 30:18

But as for me, I watch in hope for the LORD,
  I wait for God my Savior;
  my God will hear me.

—MICAH 7:7

Friday

HER LEGACY OF PRAYER

God also said to Abraham, "As for Sarai your wife, you are no longer to call her Sarai; her name will be Sarah. I will bless her and will surely give you a son by her. I will bless her so that she will be the mother of nations; kings of peoples will come from her."

—GENESIS 17:15–16

REFLECT ON: Genesis 17:1–22.

PRAISE GOD: Because he keeps his promises.

OFFER THANKS: That God has a gracious plan for you that will unfold in his time, according to his way.

CONFESS: Your anxiety and self-reliance.

ASK GOD: To help you wait with a listening ear and a ready heart to do his will.

Lift Your Heart

God hints at his purpose for you by planting dreams within your heart. Sarah's dream was to give birth to a son. Find a quiet place and spend some time focusing on your dreams. Ask yourself what dreams you've been too busy, too afraid, or too disappointed to pursue. Write them down and pray about each one. God may be telling you to wait, or he may be giving you the go-ahead to pursue one in particular. If it's time to take the plunge, you might just find yourself joyfully echoing Sarah's words in Genesis 21:6: "God has brought me laughter."

Father, thank you for loving me despite the fact that my soul still contains shadows that sometimes block the light of your Spirit. As I grow older, may I trust you more completely for the dreams you've implanted in my soul, the promises you've made to me. Like Sarah, may I be surrounded by laughter at the wonderful way you accomplish your purpose despite my weakness. In Jesus' name. Amen.

Hagar

HER CHARACTER: A foreigner and slave, Hagar let pride overtake her when she became Abraham's wife. A lonely woman with few resources, she suffered harsh punishment for her mistake. She obeyed God's voice as soon as she heard it and was given a promise that her son would become the father of a great nation.

HER SORROW: That she was taken from her homeland to become a slave in a foreign land, where she was mistreated for many years.

HER JOY: To know that God cared, that he saw her suffering and heard her cry, and that he helped her when she needed him most.

KEY SCRIPTURES: Genesis 16; 21:8−21; Galatians 4:22−31

Monday

HER STORY

An Egyptian slave and Sarah's bitter rival, Hagar still had one thing going for her that her mistress never enjoyed: a personal revelation of God, who lovingly intervened on her behalf, not once but twice. It happened when she was alone and afraid, without a shekel to her name—but that's getting ahead of the story.

You may remember that Abraham, whom we honor as the father of faith, showed little evidence of that faith when he and Sarah first entered Egypt to escape a famine in Canaan. Certain the Egyptians would kill him once they caught sight of his beautiful wife, he advised her to pose as his sister. Soon enough, Pharaoh added Sarah to his harem and rewarded Abraham with an abundance of camels, sheep, cattle, donkeys, and servants. But God punished Pharaoh for his unwitting error so effectively that, when he found out that Sarah was actually Abraham's wife, he ordered the two of them to leave Egypt with all their belongings. Possibly, Hagar was part of the booty Abraham and Sarah took with them—a gift they later regretted.

Still, of the three parties involved in the scheme to make Hagar a surrogate mother, she was perhaps the only innocent one, a slave with little power to resist. When Sarah told Abraham to sleep with her maid, she opened the door to spiritual catastrophe. As soon as Hagar discovered her pregnancy, she began lording it over her mistress, hardly a smart move for a young foreigner up against a woman entrenched in her husband's affections.

In fact, Sarah made life so difficult for Hagar that she fled into the desert, a desperate move for a pregnant woman who was so far from home. She hadn't gotten far before she heard a voice calling, "Hagar, servant of Sarai, where have you come from, and where are you going? Go back to your mistress and submit to her." But then, as if to sweeten the order, came a word of assurance: "You will have a son. You shall name him Ishmael, for the LORD has heard of your misery."

Remarkably, Hagar didn't argue but returned to Abraham and Sarah. Like a stream of water in the desert, God's word had penetrated the wilderness of her heart. Her bondage, her bitterness, her anxiety about the future—God had seen every bit of it. He knew about the child in her womb, naming him Ishmael, meaning "God Hears." In the years to come, whenever Hagar would hold her son close, watch him play, or worry about his future, she would remember that God was near, listening for the child's cry. Little wonder that she had responded to the voice in the desert by calling the Lord "the God who sees me."

Some sixteen years later, Hagar found herself once again in the wilderness, this time by force rather than by choice. In a crescendo of bitterness against her younger rival, Sarah had expelled Hagar and Ishmael from their home. Dying from thirst, Hagar placed her son under a bush and withdrew, unable to witness his agony.

Her weeping was soon broken by an angel's voice, "Do not be afraid; God has heard the boy crying as he lies there. Lift the boy up and take him by the hand, for I will make him into a great nation." With that, the angel of the Lord opened Hagar's eyes so that she discovered a well of water nearby that would save her son's life.

The last we see of Hagar, she is living in the Desert of Paran in the Sinai Peninsula, busy securing a wife, and, therefore, a future, for Ishmael. God had made a way in the wilderness for a single woman and her son, without friends, family, or resources to help her. He had seen, he had heard, and he had indeed been faithful.

Tuesday

HER LIFE AND TIMES

SLAVERY

*S*lavery was a common practice in ancient Near Eastern culture, so common that God's laws made provision for its safe and fair practice but not for its destruction. Slaves were obtained in any of a number of ways: Captives from war became slaves, particularly virgin women (Numbers 31:7–32); men and women and their children went into slavery to pay debts (Leviticus 25:39); slaves could be purchased (Leviticus 25:44); and sometimes slavery was even voluntary, as when a male slave who could have gone free remained in servitude in order to stay with a wife he loved (Exodus 21:2–6).

Hagar, an Egyptian, probably became a slave to Abraham and Sarah when they left Egypt (Genesis 12:20). Leaving her homeland behind, she made herself useful and proved herself trustworthy, thereby becoming Sarah's maidservant, a position of some importance in the household.

Sarah must have had some confidence and perhaps even affection for Hagar to want her to be the surrogate mother of her son. Such practices were fairly common in that day. Infertile women urged their husbands to take their maidservants in order to gain a child and heir for the family. Female slaves were often made the concubines or wives of the master or one of his sons. Their children became the property and sometimes the heirs of their masters. As female slaves, they had no choice in the matter. They were alone, with no rights and no one to defend them.

Many women today are in a position similar to Hagar's. They may not be actual slaves, but they are in positions of weakness, with no one to defend them. No one except God. The same God who defended Hagar and heard the cries of her son in the desert hears the cries of helpless women and their children today. When we are at our weakest, God is at his best, ready to step in and say to us as he said to Hagar, "Do not be afraid" (Genesis 21:17).

Wednesday

HER LEGACY IN SCRIPTURE

Read Genesis 16:1–16.

1. Sarah's proposition was a customary one of that day. When she asked Hagar to be a surrogate mother, what do you think Hagar's reactions might have been?

2. How do you respond to situations over which you have no control? How can God help you when you are in such a position?

3. Hagar ran away to a barren and sparsely populated area. Have you ever been that desperate? If so, what were the circumstances?

4. What impressions of God do you get from this story?

Read Genesis 21:8–21.

5. How is this incident like the previous one? How is it different?

6. Are you or is someone in your group in a desperate situation right now? Read Genesis 21:19 again. Might there be a "well" for sustenance, if only you could see it? Pray alone or together, asking God to open your eyes just as he opened Hagar's and aided her in her desperation.

Thursday

HER PROMISE

A thin young woman sits huddled in the front seat of her car. She covers her ears to block out the sound of her little son as he whimpers with cold in the backseat. Her husband abandoned her and the boy two months before. Left without resources, she was soon turned out of her apartment. The car is now their only home. It has long since seen its last drop of gasoline, and its worn interior provides little protection from the winter winds outside.

This modern-day Hagar is no further from God's promises than was Hagar herself as she poured out her sorrow in the desert. God sees her heartache, just as he saw Hagar's. Though you may not be as desperate as Hagar or her modern counterpart, you may have experienced times in your life that made you fear for the future. Whether you are living in a wilderness of poverty or loneliness or sorrow, God's promises, love, and protection are just as available to you now as they were to Hagar.

Promises in Scripture

I will lie down and sleep in peace,
for you alone, O Lord,
make me dwell in safety.

—Psalm 4:8

My comfort in my suffering is this:
Your promise preserves my life.

—Psalm 119:50

Though I walk in the midst of trouble,
you preserve my life;
you stretch out your hand against the anger of my foes,
with your right hand you save me.

—Psalm 138:7

Friday

HER LEGACY OF PRAYER

*What is the matter, Hagar? Do not be afraid; God has heard the boy
crying as he lies there. Lift the boy up and take him by the hand, for
I will make him into a great nation.*

—GENESIS 21:17–18

REFLECT ON: Genesis 21:8–21.

PRAISE GOD: Because he is an all-knowing Father who hears the
cries of his children. Nothing that happens to us can
ever escape his notice.

OFFER THANKS: That the Lord runs after the weak and the helpless, to
show them his mercy and his plan of blessing for their
lives.

CONFESS: Any pride, selfishness, or other sin that may have contributed to difficulties in your life.

ASK GOD: To open your eyes to the way he is protecting and
providing for you and your children. Ask him to help
you live each day, not as a slave to the law but as a
child of grace.

Lift Your Heart

*I*nvite a couple of close friends to share a Middle Eastern feast
with olives, figs, pita bread, nuts, hummus, tabbouleh, and your
favorite drink. Pray a special grace thanking God for providing so richly
for you even when you felt you were living through a desert season in
your life. Share stories with each other about how God has provided
even when you weren't sure he was listening to your prayers.

Hummus

In a food processor blend 2 cups of cooked or canned chickpeas,
drained, with ⅔ cup sesame paste (tahini), ¾ cup lemon juice, salt
and freshly ground pepper to taste, and 2 peeled garlic cloves. Stir in
¼ cup finely chopped scallions. Makes about 3 cups. A great dip for
bread, chips, or fresh vegetables.

Tabbouleh

1. Place ¾ cup uncooked cracked wheat in a glass bowl and cover with cold water for 30 minutes; then drain completely. (For a softer texture, cover with boiling water and let stand for one hour before draining.)

2. Add 1½ cups chopped fresh parsley; 3 medium tomatoes, chopped; 5 green onions, thinly sliced (with tops); and 2 tablespoons chopped fresh (or 2 teaspoons crushed dried) mint leaves.

3. In a separate bowl, mix ¼ cup olive oil, ¼ cup lemon juice, ¾ teaspoon salt, and ¼ teaspoon pepper. Pour over cracked wheat mixture and toss.

4. Cover and refrigerate at least one hour. Serve with a garnish of mint leaf. Makes 6 servings, about ¾ cup each.

———————

Lord, sometimes I feel abandoned, as though no one understands or cares about me. Please show me that you really are near and that you see and hear everything that happens. Refresh me with your presence even when I am walking through a desert experience. And help me, in turn, to comfort others when they feel hopeless and alone. In Jesus' name. Amen.

Lot's Wife

HER CHARACTER: She was a prosperous woman who may have been more attached to the good life than was good for her. Though there is no indication she participated in the sin of Sodom, her story implies she had learned to tolerate it and that her heart had become divided as a result.

HER TRAGEDY: That her heart's choice led to judgment rather than mercy, and that she ultimately refused God's attempts to save her.

KEY SCRIPTURES: Genesis 18:16–19:29; Luke 17:28–33

Monday

HER STORY

*L*ot's wife had only hours to live, though she never suspected it. She must have gone about her business as usual, tidying the house, cooking and kibitzing with the neighbors, unaware of the tragedy about to overtake her.

Years earlier she had married Abraham's nephew, and the two had amassed a fortune in land and livestock. Eventually, they settled in Sodom, uncomfortably comfortable in a city so wicked that heaven itself dispatched angels to investigate the allegations against it.

Lot, it so happened, was at the city gate at the very moment the angels arrived. Greeting the strangers, he quickly implored them to spend the night in his home, anxious about what might happen to them once night had fallen.

Lot's wife must have welcomed the strangers warmly, too, for hospitality was a sacred trust in the ancient world. Then, just before bedtime, she would have heard the voices. At first a few muffled words and then echoing laughter and finally an ugly clamor as a noose of men tightened around the house. Rough voices shouted for her husband to open the door and surrender his guests to their pleasure.

"No, my friends. Don't do this wicked thing!" Lot screamed back. But the crowd was furious for its own way. Then he attempted an appalling bargain. "Look, I have two daughters who have never slept with a man. Let me bring them out to you, and you can do what you like with them. But don't do anything to these men, for they have come under the protection of my roof." But the men of Sodom would not be thwarted and rushed the door to force their way in.

Suddenly, the angels reached out, pulled Lot back into the house, and struck the men at the door blind. Then they turned to Lot, urging him, "Do you have anyone else here—sons-in-law, sons or daughters, or anyone else in the city who belongs to you? Get them out of here, because we are going to destroy this place."

But Lot's sons-in-law thought he was joking and refused to leave.

At dawn the angels again urged Lot to hurry lest he and his wife and daughters perish with the rest of the city. Still, the family hesitated until the angels finally grabbed their hands and dragged them out, urging, "Flee for your lives! Don't look back, and don't stop anywhere in the plain! Flee to the mountains, or you will be swept away!"

By the time Lot and his family reached the small city of Zoar, the sun had risen over the land and everything in Sodom was engulfed in burning sulfur. Men, women, children, and livestock were all obliterated. A terrible judgment for terrible sin.

But the judgment was even worse than either Lot or his daughters first realized. Safe at last, they must have turned to each other in relief at their escape and then turned again in shock, realizing one of their number was missing. They would have searched, hoping against hope, until they finally caught sight of the white salt pillar, silhouetted against the sky, a lonely monument in the shape of a woman turning around toward Sodom.

If you have ever seen pictures of ancient Pompeii, destroyed by the eruption of Mount Vesuvius in AD 79, where human shapes are preserved to this day by the lava that stopped them dead in their tracks, you might imagine the disaster that overtook Lot's wife.

Why did she turn, despite the angel's clear warning? Was her heart still attached to everything she left behind in the city — a life of comfort, ease, and pleasure? Did she still have family trapped in the city? Or was she fascinated by the tragic spectacle taking place behind her, like a gawking motorist at the scene of a bloody accident? Perhaps all these things combined were a glue that caused her feet to slow, her head to turn, and her body to be overtaken by the punishment God had meant to spare her. By her own choice — her very last choice — she cast her lot with judgment rather than with mercy.

Jesus urged his followers to remember Lot's wife: "It will be just like this on the day the Son of Man is revealed. On that day no one who is on the roof of his house, with his goods inside, should go down to get them. Likewise, no one in the field should go back for anything. Remember Lot's wife! Whoever tries to keep his life will lose it, and whoever loses his life will preserve it" (Luke 17:30–33). Sobering words recalling a sobering story. Words meant to lead us away from the compelling illusions of wickedness and safe into the arms of mercy.

Tuesday

HER LIFE AND TIMES

SALT

*N*ot much of a legacy, is it? Lot's wife is remembered less for who she was — wife, mother, daughter, sister — than for what she became — a pillar of salt. Just one irresistible but forbidden glance back at what was happening behind her, and she turned into salt. Salt! One of the world's most common, and most used, chemicals.

Palestine, in fact, possessed rich salt depositories, which accounted for such place names as the Salt Sea (also known as the Dead Sea), the Valley of Salt, and the City of Salt. The Romans probably looked on Israel as a worthy conquest simply because of the salt available there.

The Hebrews used salt to season food: "Is tasteless food eaten without salt?" (Job 6:6). Hebrew women rubbed their newborn babies with salt or washed them in it: "On the day you were born your cord was not cut, nor were you washed with water to make you clean, nor were you rubbed with salt" (Ezekiel 16:4). Salt was a required supplement to any Old Testament grain sacrifice: "Season all your grain offerings with salt" (Leviticus 2:13).

The word *salt* is used several times in the New Testament, all of them symbolic. Jesus tells us to remember that as believers we are the salt of the earth (Matthew 5:13; cf. Mark 9:50; Luke 14:34). Our attitudes and actions can cleanse and season and purify our surroundings. When we respond graciously to someone who is ungracious, we season our world with salt. When we treat an irritable child with kindness, we season our homes with salt. When we comfort the hurting, console the lonely, encourage the discouraged, or calm the unsettled, we season our world with salt. As followers of Christ, we're saltshakers (we hope full ones!), busy sprinkling our world with the salt that flavors life.

Wednesday

HER LEGACY IN SCRIPTURE

Read Genesis 19:1–26.

1. In ancient culture, when Lot opened his house to guests, he guaranteed not only their comfort but their safety. The family's honor was at stake. What do you think were his wife's thoughts and feelings when he offered his daughters instead of his guests to the raiders?

2. Given what Sodom was like, why would Lot's wife hesitate leaving there?

3. Even though warned not to do so, she couldn't resist looking back. Why do you think she turned?

4. In Lot's wife, we can see ourselves looking back, regretting decisions made, mourning lost opportunities, yearning for ended relationships. Do you spend a lot of time looking back? If so, how does that affect the way you live in the present?

5. What does leaving the past behind mean for you right now?

Thursday

HER PROMISE

*E*arlier, God had promised Abraham he would spare the city of Sodom if he could find only ten righteous people in it, but not even ten could be found. So God sent his angels to Sodom to rescue Lot and his family (Genesis 18) from the coming destruction. Hesitant to the last minute, the angels had to take Lot, his wife, and his two daughters by the hand and lead them out of the city.

Did God know Abraham was thinking of Lot when he begged for the cities to be spared if fifty, forty-five, thirty, twenty, only ten righteous people could be found? Was God's mercy extended to Lot for love of Lot or for love of Abraham? We don't know. But we do know God's mercy was available for Lot and his family. And his mercy is available to you as well, even in the worst of times, the most difficult situations, the hardest of circumstances. He's there, stretching out his hand to lead you to safety.

Promises in Scripture

> *The men grasped his hand and the hands of his wife and of his two daughters and led them safely out of the city, for the LORD was merciful to them.*

> —GENESIS 19:16

> *He will show you mercy [and] have compassion on you.*

> —DEUTERONOMY 13:17

> *Remember, O LORD, your great mercy and love,*
> *for they are from of old.*

> —PSALM 25:6

> *"I will frown on you no longer,*
> *for I am merciful," declares the LORD,*
> *"I will not be angry forever."*

> —JEREMIAH 3:12

Friday

HER LEGACY OF PRAYER

When he [Lot] hesitated, the men grasped his hand and the hands of his wife and of his two daughters and led them safely out of the city, for the LORD was merciful to them. As soon as they had brought them out, one of them said, "Flee for your lives! Don't look back, and don't stop anywhere in the plain!"

—GENESIS 19:16–17

REFLECT ON: Genesis 19:1–26.

PRAISE GOD: That though he hates sin he also loves mercy.

OFFER THANKS: For ways that God has shown mercy to you and members of your family.

CONFESS: Any tendency to ignore God's voice because you prefer to go your own way.

ASK GOD: For the grace never to become rigid because of your attachments or your sin.

Lift Your Heart

*I*n a society like ours, it's rare to find someone who isn't attached to creature comforts. Test your own level of attachment by taking a week-long retreat from television, newspapers, magazines, catalogs, and shopping malls. Instead, carve out a time and place in your home, even if it's only a few minutes in a small corner or a closet, for silent prayer and praise. Ask God to reveal any disordered attachments or rigidity that may have developed in your own spirit. Tell him you want to be a woman who is free and flexible enough to respond quickly to his direction.

Lord, you call me to live in the world without embracing the ways of the world. Help me to live in a way that preserves my freedom to follow you wherever and however you lead. If I should leave behind a monument, may it be a reminder to others of faith and not foolishness.

Rebekah

HER CHARACTER: Hardworking and generous, her faith was so great that she left her home forever to marry a man she had never seen or met. Yet she played favorites with her sons and failed to trust God fully for the promise he had made.

HER SORROW: That she was barren for the first twenty years of her married life, and that she never again set eyes on her favorite son, Jacob, after he fled from his brother Esau.

HER JOY: That God had gone to extraordinary lengths to pursue her, to invite her to become part of his people and his promises.

KEY SCRIPTURES: Genesis 24; 25:19–34; 26:1–28:9

Monday

HER STORY

The sun was dipping beyond the western rim of the sky as the young woman approached the well outside the town of Nahor, five hundred miles northeast of Canaan. It was women's work to fetch fresh water each evening, and Rebekah hoisted the brimming jug to her shoulder, welcoming its cooling touch against her skin.

As she turned to go, a stranger greeted her, asking for a drink. Obligingly, she offered to draw water for his camels as well. Rebekah noticed the look of surprised pleasure that flashed across his face. Ten camels could put away a lot of water, she knew. But had she over-heard his whispered prayer just moments earlier, her astonishment would have exceeded his: "O Lord, God of my master Abraham, give me success today, and show kindness to my master Abraham. May it be that when I say to a girl, 'Please let down your jar that I may have a drink,' and she says, 'Drink, and I'll water your camels too'—let her be the one you have chosen for your servant Isaac."

A simple gesture. A generous response. A young woman's future altered in a moment's time. The man Rebekah encountered at the well, Abraham's servant, had embarked on a sacred mission—to find Isaac a wife from among Abraham's own people rather than from among the surrounding Canaanites. Like her great-aunt Sarah before her, Rebekah would make the journey south to embrace a future she could hardly glimpse. Betrothed to a man twice her age, whose name meant "Laughter," she felt a sudden giddiness rise inside her. The God of Abraham and Sarah was wooing her, calling her name and no other, offering a share in the promise. God was forging a new nation to be his own people.

Isaac was forty when he first set eyes on Rebekah. Perhaps his heart echoed the joy of that first man, "Here at last is bone of my bones and flesh of my flesh!" So Isaac and Rebekah entered the tent of his mother Sarah and made love. And the Bible says that Rebekah comforted Isaac after the death of his mother.

Rebekah was beautiful and strong like Sarah, yet she bore no children for the first twenty years of her life with Isaac. Would she suffer as Sarah did the curse of barrenness? Isaac prayed and God heard, giving her not one, but two sons, who wrestled inside her womb. And God told her: "Two nations are in your womb, and two peoples from within you will be separated; one people will be stronger than the other, and the older will serve the younger."

During the delivery, Jacob grasped the heel of his brother Esau, as though striving for first position. Though second by birth, he was first in his mother's affections. But his father loved Esau best.

Years later, when Isaac was old and nearly blind, he summoned his firstborn, Esau. "Take your quiver and bow and hunt some wild game for me. Prepare the kind of meal I like, and I will give you my blessing before I die."

But the clever Rebekah overheard and called quickly to Jacob, suggesting a scheme to trick the blessing from Isaac. Disguised as Esau, Jacob presented himself to his father for the much-coveted blessing.

Isaac then blessed Jacob, thinking he was blessing Esau: "May nations serve you and peoples bow down to you. Be lord over your brothers, and may the sons of your mother bow down to you. May those who curse you be cursed and those who bless you be blessed."

Isaac had stretched out his hand and passed the choicest blessing to his younger son, thus recalling the words spoken about the two children jostling for position in Rebekah's womb. The benediction thus given could not be withdrawn, despite the deceit, despite Esau's tears, and despite his vow to kill Jacob.

Afraid lest Esau take revenge, Rebekah persuaded Isaac to send Jacob north to find a wife from among her brother Laban's daughters.

As the years passed, Rebekah must have longed to embrace her younger son, hoping for the privilege of enfolding his children in her embrace. But more than twenty years would pass before Jacob returned. And though Isaac would live to welcome his son, Rebekah would not.

When Rebekah was a young girl, God had invited her to play a vital role in the story of his people. He had gone to great lengths to pursue her. Like Sarah, she would become a matriarch of God's people, and like Sarah, her heart would divide itself between faith and doubt, believing that God's promise required her intervention. Finding it difficult to rest in the promise God had made, she resorted to trickery to achieve it.

The results, mirroring her own heart, were mixed. Though Jacob indeed became heir to the promise, he was driven from his home and the mother who loved him too well. In addition, he and his descendants would forever be at odds with Esau and his people, the Edomites. Two thousand years later, Herod the Great, who hailed from Idumea (the Greek and Roman name for Edom) would slaughter many innocent children in his attempt to destroy the infant Jesus.

Yet God was still at work, graciously using a woman whose response to him was far less than perfect, in order to accomplish his purposes.

Tuesday

HER LIFE AND TIMES

JEWELRY

"Then I put the ring in her nose and the bracelets on her arms." ...
Then the servant brought out gold and silver jewelry and articles of
clothing and gave them to Rebekah.

—Genesis 24:47, 53

A nose ring! Often taken as a sign of rebellious youth today, a nose ring was an acceptable form of adornment in ancient times. When Abraham's servant realized Rebekah was the woman Isaac was to marry, he immediately got out the jewels he had brought along for the occasion. He gave her two gold bracelets and a gold nose ring. Rebekah quickly slipped the jewelry on and ran home with shining eyes to tell her family what had occurred.

A nose ring is mentioned only two other times in Scripture—in Proverbs 11 and Ezekiel 16. In Ezekiel 16, God is describing in allegorical terms how much he loves the city of Jerusalem. He lovingly bathes her, then dresses her in wonderfully rich clothing and soft leather sandals. He then tenderly adorns her with jewelry. "I put bracelets on your arms and a necklace around your neck, and I put a ring on your nose, earrings on your ears and a beautiful crown on your head. So you were adorned with gold and silver" (Ezekiel 16:11–13).

The Old Testament mentions jewels and jewelry numerous times. Women and men both wore earrings (Exodus 32:2). They also commonly wore "armlets, bracelets, signet rings, earrings and necklaces" (Numbers 31:50). The Israelites took most of their jewelry from others while at war; gold and silver and gemstones are often listed among the booty taken during a raid. According to 2 Samuel 8:11, David gained enormous amounts of gold and silver and bronze when he conquered the nations surrounding Israel. He dedicated all of it to the Lord, and his son Solomon used it to build the fabulous temple in Jerusalem. Believe it or not, Solomon had so much wealth in his kingdom that he "made silver and gold as common in Jerusalem as stones" (2 Chronicles 1:15).

In the NIV, the Greek word for various female adornments is translated "jewelry" only once. In speaking to wives, Peter urges them to pay more attention to their inner beauty than their outward beauty. "Your beauty should not come from outward adornment, such as braided hair and the wearing of gold jewelry and fine clothes," he says. "Instead, it should be that of your inner self, the unfading beauty of a gentle and quiet spirit, which is of great worth in God's sight" (1 Peter 3:3–4). Evidently, the women of New Testament times were as fascinated with jewelry as the women of Old Testament times—and the women of our times. How easy it is to look in the mirror to assess our outward appearance, forgetting to spend much time at all examining our inner appearance.

Tomorrow morning, when you put your rings on your fingers, also put on a spirit of peace. When you put your earrings on your ears, put them on with a cheerful attitude. When you clasp your necklace around your neck, clasp a sweet spirit to your heart also. The jewelry you wear won't make much difference in your day, but the spirit you wear will.

Wednesday

HER LEGACY IN SCRIPTURE

Read Genesis 24:15–27.

1. What do you notice about young Rebekah's looks and character?

Read Genesis 24:67.

2. These are some of the sweetest words about marriage found in the Bible. In your own words, describe what you think Isaac and Rebekah's marriage was like in these early days.

Read Genesis 25:21–28.

3. Verse 28 contains some of the saddest words about parenting found in the Bible. How do you think their parents' favoritism affected Jacob and Esau?

Read Genesis 27:1–13.

4. Why do you think Rebekah resorted to trickery to gain what God promised her when she was pregnant?

5. Do you see yourself anywhere in Rebekah's story? How are you like or unlike her?

Thursday

HER PROMISE

*R*ebekah heard Abraham's servant describe how he had prayed and how he was sure she was the woman God intended for Isaac. God himself had divinely orchestrated the events. Rebekah seemed to have known that and, when asked, answered simply, "I will go."

Did Rebekah fully realize God's plan for her? Was she open to following that plan? Or was she simply entranced with the romantic notions of a young girl looking for her knight in shining armor? Whatever her motivation, the events *were* planned by God, and he was able and willing to faithfully continue to fulfill his promises through her.

God's faithfulness, despite our waywardness and contrariness, is evident both throughout Scripture and throughout our lives. He will be faithful; he promises.

Promises in Scripture

Know therefore that the LORD your God is God; he is the faithful God, keeping his covenant of love to a thousand generations of those who love him and keep his commands.

—DEUTERONOMY 7:9

*The LORD is faithful to all his promises
and loving toward all he has made.*

—PSALM 145:13

Let us hold unswervingly to the hope we profess, for he who promised is faithful.

—HEBREWS 10:23

Friday

HER LEGACY OF PRAYER

Our sister, may you increase to thousands upon thousands; may your offspring possess the gates of their enemies.

—GENESIS 24:60

REFLECT ON: Genesis 27.

PRAISE GOD: Because unlike Isaac, who had only one blessing to give his children, God has blessings uniquely designed for each of us.

OFFER THANKS: That God doesn't wait until we are perfect to involve us in his plans.

CONFESS: Any tendency to try to control the future rather than trusting God to shape it according to his timetable.

ASK GOD: To protect you from playing favorites with your own children and to trust that he has a generous plan for each one.

Lift Your Heart

*T*ake a few minutes this week to write a blessing card for each of your children. Use a simple index card or decorate the card with stickers, stencils, or line drawings. (If you don't have children of your own, you can do this for a niece or nephew or another special child in your life.)

Start by praying for each child, asking God's blessing on their lives. Then write out the blessings you sense God wants for them. Tuck the blessing cards under their pillows or place them next to their dinner plates. Tell them these are some of the ways you are asking God to bless them. Be sure to keep a copy of each card for yourself so you can make those blessings a subject of frequent prayer.

Lord, you give us the power to bless our children, through our example, our teaching, our love, and our prayers. May our children surpass us in faith. In all their struggles may they sense your nearness, and may their joy be renewed each morning. May each of them become the kind of person who attracts others to you. I pray this in the name of Jesus. Amen.

Rachel
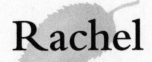

HER NAME MEANS
"Ewe"

HER CHARACTER: Manipulated by her father, she had little say over her own life circumstances and relationships. But rather than dealing creatively with a difficult situation, Rachel behaved like a perpetual victim, responding to sin with yet more sin, making things worse by competing with her sister, and deceiving her father in return.

HER SORROW: That her longing for children ultimately led to her death in childbirth.

HER JOY: That her husband cherished her and would do whatever was in his power to make her happy.

KEY SCRIPTURES: Genesis 29–35; Jeremiah 31:15; Matthew 2:18

Monday

HER STORY

*W*as it better to have love but no children or to be unloved and yet mother to a house full of sons? The question battered Rachel like a strong wind slamming the same door over and over.

Leah had just given birth to her fourth son, Judah. In her joy she had shouted, "I will praise the LORD!" Her firstborn, Reuben, meant "See, a Son"; Simeon, "One Who Hears"; and Levi, "Attached," as though Jacob could ever be attached to his plain wife! Rachel was sick to death of this habit her sister had of naming her sons in ways that emphasized Rachel's own barrenness.

Leah had become Jacob's wife through her father's treachery, but Rachel had captured his love from their first meeting at the well outside Haran. Every touch communicated his favor. Yet favor could not make children any more than wishing could make wealth. Rachel should have been his first, his only wife, just as Aunt Rebekah was Uncle Isaac's only wife.

Rachel's father, Laban, had promised her to his nephew, Jacob, provided he work for him for seven years. Seven years was a long time to wait for a wife, yet Jacob had thought it a good bargain. And that made Rachel love him all the more.

But as the wedding day approached, Laban hatched a scheme to trick seven more years of labor out of Jacob. Rachel's day of happiness dissolved the moment Laban instructed her older sister, Leah, to disguise herself in Rachel's wedding garments.

After dark he led Leah, veiled, to Jacob's tent, and the two slept together as man and wife. As the first light crept across the tent floor, Jacob reached again for Rachel only to find Leah at his side. Laban's treachery stung him. It was beyond belief. Even so, despite the recriminations and the tears, the marriage could not be undone.

But Rachel felt undone, her blessing seized by stealth. Laban's convoluted plan, however, was still unfolding. He struck another bargain, giving Rachel to Jacob the very next week in exchange for seven more years of labor. So now the two sisters lived uneasily together, Leah's sons a grating reminder that Rachel, the second wife, was cheated still.

"Give me children, or I'll die," Rachel screamed at Jacob one day—as though he could take the place of God and open her womb. So she gave him Bilhah, her maid, who conceived and bore her two sons. When Napthali, the second son, was born, Rachel proclaimed to anyone who would listen, "I have had a great struggle with my sister, and I have won." But the wrestling match between Rachel and Leah was far from over.

Rachel's bitterness again eased when she herself gave birth to a son, naming him Joseph, meaning "May He Add"—a prophetic prayer that God would add yet another child to her line.

Then one day God spoke to Jacob, telling him to return to the land of Isaac, his father. More than twenty years earlier, Jacob had wrestled the blessing from Esau and then had fled his murderous wrath. Had the long years paid him back twofold? Had Laban's treachery and the wrestling match between Rachel and Leah reminded him of his own struggles with his brother? Would God—and Esau—call it even? Only the Lord could protect him in this matter with his brother.

As Jacob gathered his flocks, his servants, and his children, preparing to leave, Rachel stole her father's household gods, small idols thought to ensure prosperity. After ten days on the road, Laban overtook them in the hill country of Gilead, accusing his son-in-law of theft. Unaware of Rachel's deceit, Jacob invited Laban to search the camp, promising to put to death anyone discovered with the idols.

Having learned a trick or two from her crafty father, Rachel tucked the idols into a saddle and then sat on it. When Laban entered her tent, she greeted him with a woman's ruse, saying, "Don't be angry, my lord, that I cannot stand up in your presence; I'm having my period." Her trick worked, much as Jacob's had when he deceived his own father, and Laban finally gave up the search. Later, Jacob made sure that all the old idols were purged from his household.

As they made their way across the desert, Jacob faced his brother Esau, and the two reconciled. But tragedy soon overtook them as Rachel struggled to give birth to a second son, the answer to her many prayers. Ironically, the woman who once said she would die unless she had children was now dying because of a child. Rachel's last words, "He is Ben-Oni, the son of my trouble," capture her anguish at the birth of this son.

But Jacob gathered the infant in his arms and with a father's tenderness renamed him Benjamin, "Son of My Right Hand."

Like her husband, the beautiful Rachel had been both a schemer and the victim of schemes. Tricked by her own father, she viewed her children as weapons in the struggle with her sister. As so often happens, the lessons of treachery and competition were passed from generation to generation. Rachel's own son, Joseph, would suffer grievously as a result, being sold into slavery by his half brothers, Leah's sons.

Yet God would remain faithful. Through a remarkable set of twists and turns, Rachel's Joseph would one day rule Egypt, providing a refuge for his father and brothers in the midst of famine. Step by step, in ways impossible to foresee, God's plan was unfolding—a plan to heal divisions, put an end to striving, and restore hope. Using people with mixed motives and confused desires (the only kind of people there are), he was revealing his grace and mercy, never once forsaking his promise.

Tuesday

HER LIFE AND TIMES

MENSTRUAL CYCLES

*R*achel said to her father, 'Don't be angry, my lord, that I cannot stand up in your presence; I'm having my period.' So [Laban] searched but could not find the household gods" (Genesis 31:35). Rachel's words here are the only mention in Scripture of a typical monthly menstrual cycle, other than the ceremonial laws covering menstruation found in Leviticus and referred to again in Ezekiel.

Rachel knew without a doubt that her ploy would successfully deter her father. By claiming to have her period, she not only kept the false gods she had stolen, she kept her very life, since Jacob had promised to kill whoever had stolen the idols from Laban.

During the time a Hebrew woman had her period, she was considered "unclean," not really surprising considering the untidy nature of a monthly flow, especially in those days, long before the invention of feminine sanitary products. But the laws were more stringent than just to cover the very personal nature of a monthly period. Those who touched a woman at this time, even by chance, became unclean until evening. Wherever the woman slept or sat also became unclean. Anyone who touched her bedding or her seat was considered unclean until they washed their clothes, bathed, and waited until evening.

A woman was considered unclean for seven days, the normal length of a woman's monthly period. She then customarily bathed in order to cleanse herself. This is probably the bath that Bathsheba was taking when spotted by King David (2 Samuel 11:2–4). Since she had just had her period, David could be sure Bathsheba's child was his when she told him she was pregnant (her husband was a soldier off to war).

The natural flow of a woman's period didn't require sacrifices for her to be cleansed; merely bathing and waiting for a prescribed time was enough. A longer, less natural flow, usually caused by some infection or disease, required a sacrifice in order for the woman to be clean. Neither implied any moral failing on the part of the woman, but since blood was seen as a source of life, anything surrounding it became an important part of ceremonial law.

Many women consider their monthly period, and the discomfort and irritability that often come along with it, a monthly trial—something women must bear, and men, lucky creatures, are spared. However, it is only through this particular function of her body that a woman can reproduce and carry a child. Although at times messy, at times a nuisance, at times downright painful, only through this process does a woman have the opportunity afforded to no man—the opportunity to bear new life. And in so doing, to be uniquely linked to the Creator of all life.

Wednesday

HER LEGACY IN SCRIPTURE

Read Genesis 29:26–30:24.

1. How do you think most women would respond to the situation in which Rachel found herself at the beginning of her marriage (Genesis 29:30)? How would they treat the other sister/wife?

2. Many women over the centuries have suffered the agony Rachel expresses in Genesis 30:1. How did Rachel's close relationship with Leah increase her pain? How could their relationship have eased her pain instead?

3. Discontentment is insidious. It traps us into thinking what was enough is no longer enough. Yet it's normal to long for things like love and children. What do you long for that you don't have? How can you tell if your longing has crossed the line from good desire to harmful discontentment?

Read Genesis 35:16–20.

4. Given that they were on a journey, how would you describe the situation under which Rachel likely gave birth?

5. What Rachel most wanted—a child—cost her life. Think about what you long for. What price would you pay? What price, to yourself or others, is too high?

Thursday

*G*enesis 30:22 says, "God remembered Rachel; he listened to her and opened her womb." God *remembered* Rachel, but he had never really forgotten her. When the Bible uses the word *remember*, it doesn't mean that God forgets and then suddenly recalls—as if the all-knowing, all-powerful God of the universe suddenly hits his forehead with the heel of his hand and says, "Oops! I forgot all about Rachel. I'd better do something quickly!"

No, when the Bible says God remembers something, it expresses God's love and compassion for his people. It reminds us of God's promise never to abandon us or leave us without support or relief. He will never forsake us. He will never forget us. He will always *remember* us.

Promises in Scripture

Then God remembered Rachel; he listened to her and opened her womb.

—GENESIS 30:22

Remember, O LORD, your great mercy and love,
for they are from of old.

—PSALM 25:6

You understand, O LORD;
remember me and care for me.

—JEREMIAH 15:15

The Mighty One has done great things for me—holy is his name.

—LUKE 1:49

Friday

HER LEGACY OF PRAYER

Then God remembered Rachel; he listened to her and opened her womb.

—GENESIS 30:22

REFLECT ON: Genesis 30:1–24.

PRAISE GOD: Because he never for a moment forgets about us. He is present and attentive, aware of our deepest desires, even when we're certain he's lost track of us.

OFFER THANKS: That God alone is the Creator. Because of him, every human life is sacred.

CONFESS: That we sometimes use our children, our husbands, our homes, or even the size of our paychecks to compete with other women.

ASK GOD: To help you form deep and loyal friendships with other women so you can know the joy that comes from being sisters in Christ.

Lift Your Heart

Think of one woman you would like to get to know better in the next few months. Then pick up the phone and make a lunch date, or invite her to a play, movie, or concert. Make sure you build in a little time to chat so you can begin to build a relationship. One expert says it takes an average of three years to form a solid friendship. Don't waste another moment!

Father, forgive me for letting my identity rest on whose wife or mother I am or what kind of job I have. I don't want to view other women as my rivals but as potential friends and even soul mates. Please lead me to the friendships I desire, and help me to be patient with the process. Amen.

Leah

HER NAME MAY MEAN
"Impatient" or "Wild Cow"

HER CHARACTER: Capable of both strong and enduring love, she was a faithful mother and wife. Manipulated by her father, she became jealous of her sister, with whom, it seems, she never reconciled.

HER SORROW: That she lacked her sister's beauty, and that her love for her husband was one-sided.

HER JOY: That she bore Jacob six sons and one daughter.

KEY SCRIPTURES: Genesis 29–35; Ruth 4:11

Monday

HER STORY

We buried my sister Rachel today. But she is still alive. I catch glimpses of her in Jacob's broken heart, in dark-eyed Joseph and squalling little Benjamin, his favorite sons. Rachel's sons. I can hear my beautiful, determined sister weeping loudly for the children she might have had, stubbornly refusing to be comforted. Yet who takes note of my tears? Should they flood the desert, no one would notice.

Reuben, Simeon, Levi, Judah, Issachar, Zebulun, Dinah, and then Gad and Asher by my maid—these are the children God has given me and I have given my beloved Jacob. And still he loves her best. Should my husband and I live another hundred years, I will never be his only wife.

Contrary to what Leah may have felt, God *had* taken note of her sorrow. Knowing well that Jacob's heart was too cramped a space to harbor both Rachel and Leah, he made Leah a mother, not once, but seven times, extending her influence in Jacob's household.

With the birth of each child the unhappy Leah hoped to secure her husband's affection. But each time her disappointment grew. She felt the old curse asserting itself: "Your desire will be for your husband and he will rule over you" (Genesis 3:16).

Perhaps Jacob still resented Leah for tricking him on their wedding night, disguising herself as his beloved Rachel. Surely Leah's love had been passionate enough to deceive him until morning. She felt both glad and guilty for her part; though, truth to tell, she had little choice but to obey her father, Laban, in the matter. And she thanked God each day for enabling her to bear Jacob's children. Still, children often caused a mother untold sorrow.

Dinah, her only daughter, had been raped by a local prince on their return to Jacob's homeland. Leah hardly knew how to comfort her. To make matters worse, her sons Levi and Simeon avenged their sister by savagely murdering a town-full of people. Then Reuben disgraced himself by sleeping with his father's concubine Bilhah.

Hadn't God promised to protect us if we returned to this land of promise? How, then, could such things happen? Leah wondered. True, God had watched over them as they faced Esau and his four hundred men. But Leah's joy at the brothers' friendly reunion was eclipsed by her sorrow at once again being proved the lesser-loved wife. Jacob had made it plain enough by placing Rachel and her children last in their long caravan, giving them the best chance of escape should Esau prove violent.

But Jacob's love could not prevent Rachel from dying in childbirth. Leah, not Rachel, was destined to be his first and last wife. Alongside her husband, the father of Israel, she would be revered as a mother of Israel. In fact, the promise of a Savior was carried not through Rachel's Joseph but through Leah's Judah, whose descendants would include David, Israel's great king, and Jesus, the long-awaited Messiah. In the end, Jacob was laid to rest in the cave of Machpelah, next to his first wife, Leah, rather than his favorite wife, Rachel, who was buried somewhere near Ephrath.

The two sisters, Rachel and Leah, remind us that life is fraught with sorrow and peril, much of it caused by sin and selfishness. Both women suffered—each in her own way—the curse of Eve after she was expelled from her garden paradise. While Rachel experienced great pain in giving birth to children, Leah experienced the anguish of loving a man who seemed indifferent to her. Yet both women became mothers in Israel, leaving their homeland to play essential roles in the story of God's great plan for his people.

Tuesday

HER LIFE AND TIMES

MARRIAGE CUSTOMS

The customs of marriage were far different in ancient biblical times from our own modern customs. Seldom did a man or woman marry for love. Jacob is a notable exception by expressing his love for Rachel and his desire to marry her. Jacob married both Rachel and her sister, Leah, a practice that was later forbidden by law (Leviticus 18:18).

Usually the bride and groom were very young when they married. The bride was often only around twelve and the groom around thirteen. Their marriage was arranged by parents, and their consent was neither requested nor required. Even so, such marriages could prove to be love matches, like that between Isaac and Rebekah (Genesis 24:67).

By New Testament times, the marriage ceremony itself was usually very short, but the festivities connected with it could go on for many days. The groom dressed in colorful clothing and set out just before sunset, with his friends and attendants and musicians, for the home of the bride's parents. There the bride would be waiting, washed and perfumed and bedecked in an elaborate dress and jewels. The bride and groom then led the marriage procession through the village streets, accompanied by music and torchbearers, to the groom's parents' home. The feasting and celebration began that night and often continued for seven days.

God's design for marriage to be between one husband and one wife was often not practiced in early biblical times. Leah shared her husband, Jacob, with not only her sister, Rachel, but their maids, Zilpah and Bilhah. Although polygamy was less common after the exodus from Egypt, Gideon had a number of wives (Judges 8:30), and, of course, Solomon had many (1 Kings 11:3). But, as the New Testament indicates, a union between one husband and one wife continues to be God's design and desire (1 Timothy 3:2, 12; Titus 1:6).

Wednesday

HER LEGACY IN SCRIPTURE

Read Genesis 29:20–35.

1. What do you think Leah might have felt during her wedding night, when Jacob was deceived?

2. How do you think Leah felt and acted toward Jacob as the years passed? What do you think his reaction was?

3. Many women today have husbands who love something more than their wives: their job, their position, their money, sports. Others have felt the lack of love from someone else, such as parents. Have you ever felt unloved by someone? If so, how did you feel and act?

4. God saw Leah's suffering and had compassion for her (Genesis 29:31). How aware are you of God's compassion for you? Where do you see his compassion active in your life?

5. What helps or hinders you from receiving love from God?

Thursday

HER PROMISE

When the LORD saw that Leah was not loved, he opened her womb.

—GENESIS 29:31

The Lord *noticed* Leah's misery. He looked down and saw a woman who was lonely and sad because her husband loved his other wife better than he loved her. So, to ease her sorrow, to provide her comfort, God gave her children—beautiful, intelligent, strong children, one of whom would establish the lineage of the priests of Israel and another who was an ancestor of Jesus himself.

This same God of Abraham, Isaac, Jacob, and Leah is our God. He sees our miseries, no matter how small or how large. He knows our circumstances, our feelings, our hurts. And, just as in Leah's life, he is willing to step in and create something beautiful in and through us.

Promises in Scripture

He [God] has sent me to bind up the brokenhearted,
   to proclaim freedom for the captives
   and release from darkness for the prisoners …
to comfort all who mourn
   and provide for those who grieve in Zion—
to bestow on them a crown of beauty
   instead of ashes,
the oil of gladness
   instead of mourning,
and a garment of praise
   instead of a spirit of despair.

—ISAIAH 61:1–3

I will turn their mourning into gladness;
   I will give them comfort and joy instead of sorrow.

—JEREMIAH 31:13

Friday

HER LEGACY OF PRAYER

When the LORD saw that Leah was not loved, he opened her womb, but Rachel was barren. Leah became pregnant and gave birth to a son. She named him Reuben, for she said, "It is because the LORD has seen my misery. Surely my husband will love me now."

—GENESIS 29:31–32

REFLECT ON: Genesis 29:16–31.

PRAISE GOD: That though human beings often judge by outward appearances, God always sees the heart and judges accordingly.

OFFER THANKS: That God is moved by our sorrow.

CONFESS: Your tendency to compare yourself with other women, judging them and yourself merely by appearances.

ASK GOD: To enable you to base your identity on your relationship with him rather than on what you see in the mirror.

Lift Your Heart

Take five minutes a day this week to pay yourself a compliment by thanking God for making you the woman you are. Call to mind everything you like about yourself—your quirky sense of humor, your love of great literature, your compassion for other people, your curly hair, even the shape of your toes. Resist the temptation to think about what you don't like. (Imagine for a moment how God must feel when he hears us complaining about how he has made us!) Instead, decide now to honor him by your gratitude. At the end of the week, treat yourself to lunch with a friend or a leisurely latte at your favorite café in celebration of all the natural gifts with which God has blessed you.

Lord, I don't want to be critical of how you've put me together, relying on what others think of me for my sense of well-being. Make me a woman who is confident that I am lovable, not because of any outward beauty but because you have loved me from the moment you called me into being. In Jesus' name I pray. Amen.

Tamar

Daughter-in-Law of Judah

HER NAME MEANS
"Date Tree" or "Palm Tree"

HER CHARACTER: Driven by one overwhelming need, she sacrificed her reputation and nearly her life to achieve her goals.

HER SORROW: That the men in her life failed to fulfill their responsibility, leaving her a childless widow.

HER JOY: That her daring behavior resulted, not in ruin, but in the fulfillment of her hopes to bear children.

KEY SCRIPTURES: Genesis 38; Matthew 1:3

Monday

HER STORY

Genealogies hardly make compelling reading at bedtime — or at any other time, for that matter. Perhaps you welcome them with a yawn, or skip over them entirely as you read through the Bible. But even long lists of bewildering names can reveal interesting insights into God's mysterious plan. That's the way the Scriptures work, yielding hidden riches on every page.

Take the genealogy in the first chapter of Matthew, for instance. It lists a grand total of forty-one male ancestors of Jesus, beginning with Abraham, and a mere five female ancestors, three of whose stories (those of Tamar, Rahab, and Bathsheba) are colored by such distasteful details as incest, prostitution, fornication, adultery, and murder.

Jesus, the perfect Son of the perfect Father, had plenty of imperfect branches in his family tree and enough colorful characters to populate a modern romance novel. That women should be mentioned at all in his genealogy is surprising, let alone that four of the five got pregnant out of wedlock. In addition, at least three of the women were foreigners, not Israelites.

Tamar fell into both categories. Her father-in-law, Judah (son of Jacob and Leah), had arranged for her to marry his firstborn, Er. Half Canaanite and half Hebrew, Er was a wicked man, whom God killed for his sins. That's all we know of him.

After Er came Onan, Judah's second son. As was the custom of the time, Judah gave Onan to the widowed Tamar, instructing him to sleep with her so that she could have children to carry on Er's line. But Onan was far too crafty for his own good. He slept with Tamar, but then "spilled his semen on the ground," thus ensuring Tamar's barrenness. That way he would not be saddled with the responsibility for children who would carry on his brother's line rather than his own. But God took note, and Onan, too, died for his wickedness.

Already Judah had lost two sons to Tamar. Should he risk a third? Shelah was his only remaining son, not yet fully grown. To placate his daughter-in-law, Judah instructed Tamar to return to her father's house and live as a widow until Shelah was of marriageable age. But time passed like a sluggish river, and Tamar continued to wear her widow's garments as Selah grew up.

After Judah's wife died, he set out one day for Timnah to shear his sheep. Hearing the news of her father-in-law's journey, Tamar decided to take desperate and dramatic action. If Judah would not give her his youngest son in marriage, she would do her best to propagate the family name in her own way. Shedding her widow's black, she disguised herself in a veil, impersonating a prostitute, and sat down beside the road to Timnah. Judah slept with her and gave her his personal seal and cord along with his staff in pledge of future payment.

About three months later, Judah learned that Tamar was pregnant, little realizing he was responsible for her condition. Outraged that she had prostituted herself, he ordered her burned to death. But before the sentence could be carried out, Tamar sent him a stunning message: "I am pregnant by the man who owns these. See if you recognize whose seal and cord and staff these are."

The man who had so quickly passed judgment, little heeding his own secret tryst with a prostitute, was suddenly taken up short. To his credit, he told the truth, saying, "She is more righteous than I, since I wouldn't give her to my son Shelah."

Six months later, Tamar gave birth to twins. Once again, as with Jacob and Esau, the children struggled in her womb. A tiny hand came out and then disappeared, but not before being tied with a scarlet thread by the midwife. Then a small, slippery body emerged, but with no trace of the red thread. They named the first boy Perez (meaning "Breaking Out"). Then the little one with the scarlet ribbon was born and they named him Zerah (meaning "Scarlet"). Perez was recognized as the firstborn. From his line would come King David and finally, hundreds of years later, Jesus of Nazareth.

Judah had shown little concern regarding the continuance of his line. Instead, God used a woman, shamed by her own barrenness and determined to overcome it, to ensure that the tribe of Judah would not only survive but that it would one day bear the world's Messiah.

Tuesday

HER LIFE AND TIMES

PROSTITUTION

*A*s abhorrent as it seems to us, prostitution was actually an expression of worship in the ancient Near East. Pagan peoples often believed that fertility gods granted blessings to those who practiced cultic prostitution. The sacrifices and the payments for the use of a cult prostitute brought huge amounts of money into the coffers of the god or goddess being worshiped. The sexual intercourse itself symbolized the hoped-for fertility and abundance of the harvest.

Judah, a widower who had only recently "recovered from his grief" (Genesis 38:12), traveled to Timnah during sheep shearing time to watch his own sheep being sheared of their wool. It may be that when he saw Tamar, he took her for a shrine prostitute and had intercourse with her to ensure a good crop of wool. That hardly justifies Judah's act, but it may shed light on his motives.

Shrine prostitutes usually kept themselves heavily veiled before and during the act of intercourse, an attempt to create the illusion that the participant was actually engaging in the sexual act with the goddess herself. This practice worked in Tamar's favor, giving her the perfect disguise so that her father-in-law would never recognize her.

Prostitution was the imagery used often by the biblical prophets to describe Israel's waywardness, their proneness to follow false gods. They saw God as the husband of Israel, her keeper and her true love. Whenever the Israelites turned from the true God to false gods, they "prostituted" themselves. It is a strong picture, but an accurate one, of turning away from the God who truly loved them and was willing to care for them and watch over them, if only they would remain true to him.

Tamar's story takes us by surprise, repulses us. We recoil from the sordid details of prostitution and find little to inspire us. Yet stories like Tamar's are what make the Bible so believable. Who would ever invent such a thing, then record it not only in the historical narrative but also in the lineage of the Messiah? Only the God of eternal surprises. The God who takes the unfit, the desperate, and the profane, and uses them to his eternal and holy purposes.

Wednesday

HER LEGACY IN SCRIPTURE

Read Genesis 38:1–30 and Matthew 1:3.

1. Onan was supposed to father children through Tamar for his brother Er. This is the same act as that of the "kinsman-redeemer" found in the book of Ruth. The closest of kin was to father a child to carry on the line of the deceased husband. None of the men in Tamar's life fulfilled their responsibilities to her, including her father-in-law, Judah. Describe what you think Tamar was feeling throughout the course of these events.

2. In that culture, a woman's whole worth was in bearing sons to carry on the family line. A woman who failed in that was nothing. What makes you feel you're worth a lot or not much?

3. When you consider what Tamar did in offering herself disguised as a prostitute to her father-in-law, do his words in verse 26 surprise you? Why or why not? Explain what Judah meant by those words.

4. The story of Tamar is tough to digest. There is simply no way to assimilate what she did with our current way of thinking. Yet Matthew makes a point of mentioning her in Christ's lineage. What do you think God is saying by including her story in the inspired Scriptures and her place in Jesus' human heritage?

5. How has God worked good out of the bad things that have happened to you or the bad things you've done?

Thursday

HER PROMISE

The story in Genesis 38 reveals nothing about Tamar's knowledge of God's hand in the events of her life. More than likely, she was totally unaware of the power of God at work. But he was at work nevertheless, bringing good out of tragedy and blessing out of less than honorable events.

That's the beauty of this story. God's power to bring positive things from the negative, even sinful, events of our lives is just as much at work now as in Tamar's day. We may not see it today or tomorrow — or perhaps ever — but we can trust the God we love to do what he loves: bring blessing to us in spite of ourselves.

Promises in Scripture

Not one of all the good promises the LORD *your God gave you has failed. Every promise has been fulfilled; not one has failed.*

— JOSHUA 23:14

Your ways, O God, are holy.
   What god is so great as our God?

— PSALM 77:13

And we know that in all things God works for the good of those who love him, who have been called according to his purpose.

— ROMANS 8:28

Friday

HER LEGACY OF PRAYER

Judah [was] the father of Perez and Zerah, whose mother was Tamar.

—MATTHEW 1:3 (GENEALOGY OF CHRIST)

REFLECT ON: Genesis 38.

PRAISE GOD: That he allowed his own Son to be intimately linked with fallen human beings from whom he was descended.

OFFER THANKS: That God can use everyone and everything to bring about a good result.

CONFESS: Any tendency you may have to judge others with a double standard, as Judah did Tamar.

ASK GOD: To take any desperation you may be feeling and replace it with hope, calling to mind the verse in Jeremiah 29:11: "'For I know the plans I have for you,' declares the LORD, 'plans to prosper you and not to harm you, plans to give you hope and a future.'"

Lift Your Hear

*I*f you've never sketched out your family tree, make an effort to trace your heritage, going back at least four or five generations—more if you have the time and energy. Ask older relatives to supply as much information as possible about your ancestors. Pay special attention to the women in your family tree. Take notes on everything you discover. Then transcribe all the information into a keepsake book that can be passed along to your own children after you're gone. Include any photos and news clippings you can find. You may discover some fascinating insights into your family background.

Lord, you formed me in my mother's womb. You knew then what every single day of my life would be like. You saw the great things and the hard things, the joy and the sorrow. Right now I come before you with the situation (or the memory) with which I have not yet made peace. As I look back at painful circumstances, help me to realize that you were present even in the midst of them. And now, as I surrender them to you, help me to sense your healing presence in my life.

Potiphar's Wife

HER CHARACTER: The wife of a prosperous and influential Egyptian, she was unfaithful and vindictive, ready to lie in order to protect herself and ruin an innocent man.

HER SORROW: To be rebuffed by a slave.

KEY SCRIPTURE: Genesis 39

Monday

HER STORY

We don't even know her name. She is merely presented as the spoiled wife of a prosperous Egyptian official, a miniature Cleopatra, determined to employ her charms to seduce the handsome young Hebrew slave, Joseph.

At the age of seventeen, Joseph was sold into slavery by his half brothers, the sons of Leah. The favorite child of Rachel and Jacob, Joseph seems to have unwittingly done everything possible to ensure his brothers' enmity, even recounting a dream predicting that he, the younger son, would one day rule over them. Envious, the brothers faked Joseph's death and contemptuously sold him to Midianite traders en route to Egypt.

There Potiphar, captain of Pharaoh's executioners, bought the young slave and gradually entrusted him with responsibility for his entire household. Even in his exile, everything Joseph touched prospered, as Potiphar couldn't help but notice.

But the captain of the guard wasn't the only Egyptian impressed by Joseph. His wife had taken special note as well. She made her desire plain enough by inviting Joseph to share her bed. The young slave must have surprised his wealthy mistress with his quick rebuff: "My master has withheld nothing from me except you, because you are his wife. How then could I do such a wicked thing and sin against God?"

From then on, Joseph did his best to avoid her. But with little else to occupy her time and attention, Potiphar's wife simply waited for her next opportunity, which came when Joseph entered the house one day to attend to his duties. Alone with him, she caught hold of his cloak, whispering once again, "Come to bed with me!" But Joseph could not be persuaded and instead fled from her, leaving his would-be seducer alone with her lust, furiously clutching his cloak in her hands.

She wasted no time accusing him of attempted rape. When her husband heard the news, he was outraged, quickly consigning his favorite servant to prison.

The story of Joseph and how God blessed him even in his prison cell, eventually enabling him to become master of the nation he had entered as a slave, is well known to us. But we haven't a clue about Potiphar's wife. Whatever became of her? Did her husband suspect her duplicity? Is that why he merely confined Joseph to prison rather than executing him, as he had every right to do? Compared with Joseph, the story's protagonist, Potiphar's wife was a hollow woman whose soul was steadily decaying through the corrosive power of lust and hate. Surrounded by luxury, she was spiritually impoverished. Empty of God, she was full of herself.

Tuesday

HER LIFE AND TIMES

EGYPTIAN LIFE

*J*n the ancient world, Egypt was considered the world's bread-basket. The Nile River regularly overflowed its banks, depositing rich soil and moisture along the river valley — a perfect place for abundant crops to grow. But fertile ground in Egypt could be found only as far as the Nile reached, a division so pronounced one could literally stand with one foot on rich soil and the other in sand.

Whenever famine struck other parts of the Near East, the starving inhabitants would hurry to Egypt for food: "Now there was a famine in the land, and Abram went down to Egypt to live there for a while because the famine was severe" (Genesis 12:10). "When Jacob learned that there was grain in Egypt, he said to his sons, 'Why do you just keep looking at each other?' He continued, 'I have heard that there is grain in Egypt. Go down there and buy some for us, so that we may live and not die'" (Genesis 42:1–2).

In addition to serving as the world's breadbasket, Egypt was the site of many impressive building projects. Some of the pharaohs constructed enormous tombs in which they and their families were to be ushered into the afterlife. Egyptians believed that their bodies were the eternal houses for their souls; therefore they became adept at mummification, preserving the bodies of the dead so thoroughly that some are intact today.

Egypt's building projects were completed at tremendous human cost. Egyptian pharaohs forced the Hebrews into slavery, using them to complete their temples and tombs. Most likely the Hebrew oppression took place during the Nineteenth Dynasty of Egypt under the Pharaoh Rameses. Officials during that time have left behind their notations of the numbers of bricks made each day as well as their complaints at the scarcity of straw for the bricks.

Temples and tombs were filled with furniture of ebony and ivory, elegant vases, and copper tools, as well as gold jewelry and ornaments. Artisans etched beautifully drawn scenes of daily life on the walls of tombs to provide comfort for the one buried there.

As the wife of a high-ranking Egyptian official, Potiphar's wife likely led a life of relative ease and prosperity. According to the story in Genesis 39, Potiphar's household and business matters prospered because of Joseph's influence, and "the blessing of the LORD was on everything Potiphar had, both in the house and in the field" (Genesis 39:5).

The story of seduction and desire is as old as history. Scripture doesn't record if Joseph found Potiphar's wife attractive and desirable. That detail could be considered superfluous since he rejected her because he "could not do such a wicked thing and sin against God." The jaded, older Egyptian woman and her desires provide a stunning backdrop for Joseph's purity, making Joseph and his choice to walk in a righteous manner all the clearer and more attractive.

Wednesday

HER LEGACY IN SCRIPTURE

Read Genesis 39:1–23.

1. Imagine the life you think Potiphar's wife might have led. What might drive a woman to be so consumed with lust that she'd attempt such an open seduction?

2. What might Joseph's life have been like if he'd given in to Potiphar's wife?

3. What legacy has sin or a rejection of sin left in your life?

4. Why do you think Potiphar's wife made up the story she told her husband? What does her lie tell you about her as a person?

5. Temptation is a fact of life — even Jesus was tempted. What temptations do you face? How do you deal with them?

Thursday

HER PROMISE

The promise of God is revealed in this story not so much through Potiphar's wife as through Joseph and his response to her. On the surface, if we look at Joseph's situation in this one story, it may appear that he is merely a pawn in the intrigue of the household of Potiphar. As before, he is rejected and tossed aside. He looks like the fool, the loser. However, God's continued blessing is on Joseph. Within the context of this one story, it may look as if Joseph has lost. But in the context of his life, he is nothing but a winner. Indirectly—through Potiphar's wife and her sexual advances toward Joseph—God reveals his promise to bless those who follow him with uprightness (an old-fashioned word, but a good one!) and integrity.

Promises in Scripture

I know, my God, that you test the heart and are pleased with integrity.

—1 CHRONICLES 29:17

Blessed are those
who do not walk in step with the wicked
or stand in the way that sinners take
or sit in the company of mockers,
but who delight in the law of the LORD,
and meditate on his law day and night.

—PSALM 1:1–2

Friday

HER LEGACY OF PRAYER

*Create in me a pure heart, O God,
and renew a steadfast spirit within me.*

—PSALM 51:10

REFLECT ON: Genesis 39.

PRAISE GOD: Because he not only shows us what is right, but he
gives us the strength to resist temptation.

OFFER THANKS: That he invites us to enjoy an intimate relationship
with himself rather than the empty pleasures this
world offers.

CONFESS: Any tendency toward becoming emotionally or physically involved in an off-limits relationship or any tendency to covet what does not belong to you.

ASK GOD: To help you break the habit of fantasizing about relationships you wish you had.

Lift Your Heart

We know what happened to Joseph after he was falsely accused,
but we don't know anything about Potiphar's wife. Write
a short account from your own imagination, entitled "Whatever
Became of Potiphar's Wife?" You can give her a happy ending or a
sad one, just make sure it's believable. Try to put yourself in the story.
You could be Potiphar's wife, her mother, her maid, her little sister,
or whatever character you dream up. Does anything hit you as you
ponder her story's conclusion?

---

*Lord, I don't want my soul to feed on empty pleasures, to long for
what belongs to someone else. Instead, increase my hunger for you
and create in me a pure heart, one that you will find irresistibly
beautiful.*

The Mothers of Moses

Jochebed

HER NAME MEANS
"The Lord Is Glory"

HER CHARACTER: Her fierce love for her son, coupled with her faith, enabled her to act heroically in the midst of great oppression.

HER SORROW: To live in bondage as a slave.

HER JOY: That God not only preserved the son she surrendered to him but that he restored her child to her.

KEY SCRIPTURES: Exodus 2:1–10; Hebrews 11:23

Pharaoh's Daughter

HER CHARACTER: The Jewish people honor men and women whom they designate as "righteous Gentiles." These are people who, though nonbelievers, have assisted God's people in some significant way. Surely, Pharaoh's daughter should top the list of righteous Gentiles, courageously and compassionately delivering a child from death, a child who would one day act as Israel's great deliverer.

HER SORROW: That her adopted son, whom she had taken care of for forty years, had to flee his home in Egypt in order to escape Pharaoh's wrath.

KEY SCRIPTURE: Exodus 2:1–10

Monday

THEIR STORY

Three hundred years after the death of the patriarch Joseph, a baby boy was born in Egypt, his lusty cries muffled by a woman's sobs. Jochebed's heart was a tangle of joy and fear. This son, his fingers forming a tiny fist against her breast, was so striking a child she hardly believed he was hers. Tenderly she raised the small hand to her mouth, pressing its warmth to her lips. Her gesture calmed them both. She could feel the stiffness in her back dissolving, her muscles relaxing as she watched the night shadows evaporate in the morning's light.

Slave though she was, she was yet a Levite, a woman who belonged to the God of Abraham and Sarah, of Isaac and Rebekah, of Jacob, Rachel, and Leah. She knew the stories. She believed the promises. God was faithful. Hadn't her people already grown as numerous as the sand of the sea, just as he said they would?

In fact, the Israelites were so numerous that the pharaohs feared they might one day welcome an invading army and betray the nation from within. Over time, the Egyptians had tightened their grip, finally enslaving the Israelites, until Pharaoh's paranoia produced an even greater evil—a command to murder each Hebrew male child emerging from the womb. But the Hebrew midwives feared God more than the king and refused to follow his orders, excusing themselves by claiming that Hebrew women were stronger than Egyptian women, giving birth before the midwives even arrived.

So Pharaoh commanded his soldiers to search out and smother every newborn male in the waters of the Nile. Jochebed could hear the screams of the mothers echoing regularly across the Hebrew camp as their children were torn from them. Her arms tightened around her own child as he slept quietly against her breast. This one, she vowed, would never be fodder for the Egyptian river god. She and her husband, Amram, would pray. They would plan. And they would trust God to help them.

For three months, as long as she dared, she hid the infant, managing to keep Miriam and three-year-old Aaron quiet about their new baby brother. Finally, she acted on an idea that had been growing in her mind. Pharaoh had commanded her to consign her son to the Nile River. All right then. Her own hands would put him into the water.

Remembering how God had spared the child Isaac on the mountain of sacrifice, she bent down and laid her son in a basket of papyrus, waterproofed with tar and pitch. Then, with a whispered prayer and a last caress, she wiped her eyes, begging God to preserve her baby from the crocodiles that swarmed the river.

She could not bear to watch as the child drifted away from her. Instead, young Miriam kept vigil, following at a distance to see what would become of him.

Soon Pharaoh's daughter arrived at the riverbank with some of her attendants. Spotting the basket among the reeds, she sent her slave girl to fetch it. As soon as she beheld the brown-eyed baby, she loved him. The river had brought her a child whom she would cherish as her own. She could not save all the innocent children, but she could spare one mother's son.

Was she surprised when a young slave girl, Miriam, approached, asking whether she could go after a Hebrew woman to nurse the baby for her? Did she suspect the truth when Jochebed gathered the boy in her arms, this time as his nursemaid?

Whatever was in her mind, Pharaoh's daughter named the child Moses, saying, "I drew him out of the water." For the next forty years, she educated him, a prince in the courts of Pharaoh himself.

God kept Moses safe in the midst of extraordinary evil and danger — first in crocodile-infested waters and then when he was growing up right under Pharaoh's nose. And he used the Egyptians to protect and educate him in ways that must have made Moses even more effective in his eventual role as his people's deliverer.

Year after year, Jochebed would surely have reflected on the marvelous faithfulness of God. Her ingenuity, courage, and faith should inspire even the most weak-kneed among us.

Two women — a slave and a princess — preserved the life of Israel's future deliverer and so preserved the entire Jewish race.

Tuesday

THEIR LIFE AND TIMES

BASKETS

*S*uch an ordinary object, used to such extraordinary purpose. Imagine with what love and care Jochebed coated the papyrus basket with tar and pitch before placing her precious son within it. Few baskets throughout the centuries likely received as loving and careful a touch.

Baskets were just one of the many types of vessels used to store and carry various items in the ancient world. In the home, women used baskets to store household items as well as fruit and bread. Brick makers carried their clay in baskets. Travelers used them to carry the supplies they needed for their journey. Priests in Israel used baskets to store the bread and wafers that were a part of worship in the tabernacle (Exodus 29:3, 23, 32).

Typically made from some sort of plant material—leaves, twigs, or stalks—baskets came in a variety of shapes and sizes. The smallest could be carried in one hand. Baskets just a bit larger were carried on the back or on the head and were often used to hold provisions on a trip. The disciples used twelve of these large baskets to gather up the leftovers at the feeding of the five thousand (Matthew 14:20). An even larger basket was used to let Paul escape out of a window in the wall at Damascus (Acts 9:25), so it must have been quite large and sturdy.

God's use of the ordinary to bring about the extraordinary is as much in evidence here in the early events of Exodus as anywhere in Scripture. His tendency to bring about his will through ordinary items, ordinary people, and ordinary events is no less at work today than it was in Jochebed's time. If you look for the signs of his presence, you are sure to discover them.

Wednesday

THEIR LEGACY IN SCRIPTURE

Read Exodus 2:1–10 and Hebrews 11:23.

1. What can you learn about Jochebed as a person from what she does at each point in this story?

2. Why do you think Pharaoh's daughter wanted to keep the baby as her own?

3. Why do you suppose her father (and possibly her husband, if she had one) let Pharaoh's daughter break the law and adopt this foreign baby?

4. Hebrews 11:23 says Moses' parents acted "by faith." What part does faith play in child rearing? In what ways have you had to choose between faith and fear as a mother?

5. Where was God in this story? What does this say about God in your story?

Thursday

THEIR PROMISE

*M*oses' mother, Jochebed, had one thing in mind when hiding her son and leaving him in a basket in the river. Her goal was to preserve his life for one more day, one more hour, one more moment. She could not have known how God planned to work in her life or in the life of her son. Nor did she realize he was putting into place a divine plan to rescue his people from the very oppression she was resisting.

God's ways are beautiful in the extreme. He uses the devoted, intense love of a mother for her child to bring freedom to an entire race. Like Jochebed, our goal should be to hang on, trusting that God has his own purpose at work and that we and our children are part of it.

Promises in Scripture

The plans of the LORD stand firm forever,
*   the purposes of his heart through all generations....*
The eyes of the LORD are on those who fear him,
*   on those whose hope is in his unfailing love.*

—PSALM 33:11, 18

"For I know the plans I have for you," declares the LORD, "plans to prosper you and not to harm you, plans to give you hope and a future. Then you will call upon me and come and pray to me, and I will listen to you. You will seek me and find me when you seek me with all your heart. I will be found by you," declares the LORD.

—JEREMIAH 29:11 – 14

Friday

THEIR LEGACY OF PRAYER

When she could hide him no longer, she got a papyrus basket for him and coated it with tar and pitch. Then she placed the child in it and put it among the reeds along the bank of the Nile.

—EXODUS 2:3

REFLECT ON: Exodus 2:1–10.

PRAISE GOD: That even the worst enemies we encounter are weak compared to him.

OFFER THANKS: For God's power to save.

CONFESS: Any failure to trust God for the lives of our children.

ASK GOD: To help you be an encouragement to another mother who is concerned about her children's well-being.

Lift Your Heart

Find another mother, perhaps a teenage mom or a friend who is having difficulty with her own children right now. Put together a gift basket for her, filled with small gifts like a scented candle, dried fruit, a coffee cup, and some small cards inscribed with encouraging Scripture verses. Tell her you will be praying for each of her children by name every day for the next couple of months. Don't expect her to confide in you, but if she does, cherish what she tells you by keeping it confidential and letting it shape your prayers.

Father, thank you for the gift and calling of motherhood. Help me to remember that my love for my children is merely a reflection of your own love for them. With that in mind, give me grace to surrender my anxiety. Replace it with a sense of trust and calm as I learn to depend on you for everything. Amen.

Miriam

HER NAME MAY MEAN

"Bitterness"

HER CHARACTER: Even as a young girl, she showed fortitude and wisdom. A leader of God's people at a crucial moment in history, she led the celebration after crossing the Red Sea and spoke God's word to his people, sharing their forty-year journey through the wilderness.

HER SORROW: That she was struck with leprosy for her pride and insubordination and was denied entry into the Promised Land.

HER JOY: To have played an instrumental role in the deliverance of God's people, a nation she loved.

KEY SCRIPTURES: Exodus 2:1–10; 15:20–21; Numbers 12:1–15

Monday

HER STORY

*S*even days, I must stay outside the camp of my people, an old woman, fenced in by memories of what has been.

How could I forget our years in Egypt, the cries of the mothers whose children were murdered or the moans of our brothers as they worked themselves to death? I have only to shut my eyes and see—the wall of water, the soldiers chasing us through the sea, the sounds of their noisy drowning, and, finally, the silence and the peace. How I miss the singing of the women I led that day, dancing at the sea's edge, praising God for hurling our enemies into the deep waters, certain we would never see them again.

But we did see them again—our enemies, though not the Egyptians. We let ingratitude stalk and rob us of our blessings. We preferred the garlic and leeks of Egypt, the food of our slavery, to the manna the good God gave us. Enslaved to fear, we refused to enter the land of promise.

Time and again Moses and Aaron and I exhorted the people to stand firm, to have faith, to obey God. But there came a day when Aaron and I could stand with our brother no longer. Instead we spoke against him and his Cushite wife. What part did she, a foreigner to our suffering, have in the promise? So we challenged Moses. Had the Lord spoken only through him? All Israel knew better. We deserved an equal share in his authority, an equal say in how to lead the people.

But the Lord who speaks also heard our complaint and summoned the three of us to stand before him at the Tent of Meeting. He addressed Aaron and me with terrible words.

When the cloud of his presence finally lifted, I was a leper. I could see the horror on every face turned toward me. Aaron begged Moses to forgive us both. And Moses cried out to the Lord to heal me.

The Lord replied, "If her father had spit in her face, would she not have been in disgrace for seven days? Confine her outside the camp for seven days; after that she can be brought back." Then at least I knew my banishment was temporary; my disease would be healed.

Now I see that my enemies were not merely buried in the sea but in my own heart as well. Still, God has let me live, and I believe he will heal me. Though he brings grief, he will yet show compassion. One thing I know, he has hurled my pride into the sea and for that I will also sing his praises.

Though Scripture doesn't reveal Miriam's thoughts or the attitude of her heart after she was chastened for complaining about Moses, it is not unreasonable to think she repented during the seven days of her banishment. After all, it's not easy for a person of faith, however flawed, to hear God speaking as though he were spitting on her and still to hold fast to her error.

Perhaps Miriam, and the nation itself, needed a shocking rebuke in order to recognize the seriousness of a sin that threatened the unity of God's people.

Why, you might ask, wasn't Aaron similarly afflicted for his sin? Perhaps because Miriam seemed to be the ringleader. Perhaps, also, because God didn't want the worship of the tabernacle to be disrupted by Aaron's absence as high priest.

The last we hear of Miriam is that she died and was buried in Kadesh Barnea, not all that far from where Hagar, another slave woman, had encountered an angel in the wilderness so many years earlier. Like her brothers Moses and Aaron, Miriam died shortly before the Israelites ended their forty-year sojourn in the desert. She, too, was prevented from entering the Promised Land.

Still, like them, Miriam is one of the great heroes of our faith. As a young girl, she helped save the infant Moses, Israel's future deliverer. Herself a prophetess, she exhorted and encouraged God's people and led the singing of the first psalm ever recorded in Scripture. Yet, strong though she was, she, like all of us, sinned against God and suffered a punishment designed to bring her to repentance.

Tuesday

DANCING

*I*n biblical times, people danced to celebrate happy events and to praise God. Dancing in Scripture is always linked to joy and happiness. The presence of mourning means the absence of dancing (Lamentations 5:15), and there is a time for both (Ecclesiastes 3:4).

The very first mention of dancing in Scripture is when Miriam led the Israelite women in a dance that celebrated God's miraculous defeat of the Egyptians at the Red Sea. Imagine, if you can, the emotions of these women as they walked (perhaps ran?) between the walls of water of the Red Sea, Egyptian chariots right behind them. Fearful for their lives, they breathlessly reached the eastern shore, turning around to see the waters come crashing in to drown the Egyptians and their horses—a narrow, frightening escape.

Then, quickly, fear gave way to a thrill of excitement. They were free! When Miriam went by with a tambourine, singing a song of praise to God, the women's feet moved to her rhythm, their voices joined her song, and they danced!

The Hebrews danced in worship, often in praise of God for his deliverance from enemies (1 Samuel 18:6; Psalm 149:3). They danced to celebrate happy events, like weddings and the return of loved ones (Luke 15:25). Hebrew men and women didn't dance together. The men usually danced alone, as David did before the ark (2 Samuel 6:14), while the women danced together.

There is some evidence that dancing was a part of the worship of the early Christian church. But according to several early Christian writers, it soon degenerated and no longer expressed a pure praise of the Lord. Before long it was banned.

Just as Miriam and the women couldn't help but dance with joy, so when God does a wonderful work in our lives we sometimes respond in much the same manner: Our faces break into smiles, our hands are lifted up, and our feet can't remain still! Certainly the God who created the human body delights in the pure use of that beautiful instrument to offer praise to him.

Wednesday

HER LEGACY IN SCRIPTURE

Read Exodus 15:19–21.

1. Describe what you think Miriam and the other women of Israel were thinking and feeling as they walked through the Red Sea. Why did they dance?

2. Have you ever been that joyful? If so, when? How did you express your joy? If not, why do you suppose that's the case?

Read Numbers 12:1–15.

3. Why do you think Miriam and Aaron attacked Moses? What other issues did they have besides his Cushite (non-Hebrew) wife?

4. What do you think Miriam was thinking and feeling when she was outside the camp for those seven days? What would go through your mind in that situation?

5. Even when we are forgiven, we sometimes have to pay a price for our sin. What sin have you had to pay a penalty for? How do you feel about that situation now: Forgiven? Still guilty? Angry?

Thursday

HER PROMISE

*M*iriam's story offers an extraordinary example of God's willingness to forgive those who sin. Though she had to pay the consequences for her actions—seven days of exclusion from the camp and from all those who loved her—she reentered the camp a forgiven woman. Hundreds of years later, she is remembered by the prophet Micah as a leader of Israel with Moses and Aaron (Micah 6:4).

Such liberating forgiveness is available to us as well as to Miriam. God looks with judgment at our sin, waits patiently for our repentance, and then eagerly offers his forgiveness and acceptance. We reenter fellowship with him renewed and clean and forgiven. Our repentance turns a legacy of judgment and punishment into a legacy of forgiveness and worthiness before God.

Promises in Scripture

> *Praise the* LORD, *O my soul,*
> *and forget not all his benefits—*
> *who forgives all your sins.*

—PSALM 103:2–3

> *Who is a God like you,*
> *who pardons sin and forgives transgression?*

—MICAH 7:18

> *If we confess our sins, he is faithful and just and will forgive us our sins and purify us from all unrighteousness.*

—1 JOHN 1:9

Friday

HER LEGACY OF PRAYER

Sing to the LORD,
  for he is highly exalted.
The horse and its rider
  he has hurled into the sea.

—EXODUS 15:21

REFLECT ON: Numbers 12:1–15.

PRAISE GOD: That he disciplines those he loves, every child who belongs to him.

OFFER THANKS: That God's anger lasts only for a moment but his favor lasts forever.

CONFESS: Any arrogance that may have crept into your heart, especially as it relates to your role at church or at work.

ASK GOD: To help you remember that discipline is an expression of his love for his children.

Lift Your Heart

If a woman like Miriam could act in a way so displeasing to God, certainly we, too, are capable of sinning, no matter what we have done for him in the past. Take time this week to do some honest soul-searching. If you discover anything displeasing to God, ask for his forgiveness. Don't just whisper a quick prayer and be done with it; let him know your repentance is sincere. Consider collecting a few small stones and then driving to the nearest river, lake, or pond. Take a leisurely walk along the water and tell God again of your sorrow. Then deliberately hurl each stone into the water, remembering Miriam's song of praise. Thank God for delivering you from your sins just as he delivered the Israelites from Pharaoh's pursuing army.

Father, thank you for the times you've brought me up short, for loving me enough to discipline me. Help me to be quick to repent, to see my sin so that you needn't rub my face in it. Then let me experience the joy that comes from receiving your forgiveness.

Rahab

HER CHARACTER: Rahab was both clever and wise. She saw judgment coming and was able to devise an escape plan for herself and her family. As soon as she heard what God had done for the Israelites, she cast her lot with his people, risking her life in an act of faith.

HER SORROW: To see her own people destroyed and her city demolished.

HER JOY: That God had given her, an idolater and prostitute, the opportunity to know him and belong to his people.

KEY SCRIPTURES: Joshua 2:1–21; 6:17–25; Matthew 1:5; Hebrews 11:31; James 2:25

Monday

HER STORY

Jericho may be the world's oldest city. Established nearly six thousand years before Miriam and Moses completed their desert wanderings, its ancient ruins can be found just seventeen miles northeast of Jerusalem. Gateway to Canaan, it was also the home of a prostitute named Rahab, whose house nestled snugly into its thick surrounding walls.

As well as entertaining locals, Rahab welcomed guests from various caravans whose routes crisscrossed Jericho. Men from all over the

East brought news of a swarm of people encamped east of the Jordan. Rahab heard marvelous stories about the exploits of the God of the Israelites—how he had dried up the Red Sea so they could escape their Egyptian slave masters, and how he had given them victory in battle against Sihon and Og, two kings of the Amorites. For forty years the God of the Israelites had trained and toughened them in the desert. Such rumors spread fear in Jericho.

While men talked, another man planned. Moses was dead, and Joshua, son of Nun, had been appointed leader of the Israelites. Nearly forty years earlier Joshua had spied out the land along with Caleb and a group of others, urging the Israelites to take hold of the land of promise. This time there would be no shrinking back. Once the Israelites crossed the Jordan River and destroyed Jericho, the land would open like a melon with the rind peeled back. He could taste the victory.

Joshua sent two spies to Jericho to probe its secrets. The spies soon made their way to Rahab's house, where she hid them beneath stalks of flax drying on the roof. Later that day, Rahab received a message from the king of Jericho, asking her about the spies who had taken refuge in her house.

"Yes, the men came to me, but I did not know where they had come from," she lied to the king's messenger. "At dusk, when it was time to close the city gate, the men left. I don't know which way they went. Go after them quickly. You may catch up with them."

As soon as the king's men left, she hurried to the roof, quickly warning her two guests: "I know that the LORD has given this land to you and that a great fear of you has fallen on us....The LORD your God is God in heaven above and on the earth below. Now then, please swear to me by the LORD that you will show kindness to my family, because I have shown kindness to you. Give me a sure sign that you will spare the lives of my father and mother, my brothers and sisters, and all who belong to them, and that you will save us from death."

To this remarkable statement of faith, the men replied: "Our lives for your lives!" thus sealing the bargain.

Quickly, the two spies handed Rahab a scarlet cord, instructing her to tie it in the window on the side of the house built into the city wall. The invading Israelites would see it and spare everyone inside. Then Rahab instructed the men to hide themselves in the hills for three days until their pursuers abandoned the chase. With that, they slipped out the window and scrambled down the walls of Jericho.

Joshua was smiling long after the spies had left him with their good report. Now was the time to move. He marshaled the people and led them across the Jordan. Though the river was at flood stage, a massive army of Israelites crossed on dry ground. God was with them just as he had been when they left Egypt. Only this time, no one was chasing them — Israel had become the pursuing army, ready for battle!

The news that the waters of the River Jordan had parted for the Israelites terrified the inhabitants of Jericho. Rahab watched anxiously from her window in the wall as the Israelites gathered around the city like a growing storm. Would these fierce warriors with their powerful God remember the scarlet cord? For the thousandth time she reminded her family, especially the little ones, not to take even one step outside the house, lest they perish.

That first day Rahab watched as seven priests carrying an ark led thousands of men around the city. She braced herself, but nothing happened. The next day and the next, for five more days it continued. Then, as the sun was rising on the seventh day, the men of Israel marched again, encircling Jericho seven times. Suddenly, she heard the ram's horn sound and then a thunderous cry, loud enough to split a mountain. The city walls shattered and the Israelites rushed in. Rahab tried to plug her ears to the mayhem outside her home. When the battle of Jericho was over, Rahab and those she loved were spared. Her faith had saved not only herself but her entire household from the terrible judgment decreed for her city.

Jericho's end reminds us of Sodom's. In Sodom, Lot and his daughters were spared; in Jericho, it was Rahab and her family who were spared. But unlike Lot or his wife, Rahab never once hesitated. She is the only woman singled out by name and commended for her faith as part of the great "cloud of witnesses" mentioned in the book of Hebrews. A prostitute living in the midst of an idolatrous people, Rahab was like a brand plucked from the fire. Her own people destroyed, she left everything behind, becoming an ancestor of King David and, therefore, one of Jesus' ancestors as well.

Rahab's story is a dramatic one. It shows us that God's grace accepts no boundaries. The red cord that saved Rahab and her family reminds us of the red blood of Jesus, who still saves us today, and of Isaiah's words, that "though your sins may be as scarlet, they shall be as white as snow." Rahab put her faith in the God of Israel and was not disappointed.

Tuesday

HER LIFE AND TIMES

CITY WALLS

*J*ericho is probably best known today for its enormous walls, walls that fell because of the faith of the people of Israel (Hebrews 11:30). A wall around a city was its chief distinguishing mark. Anything without a wall was merely a village whose inhabitants would run to the nearest walled city for protection during a battle or war.

Rahab lived in a house on the wall of Jericho. She probably had a view not only of the city itself but also of the area outside of the protective walls. This view, which gave her the perfect vantage point for spotting potential customers as they entered and left Jericho, may have given her an advantage in running her business of prostitution.

Homes, businesses, watchtowers, archer positions—all could be built on top of or within walls that were as much as twenty to thirty feet thick. The stronger the system of walls around a city (some cities had both an inner and an outer wall), the more defensible the city was against invaders who came across the plains.

Most walls of major cities were built of huge stones and mortar. Some stones of the wall of the temple in Jerusalem still exist. Their dimensions: thirty feet long, eight feet wide, and three and a half feet high. Each stone weighs an unbelievable eighty tons!

But no stone was large enough to protect the city of Jericho from the power of God through his people; no battering rams were needed to breach its walls. All that was necessary was the faith of God's people in what he said he would do. And the walls came tumbling down!

Wednesday

HER LEGACY IN SCRIPTURE

Read Joshua 2:1–21.

1. God commanded the complete destruction of Jericho and other Canaanite cities because of their extreme sins, including child sacrifice, shrine prostitution, and injustice of the powerful against the weak. What does it say about him, then, that out of the whole city he spared a prostitute and her family?

2. Rahab betrayed her city. What reasons did she give for doing this? Can you think of any additional reasons she might have had?

3. Why do you think the spies made a deal with her?

Read James 2:25–26.

4. James said Rahab was an example of the principle that real faith is linked to action. How did she demonstrate this?

5. What risks have you been willing to take for your faith? What risks haven't you been willing to take for your faith? Why?

Thursday

HER PROMISE

The story of Rahab reveals again God's willingness to use the less than perfect, the outcast, what we might see as the unsuitable to accomplish his holy purposes. Throughout Scripture, with what can almost be seen as divine humor, God chooses a stutterer to speak for him (Moses), an infertile woman to be the mother of a nation (Sarah), a weakling to defend him (Gideon), a forgettable youngest son to be the most unforgettable king of his people (David), an unknown youngster to be the mother of his son (Mary), and a persecutor to take the gospel to the nations (Paul).

God doesn't wait for us to become spotlessly clean or totally mature in our faith in order to use us. Instead, he takes ordinary, willing people and accomplishes the extraordinary, both in their lives and in the lives of those around them. As he did with Rahab, he promises to use us, and through that experience to perfect us.

Promises in Scripture

> *He gives strength to the weary*
> *and increases the power of the weak.*
> *Even youths grow tired and weary,*
> *and young men stumble and fall;*
> *but those who hope in the LORD*
> *will renew their strength.*
> *They will soar on wings like eagles;*
> *they will run and not grow weary,*
> *they will walk and not be faint.*

> —ISAIAH 40:29–31

> *When they saw the courage of Peter and John and realized that they were unschooled, ordinary men, they were astonished and they took note that these men had been with Jesus.*

> —ACTS 4:13

> *When I am weak, then I am strong.*

> —2 CORINTHIANS 12:10

Friday

HER LEGACY OF PRAYER

I know that the LORD has given this land to you and that a great fear of you has fallen on us, so that all who live in this country are melting in fear because of you. We have heard how the LORD dried up the water of the Red Sea for you when you came out of Egypt.... Now then, please swear to me by the LORD that you will show kindness to my family, because I have shown kindness to you.

—JOSHUA 2:9–10, 12

REFLECT ON: Joshua 2:1–21.

PRAISE GOD: For giving women key roles in his plan of salvation.

OFFER THANKS: That no one, including ourselves, is beyond the reach of grace.

CONFESS: Any unwillingness to take risks in order to follow God.

ASK GOD: To increase your awe of him.

Lift Your Heart

Use a small red ribbon as a bookmark, tie a red ribbon around the pot of a favorite plant, or place some decorative red roping around a dried floral arrangement to remind you of the vital importance of living by faith. Each time you notice your scarlet cord, let it remind you of the lengths Jesus went to rescue you. Ask him, as Rahab asked the Israelites, to watch over and protect every member of your family. Say a silent prayer, asking God to increase your faith. Faith, after all, is what your life and the vitality of your relationship with God depend on.

Father, I praise you for the wonderful and unexpected ways you have acted in my life. Let the knowledge of your faithfulness increase my courage to take the risks that faith demands.

Deborah

HER NAME MEANS
"Honey Bee"

HER CHARACTER: Her vision of the world was shaped not by the political situation of her day but by her relationship with God. Though women in the ancient world did not usually become political leaders, Deborah was just the leader Israel needed—a prophetess who heard God and believed him and whose courage aroused the people, enabling them to throw off foreign oppression.

HER SORROW: That her people had sunk into despair because of their idolatry, forgetting God's promises and the faith of their ancestors.

HER JOY: That God turned the enemy's strength on its head, bestowing power to the weak and blessing the land with peace for forty years.

KEY SCRIPTURE: Judges 4–5

Monday

HER STORY

Jericho, gateway to Canaan, had lain in ruins for two hundred years. From there, the Israelites had swept across the country like a storm of locusts, devouring everything in their path. But the native peoples had somehow managed to survive, and like well-rooted weeds, their idolatry spread until it began to strangle Israel's faith.

Rahab and Joshua were the palest of memories now, and the slaves-turned-warriors were once again underdogs, oppressed for twenty years by a coalition of Canaanite rulers, whose chief warrior was Sisera. His nine hundred iron-plated chariots terrified the ill-armed Israelite people, threatening to sweep over them with invincible force. Small wonder no one challenged him.

Sisera must have felt smugly secure, especially since Israel was now led by a woman. But his military calculations failed to account for one key variable: the strategic power of that woman's faith. Deborah was a prophetess who held court under a palm tree several miles northwest of Jericho. Though much of Israel was divided and dispirited, she refused to lose heart. How could she forget God's faithfulness, living so close to ruined Jericho?

She summoned Barak, a Hebrew from the north, and told him plainly: "The LORD, the God of Israel, commands you: 'Go, take with you ten thousand men of Naphtali and Zebulun and lead the way to Mount Tabor. I will lure Sisera, the commander of Jabin's army, with his chariots and his troops to the Kishon River and give him into your hands.'"

But, like every other man of Israel, Barak was terrified of Sisera, and he refused to comply unless one condition was met: Deborah must accompany him in battle. She would be his talisman in the fight. "Very well," she replied, "I will go with you. But because of the way you are going about this, the honor will not be yours, for the LORD will hand Sisera over to a woman."

Hearing of the plot, Sisera led his troops and chariots to the Kishon Wadi, a dry riverbed, determined to crush the uprising. But his very strength turned against him as rain swelled the valley to floodtide. Suddenly, nine hundred iron chariots became a huge liability. No matter how furiously the soldiers flogged their horses, urging them onward, oozing mud held them. They became easy targets for Barak's troops sweeping down from Mount Tabor, putting every man but Sisera to the sword.

Once again, God had heard his people's cries and had sent a deliverer—this time a woman whose faith stilled the nattering voices of doubt and timidity so that the people could hear the one Voice that mattered. On their day of victory, Deborah and Barak sang this song:

When the princes in Israel take the lead,
    when the people willingly offer themselves—
    praise the LORD!
Hear this, you kings! Listen, you rulers!
    I will sing to the LORD, I will sing;
    I will make music to the LORD, the God of Israel....
Village life in Israel ceased,
    ceased until I, Deborah, arose,
    arose a mother in Israel.

Judges 5:2–3, 7

Indeed, a mother in Israel had arisen, a woman whose strong faith gave birth to hope and freedom and a peace that lasted forty years. Never again would the Canaanites join forces against Israel. Like an ancient Joan of Arc, Deborah arose and called the people to battle, leading them out of idolatry and restoring their dignity as God's chosen ones.

Tuesday

HER LIFE AND TIMES

WOMEN AS LEADERS

While women leaders were uncommon in Israelite society, they were not unheard of. In this time of the judges, when Israel was spiritually malnourished, in a state of civic disorder, and oppressed by its enemies, Deborah stepped up to the challenge. Her leadership role probably evolved gradually, as her wisdom became known. When God spoke to Deborah, she immediately responded by calling to Barak to lead the people in a battle against their oppressor of twenty years. Barak's reluctance to go without Deborah starkly revealed Israel's lack of strong male leadership.

Deborah was the only female to hold the position of judge in Israel, but she was not the only female prophet noted in the Bible. Several others are listed: Miriam (Exodus 15:20), Huldah (2 Kings 22:14), Noadiah (Nehemiah 6:14), Anna (Luke 2:36), and four unmarried daughters of Philip the evangelist (Acts 21:9).

Scripture describes Deborah as "a prophetess, the wife of Lappidoth." Interestingly, when Deborah described herself, she didn't use terms like prophet or wife or judge or general or leader or any other term of influence and power. She described herself as "a mother in Israel" (Judges 5:7). Her position was one of mother not only to her own biological children, but mother to all the children of Israel. Though they had forgotten not only who they were but also whom they served, their mother Deborah reminded them and led them in a victory procession to peace.

Perhaps you're not in an influential position of authority—you can still be a mother to your children and the children in your neighborhood and lead them in the right direction. Perhaps you have little power in your job or position—you can still be a mother to those around you and inspire them to righteousness. Perhaps your life allows little time or opportunity for significant positions of leadership—you can still be a mother in your sphere, whether big or small, wielding influence far beyond your lowly position. You can be like Deborah, used of God to be a mother in Israel.

Wednesday

HER LEGACY IN SCRIPTURE

Read Judges 4:1–10; 5:7.

1. What do you think life was like for a family in Israel at this time (Judges 4:1–3)?

2. What was Barak afraid of? Why would having Deborah along alleviate those fears?

3. In Judges 4:9, Deborah talks about honor going to a woman instead of to the men. When a woman succeeds today, how do the men around her typically respond? Why?

4. Which of Deborah's characteristics would you most like to have? What would you do if you had that characteristic?

5. What can you do to become more like Deborah?

Thursday

HER PROMISE

*G*odly Deborah has been an encouragement to women throughout the centuries. When women feel confined or mistreated, when
they are unsure of what is right or which way to proceed, when
they are entering unknown territory, when they feel overlooked or
ignored—they gain stability and help from remembering Deborah.

Whatever Deborah had is available to you today. Her wisdom is
discovered in the Scriptures. Her confidence in God is found in a
relationship with him. Her bravery is achievable when you put your
trust in God and his promises. Her inner strength and calm leadership are characteristic of confidence not in herself but in her God.
All Deborah offered to Israel she offers to you as an example of a
woman willing to be used by God.

Promises in Scripture

Village life in Israel ceased,
ceased until I, Deborah, arose,
arose a mother in Israel.

—JUDGES 5:7

Some trust in chariots and some in horses,
but we trust in the name of the LORD our God.

—PSALM 20:7

Who among you fears the LORD
and obeys the word of his servant?
Let those who walk in the dark,
who have no light,
trust in the name of the LORD
and rely on their God.

—ISAIAH 50:10

Friday

HER LEGACY OF PRAYER

Hear this, you kings! Listen, you rulers!
  I will sing to the LORD, I will sing;
  I will make music to the LORD, the God of Israel.

—JUDGES 5:3

REFLECT ON: Judges 4.

PRAISE GOD: For speaking clearly to his people.

OFFER THANKS: That God gives prophets to the church, women as
                 well as men.

CONFESS: Anything that makes you reluctant to listen for God's
                 voice.

ASK GOD: To help you discern his voice.

Lift Your Heart

*I*t's difficult, even unpleasant, to listen to two pieces of music
at once. Likewise, it's hard to listen to God's voice at the same
time you are listening to voices of confusion, discouragement, and
condemnation. Deborah's peace and confidence as a leader stemmed
in part from her ability to hear God clearly. This week ask the Holy
Spirit to help you distinguish God's voice from all the background
noise. Ask for grace to discipline your thoughts in order to hear God
better. As you pray, put on some quiet background music to remind
you to tune in to the one Voice worth listening to.

Lord, I want to hear your voice. Help me to recognize and resist all
the phony voices that masquerade as yours. Help me to distinguish
yours from all the others. Make me a woman who both listens and
speaks your Word.

Jael

HER NAME MEANS

"A Wild or Mountain Goat"

HER CHARACTER: Decisive and courageous, she seized the opportunity to slay an enemy of God's people.

HER JOY: To be lauded by Deborah and Barak for her part in a decisive victory.

KEY SCRIPTURE: Judges 4–5

Monday

HER STORY

*J*ael watched uneasily through the flaps of her tent as clouds swept the blue from the sky and rain fell like a shroud across the horizon. Sisera, she knew, had marched to Tabor. *But what good were iron chariots in a flooded valley?* she wondered. Yet the Israelites were poorly armed, with little chance of prevailing. Still, she remembered the stories of Moses and the people he had led across the wilderness. Had their God, she wonderd, been asleep these many years?

The sight of a man running, then stumbling toward her interrupted her thoughts. A soldier fleeing? Was he Israelite or Canaanite? His identity might reveal the way the winds of battle were blowing. She went out to meet him, surprised to find that Sisera himself was approaching, dirty and bleeding.

"Come, my lord, come right in. Don't be afraid," she welcomed him.

"I'm thirsty," he said. "Please give me some water." Instead Jael opened a skin of milk and gave him a drink.

"Stand in the doorway of the tent," he told her. "If someone comes by and asks you, 'Is anyone here?' say 'No.'"

As soon as Sisera fell into an exhausted asleep, Jael picked up a tent peg and hammer. Her arm was steady, her aim sure. Hadn't she been in charge of the tents all these years? Quickly, she thrust the peg through his temple and into the ground. Like a piece of canvas fixed in place, Sisera, the great general, lay dead, slain by a woman's hand, just as Deborah had prophesied to Barak.

Was Jael a hero, an opportunist, or merely a treacherous woman? It is difficult to know. She and her husband, Heber, were Kenites, members of a nomadic tribe whose survival depended on its ability to stay clear of local disputes. Her husband had made his peace with the Canaanites despite his descent from Hobab, Moses' brother-in-law. Perhaps ancient ties had no longer seemed expedient, considering the power of the Canaanite rulers. But Jael may have believed in Israel's God. Or perhaps she merely wanted to curry favor with the Israelites, the day's clear winners. Certainly Barak and Deborah approved of her, singing:

Most blessed of women be Jael,
    the wife of Heber the Kenite,
    most blessed of tent-dwelling women.
He asked for water, and she gave him milk;
    in a bowl fit for nobles she brought him curdled milk.
Her hand reached for the tent peg,
    her right hand for the workman's hammer.
She struck Sisera, she crushed his head,
    she shattered and pierced his temple.
At her feet he sank,
    he fell; there he lay.
At her feet he sank, he fell;
    where he sank, there he fell—dead.

Judges 5:24–27

Jael's treachery and Deborah's gloating strike us as bloodthirsty, all the more so because we don't usually attribute such behavior to women. But by the standards of ancient warfare, both were heroes. Both were decisive and courageous women who helped God's people at a critical moment in history.

Tuesday

HER LIFE AND TIMES

BOTTLES

When Sisera asked for a drink of water and Jael instead gave him milk, she was offering the best of the house. People of the area prized this drink, which was made by putting goat's milk into an old skin bottle and shaking it. The milk then curdled, or fermented, when mixed with the bacteria that remained in the skin bottle from a prior use.

But what on earth is a skin bottle?

Nomadic desert peoples, who were frequently on the move, found skin flasks much more useful than clay bottles, which broke easily. Women sewed goat or lamb skins together with the hairy part of the skin on the outside, then sealed them so they would hold water, milk, wine, or other liquids.

Hagar carried a skin of water into the desert with her (Genesis 21:14–15). Jael offered Sisera a drink of milk from a skin bottle (Judges 4:19). Hannah brought a skin of wine along when delivering her son, Samuel, to Eli the priest (1 Samuel 1:24). David carried a skin of wine to his brothers (1 Samuel 16:20). Jesus talked about not putting new wine into old, brittle wineskins (Matthew 9:17).

Christ's decree not to put new wine in old wineskins has, of course, significant meaning for us today. Are your mind and heart like an old wineskin—brittle, hard, tough? Ready to burst when faced with new ideas or new ways of doing things? Or are your mind and heart supple, soft, and flexible like a new skin? Are you open to learning new things about your community of believers? About yourself? About your God?

Wednesday

Read Judges 4:11–22; 5:4–5, 24–27.

1. What was God's role in these events?

2. Use three adjectives to describe Jael before she kills Sisera. Pretend you don't know what she's going to do and describe her just from 4:17–20.

3. Why do you think Jael did what she did? Do you see her as brave, fearful, desperate, treacherous? How much do you think her life experience in a brutal culture had to do with it?

4. Why do you think Deborah praised Jael for such a savage deed?

5. What do you think God wants us to take away from the story of Deborah, Barak, and Jael and all of the death woven within it?

Thursday

HER PROMISE

*B*ehind the story of Jael and the death of Sisera is a God who promised never to forget his people and who holds to that promise. When hope seems dim and the prospect of victory seems close to impossible, God is at work, bringing about his plan.

The people of Israel during the time of the judges must have worn God to exasperation with their continual wavering. When times were good, they easily forgot God and went their own way. But as soon as times got tough, they went running to him for deliverance.

Sound like anyone you know? The story of the wavering of God's people continues even today. We so easily move forward on our own, thinking we can handle it all, until we run up against something too hard for us. Only then do we run to God for help.

But what an amazing God he is. Always there. Always willing to rescue us when we call. Always willing to forgive.

Promises in Scripture

When they cried out to you again, you heard from heaven, and in your compassion you delivered them time after time.

—NEHEMIAH 9:28

I love you, O LORD, my strength....
I call to the LORD, who is worthy of praise,
and I am saved from my enemies.

—PSALM 18:1, 3

We were under great pressure, far beyond our ability to endure, so that we despaired even of life. Indeed, in our hearts we felt the sentence of death. But this happened that we might not rely on ourselves but on God, who raises the dead. He has delivered us from such a deadly peril, and he will deliver us. On him we have set our hope that he will continue to deliver us, as you help us by your prayers.

—2 CORINTHIANS 1:8–11

Friday

HER LEGACY OF PRAYER

Most blessed of women be Jael....
She struck Sisera, she crushed his head,
*   she shattered and pierced his temple.*
At her feet he sank,
*   he fell; there he lay.*

—JUDGES 5:24–27

REFLECT ON: Judges 5.

PRAISE GOD: That he defeats the enemies of our soul.

OFFER THANKS: That we can be instruments of deliverance for others.

CONFESS: Any tendency toward passivity in your struggle
against sin and Satan.

ASK GOD: To give you wisdom and discernment in the spiritual
battle.

Lift Your Heart

*S*ometimes we are naive about the kinds of spiritual struggles that we face as Christians. Ephesians 6 talks about the
importance of putting on the full armor of God in order to successfully engage in battle. This week take some time for a wardrobe
check—make sure you aren't missing anything vital, without which
you will be more vulnerable to attack. Here's a quick checklist for
the well-dressed spiritual warrior:

The Belt of Truth—Have any small dishonesties crept into your
life?
The Breastplate of Righteousness—Are you cooperating with
grace to become more Christlike?
The Shoes of the Gospel of Peace—The gospel reconciles us to
God and others. Are you willing to receive it, live by it, and
share it?

The Shield of Faith—Are you responding to life with faith or in a way that shows you really don't think God is quite as loving or as powerful as he says he is?

The Helmet of Salvation—Salvation is a gift. But like any gift, it has to be received.

The Sword of the Spirit—God's Word wounds the enemy and thwarts his purposes. Reading and praying through Scripture helps us take the offensive.

Lord, help me to be ready so that any moment I can stand against the enemy and even deal a decisive blow in the battle. Give me courage, discernment, and wisdom and help me to stay close to you in the midst of the fray.

Delilah

HER CHARACTER: A prostitute whose nationality is unknown, she used her beauty to betray her lover and enrich herself.

HER SORROW: That Samson lied to her, making her look foolish on three different occasions.

HER JOY: That she overpowered one of history's most powerful men, handing him over to his enemy, the Philistines.

KEY SCRIPTURE: Judges 16:4–22

Monday

HER STORY

Her teeth gleamed white in the dusky light as a smile parted lips soft and smooth as a scarlet ribbon. Earrings glinted gold as she threw back her head and laughed out loud. Fortune had come knocking on her door that day. No lover had ever paid Delilah as well as Samson would.

The Philistine kings hated the long-haired strongman who had set their fields afire and slain a thousand of their countrymen. Each had offered Delilah an incredible sum—eleven hundred shekels of silver! She had merely to deliver the secret of Samson's strength. His would be no match for hers, a strength born of beauty and schooled in the arts of love. Weakened by passion, he would tell her everything she needed to know.

"If anyone ties me with seven fresh thongs that have not been dried, I'll become as any other man," he replied to her persistent probing. Hiding a few Philistines in the room for good measure, Delilah waited until he slept and then carefully wrapped him with the thongs and exclaimed, "Samson, the Philistines are upon you!" But he had outsmarted her, snapping the cords as his enemies fled.

Like a man toying with a kitten, Samson repeated the ruse twice, tricking Delilah with crazy stories about new ropes and braided hair. Finally Delilah confronted him, "How can you say, 'I love you,' when you won't confide in me? This is the third time you have made a fool of me and haven't told me the secret of your great strength." Worn down by her nagging, Samson gave in.

"No razor has ever been used on my head," he confided, "because I have been a Nazirite set apart to God since birth. If my head were shaved, my strength will leave me, and I will become as weak as any other man." Years earlier, before his birth, an angel had instructed his mother that he should drink no wine, touch nothing unclean, and never cut his hair. He was to be dedicated to God in a special way, destined to play a great role in God's plan to free his people from their Philistine overlords. A strong man unable to subdue his own tempestuous nature, Samson had already broken the first two stipulations of his vow. Now he was about to break the third, preferring the good graces of a woman to the favor of his God.

Sensing she had heard the truth at last, Delilah sent word to the Philistines. After cutting his hair while he slept, she once again called, "Samson, the Philistines are upon you!" This time Samson awoke from his sleep unable to resist his enemies, who quickly seized him, gouging out his eyes. Then they imprisoned him in Gaza, where he spent his days in darkness, performing women's work grinding grain.

That's the last we hear of the lovely, treacherous, and now wealthy Delilah, but not the last we hear of her lover. Slowly Samson's hair began to grow back, first a short cap to warm his head and then a cover for his ears. *What harm can a blind man do us?* the Philistines must have reasoned.

One day they held a great celebration in honor of Dagon, god of the harvest, for delivering Samson into their hands. Oblivious to their danger, they brought him out of prison to make sport of their once-mighty enemy. But when Samson stood among the pillars of their temple, he prayed, "O Sovereign LORD, remember me. O God, please strengthen me just once more, and let me with one blow get revenge on the Philistines for my two eyes." Then he braced himself against the two central pillars of the temple and pushed. The roof buckled and collapsed, and Samson and his enemies were buried together under its rubble. By his death, Samson killed more Philistines than he had in life. Just as the angel had predicted, Samson had begun a work of deliverance that David would complete many years later.

The strange story of Samson and Delilah is hardly edifying. It's tempting to conclude that the selfish, ill-disciplined Samson had finally met his match in the greedy Delilah. A visitation by an angel, the gift of supernatural strength, a prophetic destiny—such obvious blessings could not assure Samson's devotion. Why would God use such a man, enabling him to become a judge in Israel? What a contrast to Deborah, who had ruled Israel a century earlier! Perhaps God had little promising material to choose from, given the state of his people during an era of Israel's history where "everyone did as he saw fit" (Judges 21:25).

If anything, Delilah's role in this sordid tale assures us that God will use anything and anyone to accomplish his purpose. Even our sin. Even our enemies. Our deliverance is purely a matter of grace. But how much better if we become people set apart for his service, whose inner strengths match our outer strengths, enabling us to live out our destiny assured of God's pleasure.

Tuesday

HER LIFE AND TIMES

HAIR

*S*amson's hair obviously plays a key role in the story of his rise to power and his fall from grace. He had grown it long, plaiting it in seven braids as a result of a Nazirite vow (for more on such vows, read Numbers 6).

Good-looking Absalom, King David's son, had so much hair that he had to cut it whenever "it became too heavy for him" (2 Samuel 14:26). Remarkably, his shorn curls weighed as much as five pounds! But Absalom's luxurious locks eventually got the better of him. During battle one day his head got caught in the branches of a large oak tree (2 Samuel 18:9). His mass of hair no doubt contributed to the entanglement. The man who had tried to wrench the kingdom from his own father swung helplessly from the tree, an easy target for his enemies.

Before being thrown to her death, Queen Jezebel not only painted her eyes but "arranged her hair" (2 Kings 9:30). The beautiful hair of the Beloved in Song of Songs is compared to a "flock of goats" and a "royal tapestry" (Song of Songs 4:1; 7:5), while the Lover's hair is described as "wavy and black as a raven" (Song of Songs 5:11). Often the Old Testament writers described living to old age—so old their hair turned gray—as a mark of God's favor and blessing (Proverbs 16:31; 20:29). People who were mourning would cut or pull out their hair in their grief (Ezra 9:3; Isaiah 22:12; Jeremiah 7:29). A sinful woman, full of anguish for her sins, poured perfume on Jesus' feet, washed them with her tears, and wiped them with her hair (Luke 7:38).

By New Testament times, men were wearing their hair shorter and only women allowed their hair to grow long. Paul was pretty adamant about this in 1 Corinthians 11:6, 14–15. Both Paul and Peter took time to warn the women of their day specifically against "braided hair," directing them to focus on inner beauty, not outward.

Women today spend millions of dollars cutting, coloring, perming, and styling their hair. But remember, no amount of money or primping can cover up a lack of inner beauty. Before arranging your hair into a becoming style, consider where your inner beauty needs work. Go to Galatians 5:22–23 for some attractive characteristics the Spirit is willing to work in you. Then you'll be beautiful outside and in.

Wednesday

HER LEGACY IN SCRIPTURE

Read Judges 16:4–22.

1. Why was Delilah willing to betray Samson?

2. What were her strengths? Her weaknesses? What are your strengths? Your weaknesses?

3. If you think back over the biblical women you've studied so far, you will notice that several of them used manipulation to get what they wanted. When, if ever, have you used manipulation to get what you wanted? How common a habit is it for you? Exactly what manipulative tactics have you used?

4. Why do you think God chose to work through a man like Samson? What does this say about God? About the times in which Samson and Delilah lived?

5. In what area of your life do you need renewed faith that good will triumph?

Thursday

HER PROMISE

*E*ven the sordid story of Delilah and her Hebrew lover, Samson, conveys an important truth: God loves us and will not abandon us even when we make mistakes, even when we sin. Over and over throughout the biblical narrative, we see God using people who are great sinners, people who are less than perfect, people who through their own folly fail and only then recognize their need of him. He didn't abandon people like Samson, foolish and sinful though he was, and he won't abandon us, foolish and sinful though we might be.

Promises in Scripture

> *Remember not the sins of my youth*
> *and my rebellious ways;*
> *according to your love remember me,*
> *for you are good, O* Lord.

> —Psalm 25:7

> *The* Lord *is faithful to all his promises*
> *and loving toward all he has made.*
> *The* Lord *upholds all those who fall*
> *and lifts up all who are bowed down.*

> —Psalm 145:13−14

> *The one who calls you is faithful and he will do it.*

> —1 Thessalonians 5:24

Friday

HER LEGACY OF PRAYER

"How can you say, 'I love you,' when you won't confide in me? This is the third time you have made a fool of me and haven't told me the secret of your great strength." With such nagging she prodded him day after day until he was tired to death.

—JUDGES 16:15–16

REFLECT ON: Judges 16:4–22.

PRAISE GOD: That he is sovereign, able to use our most tangled relationships to achieve his purposes.

OFFER THANKS: For calling you to be devoted to him, set apart in a special way.

CONFESS: Any tendency to manipulate others.

ASK GOD: To help you surrender any unhealthy relationship to him. Take whatever steps God is calling you to take.

Lift Your Heart

Take inventory of your most important relationships. Have you formed any unhealthy dependencies? Is a spouse or boyfriend leading you away from God rather than closer to him? Have you made compromises that diminish your desire for God? If so, find a trusted friend or counselor in whom to confide. Pray together about the best course of action and then follow it. Be faithful to marital commitments, but find a way to restore your spiritual passion. Right now, take time to write God a letter. Tell him how desirable he is and how much you long to be connected to him. Don't be afraid to wear your heart on your sleeve—God is looking for men and women who love him more than they love their own lives.

Lord, you know all the struggles of my heart. You created me in such a way that no one but you can fully satisfy my longings. Yet you also know how easily I am fooled, believing that flesh and blood relationships hold the key to all my needs. Forgive me for the times I've put my relationship with _____ above my relationship with you. Give me the wisdom, courage, and grace to love you with abandon.

Naomi
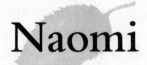

HER NAME MEANS

"My Joy" or "Pleasant"

HER CHARACTER: Suffering a threefold tragedy, Naomi refused to hide her sorrow or bitterness. Believing in God's sovereignty, she attributed her suffering to his will. But her fixation on circumstances, both past and present, led to hopelessness. A kind and loving mother-in-law, she inspired unusual love and loyalty in her daughters-in-law.

HER SORROW: To have lost a husband and two sons in a foreign land, far from family and friends.

HER JOY: To have returned safely to Bethlehem with her daughter-in-law Ruth, who would eventually rekindle her happiness and hope.

KEY SCRIPTURE: Ruth 1; 4:13–17

Monday

HER STORY

She stood like an old tree twisted against the sky. Though Naomi could see for miles from her vantage point high on the road that led from Moab to Judah, she could glimpse nothing at all of her future. She thought about robbers, rumored on the road ahead. What more, she wondered, could possibly be taken from her? Her thoughts strayed to the past.

Moses, she knew, had been buried somewhere in these mountains. But his people and hers had moved west into Canaan centuries earlier. Would she, too, be left behind, prevented from ever seeing her kinsfolk again? Was God so displeased with her?

Ten years ago, she and her husband, Elimelech, had lived happily in Bethlehem. But the city whose name meant "house of bread" suddenly had none, so they had migrated to the highlands of Moab to escape the famine. Then Elimelech had died and her sons had married Moabite women, whose race had descended from Abraham's nephew, Lot. Plenty of women lost their husbands. Like them, she would find a way to survive. But then she had suffered the worst grief a mother could—outliving her own children.

Now Ruth and Orpah, her daughters-in-law, were the only kin she had in Moab. Loving them tenderly, she felt their widowhood as a double grief. Together they had cried and comforted each other. The three women finally decided to leave Moab for Bethlehem. But once on the road, Naomi's misgivings outran her craving for companionship. It wasn't right for young women to forsake their families and friends for so uncertain a future. What chance would they, widows and strangers, have in Bethlehem, even now that the famine had run its course?

"Go back, each of you, to your mother's home," she told them. "May the LORD show kindness to you, as you have shown to your dead and to me. May the LORD grant that each of you will find rest in the home of another husband."

But Orpah and Ruth insisted, "We will go back with you to your people."

"Why would you come with me? Am I going to have any more sons, who could become your husbands? Return home, my daughters; I am too old to have another husband. Even if I thought there was still hope for me—even if I had a husband tonight and then gave birth to sons—would you wait until they grew up?"

The three women embraced, tears streaking their cheeks. Then Orpah kissed her mother-in-law good-bye. But Ruth clutched Naomi and whispered fiercely, "Where you go I will go, and where you stay I will stay. Your people will be my people and your God my God. Where you die I will die, and there I will be buried. May the LORD deal with me, be it ever so severely, if anything but death separates you and me."

The old woman's stubbornness was no match for the younger woman's love. And so Naomi and Ruth continued on to Bethlehem. After so long an absence, Naomi's return created a great commotion in the town, and all the women welcomed her, saying, "Can this be Naomi?"

"Don't call me Naomi," she told them. "Call me Mara [meaning 'bitter'], because the Almighty has made my life very bitter. I went away full, but the LORD has brought me back empty. The LORD has afflicted me; the Almighty has brought misfortune upon me."

Naomi could not see past her suffering. Like many of us, she may have felt as though her tragedies were punishment for her sins. Yet had she known the blessings in store, she might not have felt so hopeless. Instead, she may have compared herself to the tree that Job so graciously describes:

> At least there is hope for a tree:
>   If it is cut down, it will sprout again,
>   and its new shoots will not fail.
> Its roots may grow old in the ground
>   and its stump die in the soil,
> yet at the scent of water it will bud
>   and put forth shoots like a plant.
>
> Job 14:7–9

Though she didn't know it, the scent of water was in the air. Naomi's life was beginning again, her story still unfolding.

Tuesday

HER LIFE AND TIMES

FAMINE

*P*ictures of the bloated stomachs and empty eyes of children dying of hunger hover in our minds long after the television is turned off. Famine today, just as in Bible times, is the great destroyer of the weak — of helpless children and defenseless elderly. The cries of mothers unable to save their hungry children echo throughout the years, a painful reminder of our dependence on the earth for our sustenance.

There are two rainy seasons in Palestine — October – November and March – April. When rain didn't fall during these two periods, famine resulted. Famine could also occur when hail or insects destroyed the food supply or when invading armies devastated crops in order to bring a captured people into submission.

Throughout Scripture God seemed to use famine to bring about his purposes. Deuteronomy 28:22 – 24 gives a vivid description of the famine that would come if God's people disobeyed him. Abraham, Isaac, and Jacob all left Palestine because of a famine in the land. The events of a worldwide famine brought Joseph's father, Jacob, and his brothers to Egypt, where they eventually became the slaves of the pharaohs. In the book of Ruth, Naomi and her husband fled to Moab because of a famine in Israel, and, through their flight and its subsequent events, God brought Ruth into his holy plan as an ancestor of his Son, Jesus.

In the New Testament, Jesus predicted that famine would be one of the signs of the end of the ages (Matthew 24:7; Mark 13:8; Luke 21:11). In the book of Acts we learn that a believer by the name of Agabus foretold a severe famine (Acts 11:28); the next verse then reveals the opportunity this gave the believers to share with each other.

In one of Scripture's most somber prophecies, Amos told of the time when God would bring about another sort of famine: "I will send a famine through the land — not a famine of food or a thirst for water, but a famine of hearing the words of the LORD" (Amos 8:11).

In the past, God had always listened and responded when his people cried out to him, but Amos told of a time to come when their cries would be met with a frightening silence.

"Who shall separate us from the love of Christ?" asks Paul. "Shall trouble or hardship or persecution or famine or nakedness or danger or sword?" (Romans 8:35). But then Paul answers his own question with that wonderful believer's cry of victory: Nothing, not even famine, will ever separate us from God's love.

Wednesday

HER LEGACY IN SCRIPTURE

Read Ruth 1:1–22.

1. Choose three or four words to describe what Naomi experienced in 1:3–5.

2. What kind of reception do you think Naomi expected when she returned to Bethlehem with her Moabite daughter-in-law?

3. Who was at fault for Naomi's circumstances? Naomi? Her husband? God? Explain your answer. Who controlled Naomi's response to her circumstances?

4. If you suffered what Naomi suffered, would you be bitter? Why or why not?

5. What would it take for you to love and trust God in Naomi's circumstances?

Thursday

HER PROMISE

God's faithfulness to restore to fullness an empty life is revealed more in this story of Naomi than in any other biblical account. The famine and hunger that drove Naomi and her husband and sons away from Bethlehem are finally replaced with full harvests and bread baked from grain gleaned in the fields. The anguish of losing her husband and sons is replaced with the loving care and concern of her daughter-in-law Ruth, who is "better to [Naomi] than seven sons" (Ruth 4:15). And Naomi's empty mother-arms are filled with the son of Boaz and Ruth. She is no absent grandmother; the Scriptures say Naomi took Obed and "laid him in her lap and cared for him" (Ruth 4:16). (We'll hear more about this grandson in the next chapter.)

Like Naomi, we may have trouble recognizing God's goodness and his faithfulness at times. But he is still with us no matter the circumstances.

Promises in Scripture

The women said to Naomi: "Praise be to the LORD, who this day has not left you without a kinsman-redeemer. May he become famous throughout Israel! He will renew your life and sustain you in your old age. For your daughter-in-law, who loves you and who is better to you than seven sons, has given him birth."

—RUTH 4:14–15

Though you have made me see troubles, many and bitter,
 you will restore my life again.

—PSALM 71:20

I will repay you for the years the locusts have eaten....
You will have plenty to eat, until you are full,
 and you will praise the name of the LORD your God,
 who has worked wonders for you.

—JOEL 2:25–26

Friday

HER LEGACY OF PRAYER

Where you go I will go, and where you stay I will stay. Your people will be my people and your God my God. Where you die I will die, and there I will be buried. May the LORD deal with me, be it ever so severely, if anything but death separates you and me.

—RUTH 1:16–17

REFLECT ON: Ruth 1.

PRAISE GOD: For creating us with the power to form deep and lasting relationships.

OFFER THANKS: For the variety of friends God has given you.

CONFESS: Your tendency to be too busy to pay attention to your friends or too preoccupied with your own concerns to take time for theirs.

ASK GOD: To make you a more loyal and loving friend in the year ahead.

Lift Your Heart

Think about someone with whom you used to be especially close. Perhaps time or distance has eroded the friendship. Wax nostalgic as you recall the great meals, oddball jokes, late-night conversations, or crazy adventures you shared. Wouldn't it be great to have that person back in your life? Pick up the phone or write a letter to renew the friendship. If the other person seems willing, invest some energy rebuilding the relationship in the year ahead. Let your memories form a foundation for your friendship, but don't stop there—get busy making new ones. If she's nearby, have her over for a meal or a fancy dessert. If not, exchange family photos. Stay in touch by email. If you can afford to, you can even meet halfway for a weekend excursion.

Lord, thank you for the blessing of friends who, by sharing their lives with us, double our joy and halve our sorrows. Help me to cherish the friends you've given me and to become the kind of friend others will cherish: a woman who listens, encourages, and keeps confidences; a woman who knows how to laugh and how to cry, who is loyal, forgiving, and loving.

Ruth

HER NAME MEANS
"Friendship"

HER CHARACTER: Generous, loyal, and loving, she is strong and serene, able to take unusual risks, dealing actively with life circumstances.

HER SORROW: To have lost her husband, homeland, and family.

HER JOY: To discover firsthand the generous, loyal, and loving nature of God, as he provided her with a husband, a son, and a home to call her own.

KEY SCRIPTURES: Ruth 2–4; Matthew 1:5

Monday

HER STORY

*I*t was harvest time in Israel when Boaz first laid eyes on the young woman. The sun had painted the fields a tawny gold as workers swung their sickles in even rhythms through the standing grain. According to Israel's law and custom, the poor had the right to gather whatever the harvesters missed.

Ruth toiled quickly and efficiently, he noticed, stuffing grain into a coarse sack slung across her shoulder. Strands of black hair escaped her head covering, softly framing olive-colored skin, still smooth despite the sun. She rested, but only for a moment, her eyes wary for any sign of trouble from the men working the fields. Gleaning was rough work and dangerous, especially for an attractive young foreigner, alone and unprotected.

Everyone in Bethlehem had been talking about Boaz's relative, Naomi, and her unexpected return. Ruth, he knew, had come with her. He had heard of their shared tragedy and the extraordinary loyalty the young woman had displayed toward her mother-in-law, even promising to renounce Moab's idols for Israel's God. A man could wish for such a friend as Ruth had been to Naomi.

Determined to repay her kindness in some way, Boaz called to her, "My daughter, listen to me. Don't go and glean in another field and don't go away from here. Stay here with my servant girls. Watch the field where the men are harvesting, and follow along after the girls. I have told the men not to touch you." The young woman smiled her agreement.

Later he spoke to Ruth again, this time offering bread and roasted grain for her dinner. When she finished eating, Boaz instructed his men to pull out some stalks of grain and strew them in her path. It was good to see her leaving that night with a bulging harvest sack.

Day after day, he watched her, aware that the wheat and barley harvest would soon be drawing to a close. One evening, Boaz and the other men were winnowing barley on the threshing floor. After he had finished eating and drinking, he lay down under the stars at the far end of the grain pile. With so many men to guard the harvest, robbers wouldn't dare approach. But in the middle of the night he woke with a start, realizing that someone *had* dared. To his surprise, he discovered the intruder was neither a robber nor a man, but a woman who lay at his feet.

She, too, was awake. "I am your servant, Ruth," she whispered. "Spread the corner of your garment over me, since you are a kinsman-redeemer."

He could hardly believe her words. The young woman had taken a remarkable risk, appearing at night and lying down so close to him. Quickly, he covered her, saying, "The LORD bless you. This kindness is greater than that which you showed Naomi: You have not run after the younger men, whether rich or poor. And now, my daughter, don't be afraid. I will do for you all you ask." So Ruth lay at his feet until morning, rising before the early light could reveal her presence to others.

But Boaz knew there was one obstacle that could yet spoil things. Naomi had a closer relative than Boaz, a man who could play the role of kinsman-redeemer, marrying Ruth and restoring her dead husband's name. This man was entitled to purchase a field belonging to Naomi. If he purchased the field, by law he had to marry Ruth as well. That would destroy Boaz's hope of making Ruth his wife.

Boaz wasted no time putting the case before the man, who seemed interested enough in the land. But as soon as the man discovered that marriage was part of the bargain, he relinquished his rights to the land to Boaz.

So the two were married and the older man welcomed the young woman into his home. And God blessed them with a son, whom they named Obed.

Pulling Ruth close to him, Boaz watched one day as Naomi held her grandson to her breast. Surrounded by the other women of Bethlehem, she looked young again, more like the woman he remembered when her husband, Elimelech, had been alive. He watched as the women talked with Naomi regarding the child: "Praise be to the LORD, who this day has not left you without a kinsman-redeemer. May he become famous throughout Israel! He will renew your life and sustain you in your old age. For your daughter-in-law, who loves you and who is better to you than seven sons, has given him birth."

Yes, Boaz thought, his Ruth was better to Naomi than seven sons. And he was grateful for the friendship between the two women. Had Ruth and Naomi gone their separate ways, his life would have been so much the poorer.

The good-hearted Boaz felt strong and young again. But even he couldn't have realized how greatly God had blessed him in the person of Ruth. For their son, Obed, became the father of Jesse, and Jesse was the father of David. In addition to being King David's great-grandparents, both Boaz and Ruth are mentioned in the genealogy of Jesus of Nazareth, who is, after all, our own great Kinsman-Redeemer, uniting us to himself, healing our sorrows, and giving us, as well, a future full of hope.

Tuesday

HER LIFE AND TIMES

GLEANING

*W*hen Ruth and Naomi arrived in Bethlehem, it was harvest time. They would not have the opportunity to plant their own grain and harvest it. So, unless there was another way to get food, they would starve. Naomi knew the Mosaic laws and urged Ruth to follow the harvesters and "glean," or gather, what they left behind. In this way, Ruth would be able to provide food for both Naomi and for herself.

The laws of Moses directed landowners to leave some of the harvest behind for the "poor and aliens." As a Moabite with no one to support her, Ruth fit both categories. Harvesters were not to reap to the very edges of their fields, nor were they to go over a field a second time to pick up what was missed the first time. This grain was to be left for the poor (Leviticus 19:9; 23:22; Deuteronomy 24:19–22). This "welfare system," set up by Moses, took care of the needy by encouraging the rich to share their bounty with those less fortunate.

But it wasn't a handout. The poor still had to work for their food, following along behind the harvesters and picking up what was left by them. Depending on the efficiency of the field hands and the number of fellow gleaners reaping the grain, it could be difficult to do much more than survive. When Boaz ordered his reapers to purposely leave behind stalks of grain for Ruth to pick up, he went beyond the letter of the law.

Boaz also ordered his reapers not to "embarrass" Ruth were she to glean in the wrong part of the field; that is, if she didn't follow the rules exactly. His admonishment offers a glimpse into the heart and character of this man, who took great care to follow the Mosaic law and who, with Ruth, became an ancestor of Christ.

Was it by chance that Ruth "found herself working in a field belonging to Boaz, who was from the clan of Elimelech [Ruth's father-in-law]" (Ruth 2:3)? Of course not. Even in what appeared to be a chance situation, God was at work, divinely preparing for Ruth's and Naomi's sustenance. Never assume that what happens in your life is merely a matter of chance or coincidence. Remember: God is at work, divinely orchestrating events to bring about his purposes in your life.

Wednesday

HER LEGACY IN SCRIPTURE

Read Ruth 2:1–3:18.

1. What character qualities do you see in Ruth in chapter 2? How does she act, and what is her reputation?

2. The ultimate loyalty to her late husband was for Ruth to marry one of his relatives and have a son in her late husband's name. At what point in the story do you see Ruth decide to attempt that?

3. What risk was Ruth taking when she lay down on the threshing floor at Boaz's feet? What does this say about her?

4. Where do you see God at work in this story?

5. In what areas of your life are you called upon to be loyal? What, for you, are the risks and costs of loyalty?

Thursday

HER PROMISE

*A*ll that Ruth did was done for love of her mother-in-law, and for love of Naomi's God. She made a promise on the road to Bethlehem that she was determined to keep. Though it was a promise made by one woman to another, it is often quoted in wedding ceremonies as an eloquent expression of love and loyalty between spouses.

Ruth had no way of knowing that her way of blessing Naomi would eventually become a blessing in her own life. That's just the divine irony of our God, who delights so much in seeing us love and bless others that he turns that love and blessing back on us in double measure.

Promises in Scripture

Where you go I will go, and where you stay I will stay. Your people will be my people and your God my God.

—RUTH 1:16

A generous person will prosper;
  whoever refreshes others will be refreshed.

—PROVERBS 11:25

Blessed are the merciful,
  for they will be shown mercy.
Blessed are the pure in heart,
  for they will see God.

—MATTHEW 5:7–8

Command those who are rich in this present world not to be arrogant nor to put their hope in wealth, which is so uncertain, but to put their hope in God, who richly provides us with everything for our enjoyment. Command them to do good, to be rich in good deeds, and to be generous and willing to share. In this way they will lay up treasure for themselves as a firm foundation for the coming age, so that they may take hold of the life that is truly life.

—1 TIMOTHY 6:17–19

Friday

HER LEGACY OF PRAYER

The women said to Naomi, "Praise be to the LORD, who this day has not left you without a kinsman-redeemer. May he become famous throughout Israel! He will renew your life and sustain you in your old age. For your daughter-in-law, who loves you and who is better to you than seven sons, has given him birth."

—RUTH 4:14–15

REFLECT ON: Ruth 3–4.

PRAISE GOD: That he provides for those who have no one to provide for them.

OFFER THANKS: For the way God has used other women, your mother or mother-in-law, your sisters or daughters, to provide for you.

CONFESS: Any tendency to compete with other women.

ASK GOD: To help you appreciate your own mother and mother-in-law and to give you a vision of the power of two women, linked by love and faith.

Lift Your Heart

*I*t's easy to assume the important women in our lives know how much we cherish them. But Mother's Day cards and friendship cards, nice as they are to get and give, don't really do the trick. We also need to verbalize our love sincerely and regularly. Don't wait until Mother's Day to treat your mother, mother-in-law, or an older friend to tea or a leisurely lunch. Tell her just how much you care about her. (Make sure you take time beforehand to think about all her wonderful qualities. Take notes so that you can be specific.) You might even buy a small blank book and record all the ways she's blessed you. Decorate each page with colorful stickers or stencils. Package it with scented soap and bath salts and give it as a keepsake she can treasure.

Father, I thank you for the women who have played such an important role in my life. Please bless each one in a special way today and help me find ways to express to them my love and gratitude.

Hannah

HER NAME MEANS
"Graciousness" or "Favor"

HER CHARACTER: Provoked by another woman's malice, she refused to respond in kind. Instead, she poured out her hurt and sorrow to God, allowing him to vindicate her.

HER SORROW: To be taunted and misunderstood.

HER JOY: To proclaim God's power and goodness, his habit of raising the lowly and humbling the proud.

KEY SCRIPTURES: 1 Samuel 1:1–2:11; 2:19–21

Monday

HER STORY

*I*t was only fifteen miles, but every year the journey from Ramah, to worship at the tabernacle in Shiloh, seemed longer. At home, Hannah found ways to avoid her husband's second wife, but once in Shiloh there was no escaping her taunts. Hannah felt like a leaky tent in a driving rain, unable to defend herself against the harsh weather of the other woman's heart.

Even Elkanah's arm around her provided no shelter. "Hannah, why are you weeping? Why don't you eat? Why are you downhearted? Don't I mean more to you than ten sons? Yes, she has given me children, but it's you I love. Ignore her taunts."

How could Hannah make him understand that even the best of men could not erase a woman's longing for children? His attempt to comfort her only sharpened the pain, heightening her sense of isolation.

Once inside the tabernacle Hannah stood for a long time, weeping and praying. Her lips moved without making a sound as her heart poured out its grief to God: "O LORD Almighty, if you will only look upon your servant's misery and remember me, and not forget your servant but give her a son, then I will give him to the LORD for all the days of his life, and no razor will ever be used on his head."

The priest Eli was used to people coming to Shiloh to celebrate the feasts, eating and drinking more than they should. Watching Hannah from his chair by the doorpost of the temple, he wondered why her shoulders were shaking, her lips moving without making a sound. She must be drunk, he concluded. So he interrupted her silent prayer with a rebuke: "How long will you keep on getting drunk? Get rid of your wine."

"Not so, my lord," Hannah defended herself. "I am a woman who is deeply troubled. I have not been drinking wine or beer; I was pouring out my soul to the LORD. Do not take your servant for a wicked woman; I have been praying here out of my great anguish and grief."

Satisfied by her explanation, Eli blessed her, saying, "May the God of Israel grant your request."

Early the next morning, Hannah and Elkanah returned to their home in Ramah, where Hannah at last conceived. Soon she held against her shoulder the tiny child she had yearned for, the son she had dedicated to God. After Samuel was weaned, she took him to Eli at Shiloh. Like Jochebed placing the child Moses into the waters of the Nile as though into God's own hands, she surrendered her child to the priest's care. Eventually Hannah's boy became a prophet and Israel's last judge. His hands anointed both Saul and David as Israel's first kings.

Like Sarah and Rachel, Hannah grieved over the children she couldn't have. But unlike them, she took her anguish directly to God. Misunderstood by both her husband and her priest, she could easily have turned her sorrow on herself or others, becoming bitter, hopeless, or vindictive. But instead of merely pitying herself or responding in kind, she poured out her soul to God. And God graciously answered her prayer.

Each year Hannah went up to Shiloh and presented Samuel with a little robe she had sewn. And each year, the priest Eli blessed her husband, Elkanah, saying, "May the LORD give you children by this woman to take the place of the one she prayed for and gave to the LORD." And so Hannah became the mother of three more sons and two daughters. Hannah's great prayer, echoed more than a thousand years later by Mary, the mother of Jesus (Luke 1:46–55), expresses her praise: "My heart rejoices in the LORD; in the LORD my horn is lifted high. My mouth boasts over my enemies, for I delight in your deliverance.... The Lord sends poverty and wealth; he humbles and he exalts. He raises the poor from the dust and lifts the needy from the ash heap" (1 Samuel 2:1, 7–8).

Tuesday

HER LIFE AND TIMES

INFERTILITY

*P*raying through her tears, so overwrought that Eli thought she was drunk, Hannah expresses for women throughout the ages the agonizing experience of infertility. The deep, unsatisfied longing for children, the pain of watching others bear one child after another, the anguish of watching a mother kiss her baby's face—Hannah experienced it all.

The Israelites saw children as a particular blessing from the Lord, recognizing his power to open or close a woman's womb. Women who couldn't bear children were considered subfemale, unable to fulfill their divine purpose on earth. When a woman was unable to fulfill this "duty," her emotional pain was tremendous. And more than likely, barren women also felt they were denied the possibility of being the one chosen to bear the Messiah.

Infertility brought with it not only a debilitating personal sorrow but also the reproach of a woman's husband, the disapproval of a woman's family, and the rejection of society. Husbands looked to their wives to produce many sons to help in supporting the family. A woman's extended family, both her own and her husband's, looked to her to continue the family line and saw her as one who had not fulfilled her responsibility when she didn't produce children. And the social circles of young women of childbearing years by their very nature included many other young women, women who were often producing one child after another. Their fertility mocked the infertility of the barren woman every time she went to the market or to the well or to a community social event.

Scripture tells the stories of a number of women who were barren. Sarah laughed when told she would finally have a son. Rachel clutched Jacob and begged him to give her sons, as if he could open her womb. Hannah's pain made her seek help from the only One truly capable of providing it.

If Hannah had never had a child, she would still have gone down in Scripture's narrative as a woman of faith. Hannah is not a woman of faith because she bore a child; she is a woman of faith because she sought God when she was in her deepest distress, because she realized that only he could answer her questions and that only he could provide the consolation and purpose in life she so desperately sought.

Wednesday

HER LEGACY IN SCRIPTURE

Read 1 Samuel 1:1–2:21.

1. What response does Hannah's childlessness cause in each of the people involved: In Hannah herself? In Peninnah? In Elkanah?

2. What caused the change in Hannah recorded in 1 Samuel 1:18? Was she assured of getting what she wanted? If so, how? If not, why was she comforted?

3. When have you been profoundly disappointed? What were your prayers like at that time?

4. Describe what it might have been like for Hannah to fulfill her vow to God. What does her action tell you about her?

5. What does Hannah's song of praise to the Lord (1 Samuel 2:1–10) have to do with the events of the story? What does she say about God, and why is it relevant to her life?

Thursday

HER PROMISE

When God met Hannah at the temple in Shiloh, he not only answered her prayer for a child, he answered her prayer for comfort in her misery. He gave her consolation in her disappointment and strength to face her situation. Scripture does not say that she went away sure she would bear a child, but it does make it clear that she went away comforted: "Her face was no longer downcast" (1 Samuel 1:18). What even the love and care of her husband Elkanah could not provide, God could provide.

God is willing to meet us just as he met Hannah. Whatever our distress, whatever hard situations we face, he is willing—more than that, he is eager—to meet our needs and give us his grace and comfort. No other person—not our husband, not our closest friends, not our parents, not our children—can render the relief, support, and encouragement that our God has waiting for us.

Promises in Scripture

My comfort in my suffering is this:
Your promise preserves my life.

—PSALM 119:50

We rejoice in the hope of the glory of God. Not only so, but we also rejoice in our sufferings, because we know that suffering produces perseverance; perseverance, character; and character, hope. And hope does not disappoint us, because God has poured out his love into our hearts by the Holy Spirit, whom he has given us.

—ROMANS 5:2–5

And we know that in all things God works for the good of those who love him, who have been called according to his purpose.

—ROMANS 8:28

Friday

HER LEGACY OF PRAYER

In bitterness of soul Hannah wept much and prayed to the LORD. And she made a vow, saying, "O LORD Almighty, if you will only look upon your servant's misery and remember me, and not forget your servant but give her a son, then I will give him to the LORD for all the days of his life."

— 1 SAMUEL 1:10–11

REFLECT ON: 1 Samuel 2:1–10.

PRAISE GOD: That he knows our hearts.

OFFER THANKS: For already answering so many of your prayers.

CONFESS: Your tendency to pour out your heart to everyone but God, making him a last, rather than first, resort.

ASK GOD: To give you the grace to trust his strength.

Lift Your Heart

One way to build your confidence in God is to form a habit of remembrance. It's so easy to forget everything he's already done by being preoccupied with what you want him to do right here, right now. But by forgetting his blessings, you form a habit of ingratitude. By frequently thanking God for what he's done, you build a habit of gratitude, which will also deepen your trust in God's compassion, mercy, faithfulness, and power.

Find a blank notebook or a lovely scrapbook that can become your Remembrance Book. In it, write down ways in which God has answered your prayers. Keep letters, photos of loved ones, or newspaper clippings—anything that reminds you of answered prayers. Let your Remembrance Book be a tangible way to keep God's faithfulness in the forefront of your heart.

Father, thank you for all the prayers you've answered during my lifetime. You've answered small prayers and big prayers, evening prayers and morning prayers, quiet prayers and loud prayers, anxious prayers and peaceful prayers. May my own prayers be shaped according to your faithfulness, becoming less selfish and frantic and more calm and trusting with each day that passes. In Jesus' name. Amen.

Michal

"Who Is Like God?"

HER CHARACTER: A woman of strong emotions, she was unable to control the important circumstances of her life. Forcibly separated from two husbands, she lost her father and her brother, who were savaged by their enemies.

HER SORROW: That she was ensnared in the drawn-out battle between Saul and David.

HER JOY: Though short-lived, she enjoyed a passionate love for David.

KEY SCRIPTURES: 1 Samuel 18:20–29; 19:11–17; 2 Samuel 6:16–23

Monday

HER STORY

Scene One

Michal stretched herself across the window's edge. Leaning out as far as she dared, she could see her husband running through the night shadows, his movements swift and lithe, like a young stag evading its predators. Even if her father, the king, pursued with an army, she was confident he would not catch her David.

She had loved the shepherd boy since the day he had calmed Saul's troubled soul with his harp playing. After he defeated the hideous Goliath with only a sling and a stone, all Israel fell in love with him. But it was for her alone that David had slain two hundred Philistines—to prove his worth.

153

She turned from the window, grateful for the chance to have aided her husband's escape. Quickly she dressed one of the household idols, placing it in their bed and topping it with goat's hair to make it look like a sleeping David. She was ready for her father's men when they came pounding on her door.

"David is ill," she told them.

So they returned to King Saul, who immediately ordered them back, saying, "Bring him up to me in his bed so that I may kill him."

Discovering the ruse, Saul confronted his daughter: "Why did you deceive me like this and send my enemy away so that he escaped?"

Michal lowered her eyes and replied, "He said to me, 'Let me get away. Why should I kill you?'" She held her breath, certain her father would never swallow so bold a lie.

Scene Two

$\mathcal{N}$ine years or more have passed. Michal glanced out the window, arms folded tightly against her breast, observing the scene below. David, now the king, had entered Jerusalem, leaping and dancing as the ark of the covenant was carried into Jerusalem. He looked ridiculous to Michal, more like a romping goat than a great king.

David offered the sacrifices and blessed the people. Then he entered his own house to bless it. But Saul's daughter met him with scornful eyes: "How the king of Israel has distinguished himself today, disrobing in the sight of the slave girls of his servants as any vulgar fellow would!"

"It was before the LORD, who chose me," he replied, "rather than your father or anyone from his house when he appointed me ruler over the LORD's people Israel—I will celebrate before the LORD. I will become even more undignified than this, and I will be humiliated in my own eyes. But by these slave girls you spoke of, I will be held in honor."

Twice, Michal stood at a window observing David. In the first scene, Scripture paints her as David's wife, in the second as Saul's daughter. In fact, her attitude is so changed that we feel perplexed, watching her as she watches David. To understand what may have shaped Michal's heart in the intervening years, we need to find a corridor connecting the two windows, a passageway that somehow led from love to scorn.

Michal may have expected her separation from David to be a short one, her idealism forging a happy ending to their fairy-tale love. Perhaps she believed David would find a way to protect her from her father's wrath. Was she shocked when real life intervened and her father punished her by marrying her to another man? Did her bitterness grow during David's long absence? Had she finally made peace with her new marriage only to be torn from her husband when David demanded her back after Saul's death? Did she question God's judgments, identifying more with the dead than the living after her father perished in a desperate battle with the Philistines?

Perhaps Michal's bitterness swelled to rage when she realized she had always been someone else's pawn, a mere woman manipulated by powerful men. Her own father used her, promising her to David in hopes she would prove a snare to him. And, finally, one of her brothers handed her back to David after Saul's death, further legitimizing David's claim to the throne. A princess, then a queen, she was still a slave.

Michal's story is tragic. Throughout the difficult circumstances of her life, we see little evidence of a faith to sustain her. Instead, she is tossed back and forth, her heart left to draw its own bitter conclusions. In the last scene with David, we see a woman blind with scorn, making the very mistake God cautioned the prophet Samuel against in his search for a king to succeed the wayward Saul: "Do not consider his appearance or his height, for I have rejected him. The LORD does not look at the things human beings look at. People look at the outward appearance, but the LORD looks at the heart."

The truth is, God is the only one who can see into the depths of anyone's heart, including Michal's. He knew everything that had happened, both good and bad. Still the story of Michal seems to indicate that she grew to be more like Saul than like David. As such, she reminds us that even victims have choices. No matter how much we've been sinned against, we still have the power to choose the attitude of our heart. If we cast ourselves on God's mercy, asking him to help us, he cannot refuse. Even in difficulty, he will dwell in us, shaping our own wayward hearts into the likeness of his own.

Tuesday

HER LIFE AND TIMES

WORSHIP

*W*hen David brought the ark of the covenant to Jerusalem, after it had been in Philistine hands for a number of years and after a fateful earlier attempt to move it, he did so with a deep sense of awe. The ark was moved only six steps before he stopped and sacrificed a bull and a fattened calf. Then, as the priests brought the ark into Jerusalem, David "danced before the LORD with all his might" (2 Samuel 6:14), and the people with him shouted and blew on trumpets.

There was nothing subdued or restrained about David's worship of the Lord. The psalms of praise he wrote also reveal his deep love for God, a love so all-encompassing it could not be contained, but burst forth in exuberant worship.

Sacrifices and offerings were an important part of worship in Old Testament times. Since sin separated the worshiper from God, sacrifice was needed to reestablish the relationship and make true worship possible. The response of praise to God took several forms: prayer, as when Solomon dedicated the temple (1 Kings 8); praise in singing as individuals (2 Samuel 23:1) and in choirs (Nehemiah 12); praise with musical instruments (Psalm 150); and praise with dancing (Exodus 15:20–21; 2 Samuel 6:14–16; Psalm 149:3).

But God makes it clear that he won't be satisfied with only the forms of worship. Sacrifices and music and dancing have no meaning apart from a heart and life truly dedicated to the Lord. God's words to the prophet Micah (Micah 6:6–8) clearly state this truth:

> With what shall I come before the LORD
>   and bow down before the exalted God?
> Shall I come before him with burnt offerings,
>   with calves a year old?
> Will the LORD be pleased with thousands of rams,
>   with ten thousand rivers of oil?
> Shall I offer my firstborn for my transgression,
>   the fruit of my body for the sin of my soul?

He has shown all you people what is good.
    And what does the LORD require of you?
To act justly and to love mercy
    and to walk humbly with your God.

Michal's contempt for her husband, David, revealed her own lack of true dedication. She was content to be a critical spectator rather than a true worshiper of God. Whenever anyone puts appearances or tradition or form above a true desire to worship our God and Savior, we'd best step carefully ... and read the words of God to Micah the prophet, which are as true for us today as they were for the Israelites of the prophet's day.

Wednesday

HER LEGACY IN SCRIPTURE

Read 1 Samuel 18:20–27; 19:11–17.

1. How would you describe Michal in these passages?

Read 1 Samuel 25:43–44 and 2 Samuel 3:14–16.

2. After Michal helped David escape, she didn't see him for more than nine years. How do you think these events in the intervening years affected her? How would they have affected you?

Read 2 Samuel 6:12–23.

3. Why do you think Michal responded to this scene of worship as she did? Why do you suppose she was in her room watching from the window instead of in the crowd participating?

4. What is your biggest barrier to true worship? What could bring that barrier down so that you are a participant rather than a spectator?

5. What was David trying to tell Michal in 2 Samuel 6:21–22?

6. Think about your own experience of suffering—perhaps even victimization. How have you responded? Has suffering tended to make you tough and bitter? Shattered and helpless? Strong and full of faith? Why?

Thursday

HER PROMISE

*M*ichal's contempt for true worship can be contrasted with David's love of worship. He worshiped God with abandon, with a true heart. His devotion was so deep, so real, it had to be expressed in the most extravagant praise and in dancing "with all his might." That's the sort of worship God is looking for from his people, and he responds with a promise to bless.

Promises in Scripture

> *Ascribe to the LORD the glory due his name.*
> *Bring an offering and come before him;*
> *worship the LORD in the splendor of his holiness.*

>   —1 CHRONICLES 16:29

> *Blessed be your glorious name, and may it be exalted above all bless-*
> *ing and praise. You alone are the LORD. You have made the heavens,*
> *even the highest heavens, and all their starry host, the earth and all*
> *that is on it, and seas and all that is in them. You give life to every-*
> *thing, and the multitudes of heaven worship you.*

>   —NEHEMIAH 9:5–6

> *Come, let us bow down in worship,*
> *let us kneel before the LORD our Maker;*
> *for he is our God.*

>   —PSALM 95:6–7

> *Enter his gates with thanksgiving*
> *and his courts with praise;*
> *give thanks to him and praise his name.*

>   —PSALM 100:4

Friday

HER LEGACY OF PRAYER

Now Saul's daughter Michal was in love with David, and when they told Saul about it, he was pleased. "I will give her to him," he thought, "so that she may be a snare to him and so that the hand of the Philistines may be against him."

— 1 SAMUEL 18:20–21

As the ark of the LORD was entering the City of David, Michal daughter of Saul watched from a window. And when she saw King David leaping and dancing before the LORD, she despised him in her heart.

— 2 SAMUEL 6:16

REFLECT ON: 1 Samuel 19:11–17; 2 Samuel 6:16–23.

PRAISE GOD: Because he is the same — yesterday, today, and forever.

OFFER THANKS: That God gives us the freedom to choose how we will respond to him.

CONFESS: Allowing skepticism or cynicism to infiltrate your faith.

ASK GOD: To increase your awe of him.

Lift Your Heart

avid was so exuberant that he danced in public as a way of worshiping God. You may not be quite ready to take your joy to the streets, but you can loosen up a bit by raising your hands in prayer, visiting a church whose worship style is a little outside your comfort zone, or just dancing and singing along with a praise and worship tape when no one else is home. Go ahead. Enjoy yourself in God's presence! If he's not worth getting excited about, who is?

Shout with joy to God, all the earth! Sing the glory of his name; make his praise glorious! Say to God, "How awesome are your deeds! So great is your power that your enemies cringe before you. All the earth bows down to you; they sing praise to you, they sing praise to your name" (Psalm 66:1–4).

Abigail

HER CHARACTER: Generous, quick-witted, and wise, she is one of the Bible's great peacemakers.

HER SORROW: To have been mismatched in marriage to her first husband.

HER JOY: That God used her to save lives, eventually making her the wife of David.

KEY SCRIPTURE: 1 Samuel 25:2–42

Monday

HER STORY

*B*lockhead, numskull, nincompoop—the words strike us as both harsh and humorous. But any woman married to a man worthy of such labels would have little to laugh about.

Abigail must have felt suffocated, having been paired with just such a husband. Her father may have thought the wealthy Nabal was a catch, little realizing the man's domineering attitude might one day endanger his daughter's future. But fools and ruin often keep close company, as Abigail discovered.

For some time Abigail had been hearing of David: his encounter with Goliath, his ruddy good looks, his prowess in battle, his rift with King Saul. Recently, he had become her near neighbor in the Desert of Maon, west of the Dead Sea, where he had taken refuge from

Saul. Since David had arrived with his six hundred men, marauders kept clear of her husband's livestock, and Nabal's flocks prospered as a result.

But when David sent ten of his men to ask Nabal for provisions, Nabal, who had grown richer by the day thanks to David, nearly spit in their faces. "Who is this David? Many servants are breaking away from their masters these days. Why should I take my bread and water, and the meat I have slaughtered for my shearers, and give it to men coming from who knows where?" Rich though he was, Nabal had just foolishly insulted the region's most powerful man.

Aware of their danger, one of the servants ran quickly to Abigail, begging her to intervene. As Nabal's wife, she must have suffered his arrogance every day of her life. But this time his folly jeopardized the entire household. Wasting no time, and without a word to her husband, she loaded a caravan of donkeys with gifts for David and his men—freshly baked bread, skins of wine, red meat, and various delicacies—and took them to David's camp. As soon as she saw him, she fell to the ground at his feet, making one of the longest speeches by a woman recorded in the Bible:

"My lord," she pleaded, "let the blame be on me alone. May my lord pay no attention to that wicked man Nabal. He is just like his name—his name is Fool, and folly goes with him. But as for me, your servant, I did not see the men my master sent. Please forgive your servant's offense, for the LORD will certainly make a lasting dynasty for my master, because he fights the LORD's battles. Let no wrongdoing be found in you as long as you live. Even though someone pursues you, your life will be held securely by the LORD your God. But the lives of your enemies he will hurl away as from the pocket of a sling."

Her well-chosen words, of course, reminded David of his success against Goliath, erasing his anger and enabling his gracious reply: "Praise be to the LORD, the God of Israel, who has sent you today to meet me. May you be blessed for your good judgment and for keeping me from bloodshed this day and from avenging myself with my own hands. If you had not come quickly to meet me, not one male belonging to Nabal would have been left alive by daybreak." In addition to saving lives, Abigail's wisdom had spared David from sinning, reminding him that vengeance belongs only to God.

After her encounter with David, Abigail went to Carmel, where Nabal had been shearing his sheep and celebrating his good fortune. Once again, she found him playing the fool. Oblivious to danger, he was drunkenly presiding over a festival banquet, like a great king. She waited until morning, when he was sober, to tell him what had happened. As soon as Nabal heard the news, his heart failed. Ten days later he was dead.

Arrogance, greed, and selfishness had conspired to rob Nabal of any good sense he might once have possessed. Thinking himself a great man when he was only a small one, he lost everything. Abigail was Nabal's opposite, a woman whose humility, faith, generosity, intelligence, and honesty made her wise. Rather than putting others at risk by an ungoverned tongue, her gracious words saved lives.

When David heard the news of Nabal's death, he sent word to Abigail, asking her to be his wife. This time it was Abigail's choice whether or not to marry. She accepted, becoming David's third wife and eventually mother to his second son, Kileab.

Unlike Michal, who had been a mere pawn on a chessboard, Abigail was a woman who rose above her circumstances to change the course of events. Though Scripture doesn't offer details regarding her daily life, it is logical to suppose she was a good wife to Nabal. Even her entreaty to David was the act of a good wife. Perhaps her marriage was the catalyst for her character, helping her to cultivate contrasting virtues to Nabal's vices. Regardless, through her quick-witted action, she spared her husband's life and goods. It was God, not Abigail or David, who paid Nabal back for his arrogance and greed.

Tuesday

HER LIFE AND TIMES

FOOD

*T*wo hundred loaves of bread, two skins of wine, five dressed sheep, a bushel of roasted grain, a hundred cakes of raisins, and two hundred cakes of pressed figs—what a feast! Abigail put together a marvelous meal for David and his men.

Even though famine was not unknown in the area, Palestine had the reputation of being a "land of milk and honey." The most basic food of the land was bread. The bread of biblical times was coarse, dark, and rich. Field workers often brought two small hollow loaves of bread with them, one they filled with olives and the other with cheese. Abigail's offering of two hundred loaves of such bread formed a bountiful beginning to the meal for David and his men.

Wine was the common drink in this hot land. Juices fermented quickly in bags of animal skins. Often wine was mixed with water to provide a refreshing drink with meals. Wine also was used as a disinfectant (Luke 10:34) and as a medicine (1 Timothy 5:23).

Next Abigail took five "dressed sheep." No, this didn't mean the sheep wore clothes appropriate for the trip; it meant they were killed and skinned and ready to be cooked. Because the sheep were dressed, David's men merely had to build a fire and cook parts of the sheep to eat. Sheep, both young and old, formed a major part of the Israelites' meat diet, as did calves, goats, and different types of birds. Hunters also brought in venison, antelope, and other wild animals, and fishermen provided many types of fish for eating, something the Israelites complained about missing while they were wandering in the desert.

The bushel of roasted grain was a food that could be eaten anywhere, anytime. Since David and his men were often pursued, such food would have been a helpful addition to their diet. Such roasted grain along with a bit of wine often formed a quick lunch for field laborers (Ruth 2:14).

Now for dessert—or at least something sweet. Abigail gathered one hundred cakes of raisins and two hundred cakes of pressed figs. Palestine swelled with the produce from the vine and fig tree, so much so that the tree came to be known as a metaphor for safe, abundant living: "During Solomon's lifetime Judah and Israel, from Dan to Beersheba, lived in safety, each man under his own vine and fig tree" (1 Kings 4:25). Fresh fruit of many different kinds was available year round, but the first fresh figs of the year were considered a special delicacy. Dried figs and raisins also made excellent food for the traveler, perfect for David and his men.

The women in Israelite households (some things never change!) customarily prepared the meals. They usually prepared food in a mixed form; that is, small pieces of meat, vegetables, rice, grain, and sometimes fruits were mixed together to form the meal rather than being kept separate, as is common today. The Israelite diet could be almost as varied—depending on the season and the individual's wealth—as many of today's people have come to expect and enjoy.

New Testament writers used food as a metaphor for spiritual nourishment. Paul talks about the milk, rather than solid food, required by new Christians (1 Corinthians 3:2), and the writer to the Hebrews writes of those Christians whose spiritual growth is so slow that they still require milk rather than solid food (Hebrews 5:11–14). Jesus reminded his disciples that "life is more than food" (Luke 12:23–26), and that we shouldn't worry so much about it.

Wednesday

HER LEGACY IN SCRIPTURE

Read 1 Samuel 25:2–42.

1. What do you imagine it was like for Abigail to be married to Nabal on a day-to-day basis?

2. How would you have dealt with a husband like Nabal? What kind of person would you have become?

3. How did Abigail deal with an arrogant man (Nabal) and an angry man (David)?

4. How do you react when someone in authority over you makes a bad choice? If the choice affects you, what should you do?

5. How would you like to grow in the way you relate to men?

Thursday

HER PROMISE

A bigail was a courageous woman, who made the best out
of a difficult situation. She knew the cultural principles at work
here: Nabal—out of just plain good hospitality and out of gratitude
for the protection David's men had provided—should have given
David's men what they asked for. Yet when David sought vengeance,
Abigail interceded, realizing that vengeance wasn't something that
was up to David—or her—to give.

Years of living with Nabal did not seem to have made Abigail
bitter, nor had the years caused her to look for ways to get back at
him and seek revenge. The Lord honored Abigail for her consistency,
her generosity, and her willingness to continue on the right path, no
matter how difficult. In the same way, God continues to honor those
who are faithful even when faithfulness brings difficulty and hardship and pain. He doesn't promise to always deliver, as he delivered
Abigail, but he does promise to go with us.

Promises in Scripture

Hear, O LORD, and be merciful to me;
*   O LORD, be my help."*
You turned my wailing into dancing;
*   you removed my sackcloth and clothed me with joy,*
that my heart may sing to you and not be silent.
*   O LORD my God, I will give you thanks forever.*

—PSALM 30:10–12

Do not withhold your mercy from me, O Lord;
*   may your love and your truth always protect me.*

—PSALM 40:11

So do not fear, for I am with you;
*   do not be dismayed, for I am your God.*
I will strengthen you and help you;
*   I will uphold you with my righteous right hand.*

—ISAIAH 41:10

Friday

HER LEGACY OF PRAYER

David said to Abigail, "Praise be to the LORD, the God of Israel, who has sent you today to meet me. May you be blessed for your good judgment and for keeping me from bloodshed this day and from avenging myself with my own hands."

—1 SAMUEL 25:32–33

REFLECT ON: 1 Samuel 25:2–42.

PRAISE GOD: For calling you to be a peacemaker in your family, neighborhood, and world.

OFFER THANKS: That God knows every challenge facing your marriage.

CONFESS: Any bitterness you may have harbored about your marriage.

ASK GOD: To use your relationship with your husband to strengthen your character and increase your faith.

Lift Your Heart

*I*f you haven't yet made a commitment to pray daily for your husband, do so today. Set aside a few minutes to surrender your marriage to God, specifically asking him to bless your spouse. Try to refrain from focusing on your laundry list of complaints and instead pray for the needs you know your husband has. Ask God to shape your marriage relationship and use it for his purposes. Relinquish any desire you may have to control your husband; instead, ask God to work in his life.

Father, I ask you to bless my husband in every facet of his life—

> *his health*
> *his work*
> *his relationship with our children*
> *our relationship together*
> *and his relationship to you.*

Let nothing and no one, including myself, hinder your work in his life.

The Woman of Endor

HER CHARACTER: Compassionate to Saul on the eve of his death, she
exercised power by acting as a medium.

HER SORROW: To have delivered a hopeless message to Israel's king.

KEY SCRIPTURE: 1 Samuel 28:3–25

Monday

HER STORY

*I*t was a night for frightening apparitions. Squinting through the
open doorway, the woman stiffened, retreating a step. A face loomed
before her, floating on its own like a full white moon in the outer
darkness. Before she could close the door, she felt fingers gripping
her wrist.

"Please," the voice insisted, "consult a spirit for me, and bring up
for me the one I name."

The large man pushed through the door, followed by two more
men. She could smell his fear as he swept past her and sat down on
the couch.

"Surely you know what Saul has done. He has cut off the mediums and spiritists from the land. Why have you set a trap for my life
to bring about my death?" she replied.

"As surely as the LORD lives, you will not be punished for this,"
he swore.

"Whom shall I bring up for you?"

"Bring up Samuel," he said.

So the woman sat down and yielded herself, making her soul a bridge for the dead to walk across.

Suddenly she screamed, "Why have you deceived me? You are Saul!"

The king calmed her, saying, "Don't be afraid. What do you see?"

"An old man wearing a robe is coming up," she said.

Saul bowed down and prostrated himself, his face in the dirt.

Samuel said to Saul, "Why have you disturbed me by bringing me up?"

"I am in great distress," Saul replied. "The Philistines are fighting against me, and God has turned away from me. He no longer answers me, either by prophets or by dreams. So I have called on you to tell me what to do."

Samuel said, "Why do you consult me, now that the LORD has turned away from you and become your enemy? The LORD has done what he predicted through me. The LORD has torn the kingdom out of your hands and given it to one of your neighbors—to David. Tomorrow you and your sons will be with me. The LORD will also hand over the army of Israel to the Philistines."

The woman shuddered, the message delivered. Little wonder the king had seemed so desolate. Fear had crushed the life out of his once-strong face, hollowing the eyes, etching deep lines across cheeks and forehead.

Taking pity, she spoke to him: "Look, your maidservant has obeyed you. I took my life in my hands and did what you told me to do. Now please listen to your servant and let me give you some food so you may eat and have the strength to go on your way."

Kindly, she served what may have been Saul's last meal. The next day he was dead. Wounded in battle, he fell on his own sword, determined to finish the job before his enemies could reach him. True to form, Saul, who had always tried to control his destiny, controlled even the manner of his death. But he could not control what happened next. Discovering his body, the Philistines celebrated by severing his head and hanging it in the temple of their god. Then they tacked his naked corpse to the walls of a nearby town as a trophy. Israel's first king had become a gruesome spectacle.

The woman of Endor is a strange character, steeped in the occult yet kind and motherly in her attitude toward the tormented king. For some reason, God allowed her to call up the prophet Samuel even though necromancy (conjuring spirits for the purpose of knowing or influencing future events) was strictly forbidden in Israel.

Perhaps she had become a medium because women in those days had so little power. Or perhaps it seemed an outlet for her helpful nature. But by yielding her soul to spirits, she was abusing herself in the deepest possible way, distorting her dignity as a person for the sake of obtaining power. How fitting that Saul, who had always tried to control the future, spent his last moments consulting her, breaking his own law in the process. Step-by-step, his insecurities had taken control of him, reducing his soul and disabling his ability to depend on God rather than on himself.

That night the woman of Endor had looked into the eyes of the most powerful man in Israel and had seen the terror there. Did the vision shake her? Did she recognize herself in him? Did her encounter with a true prophet cause her to forsake her trade as a medium? We have no idea what became of her. Sadly, her meeting with Saul marks one of the lowest moments in the life of Israel's first king, revealing his disintegration as a man whose future was destroyed by disobedience.

Saul's tragic ending reminds us that the antidote to fear is always trust. Only faith can cure our worst nightmares, and faith is a gift that is either fed by obedience or starved by disobedience. Forsaking our own desire to manipulate and control people and circumstances, we must trust God to use his power on our behalf.

Tuesday

HER LIFE AND TIMES

WITCHCRAFT

*I*ronic, isn't it, that the same Saul who refused to heed Samuel's prophetic words when he was alive now disobeyed the very laws he had put into effect in order to hear from Samuel one last time. Saul's desperation must have been very great for him to consult with a medium, to dabble in the occult.

Ancient peoples felt as though they were living in close contact with the spirit world around them. They depended on divination — foretelling the future — to help them avoid possible troubles ahead, and used occult rituals to attempt to gain control over people, objects, and even nature.

Magicians studied the entrails of animals and the flights of birds to discover information about the future. They examined the stars and interpreted dreams. They called on the dead to make use of their wisdom. At times, they even gathered information from such common occurrences as a sneeze.

Right from the start, God commanded his people not to have anything to do with witchcraft in any form. His words are clear and firm — we might even think harsh: "A man or woman who is a medium or spiritist among you must be put to death. You are to stone them; their blood will be on their own heads" (Leviticus 20:27).

Today, when the interest in spiritism and mediums is once again strong, it is good to consider what may be fueling the fascination. Words like *waiting*, *depending*, *surrendering*, and *obeying* rankle. We would much rather find ways to control the course of events. Yet the spiritual life is often counterintuitive. When we embrace the way of faith and trust in God, following him even when the path is unfamiliar or unknown, what seems like it should diminish us actually enlarges us. The story of Saul and the woman of Endor reminds us that there's really nothing new about human behavior. Under the skin we all experience the same desires, temptations, and needs. Then, as now, our happiness lies in faith and trust.

Wednesday

HER LEGACY IN SCRIPTURE

Read 1 Samuel 28:3–25.

1. The woman of Endor enters this story fearfully. Why was she afraid?

2. Who do you think appears in 1 Samuel 28:13? Is it really Samuel or a spirit impersonating Samuel? Explain why you think so.

3. What do you learn about occult practices from this story?

4. How, if ever, have you consulted spirits (horoscopes, cards, books, fortune-tellers, Ouija boards) to plan your future or just for "fun"? Why do you think the Bible says that nothing like this should ever be done, even for fun?

5. Consider how kind the woman is to Saul in 1 Samuel 28:21–25. If someone who practices the occult can also be such a kind person, how do you think that should affect your views on occult practice and practitioners? Why?

Thursday

HER PROMISE

*I*n a backhanded sort of way, the woman of Endor reveals for us our need to trust God. As human beings, many of us are like Saul, afraid of the future, estranged from our loved ones and God, willing to go anywhere for help. But God is our only true source of help and comfort. He has promised to guide and direct us and plan our steps. He doesn't promise to reveal the future to us, but he does promise to go with us as we step into it.

Promises in Scripture

O people of Zion, who live in Jerusalem, you will weep no more. How gracious he will be when you cry for help! As soon as he hears, he will answer you. Although the LORD gives you the bread of adversity and the water of affliction, your teachers will be hidden no more; with your own eyes you will see them. Whether you turn to the right or to the left, your ears will hear a voice behind you, saying, "This is the way; walk in it."

—ISAIAH 30:19–21

Strengthen the feeble hands,
    steady the knees that give way;
say to those with fearful hearts,
    "Be strong, do not fear;
your God will come …
    he will come to save you." …
And a highway will be there;
    it will be called the Way of Holiness.…
Only the redeemed will walk there.

—ISAIAH 35:3–4, 8–9

This is what the LORD says:

"Stand at the crossroads and look;
    ask for the ancient paths,
ask where the good way is, and walk in it,
    and you will find rest for your souls."

—JEREMIAH 6:16

Friday

HER LEGACY OF PRAYER

Do not turn to mediums or seek out spiritists, for you will be defiled by them. I am the LORD your God.

—LEVITICUS 19:31

REFLECT ON: 1 Samuel 28:3–25.

PRAISE GOD: That he protects us against evil.

OFFER THANKS: That God doesn't hide himself from those who love and follow him.

CONFESS: Any dealings you may have had with the occult: using tarot cards, consulting horoscopes, visiting fortune-tellers, reading occult books.

ASK GOD: To cleanse and free you from any ill effect of your contact with the occult.

Lift Your Heart

Sometimes we expose ourselves to the occult naively—reading horoscopes in the daily paper, consulting a medium on a whim, or thinking tarot cards simply an innocent game. At other times our interest is more serious, based on a desire for knowledge, healing, or power over others and ourselves. If you have ever dabbled in the occult, now is the time to come clean before God. Express your sorrow and your resolve to follow God by removing from your home anything remotely related to the occult. Confide in your pastor or a mature Christian friend about your involvement, asking them to pray with you as you seek God's protection and forgiveness.

Father, forgive me for my involvement in the occult. I want nothing whatever to do with the realm of evil. Draw me out of the darkness and into the light of your presence. Free me from any lingering effects of my involvement and help me to trust you completely for my future.

Bathsheba

HER NAME MEANS

"The Seventh Daughter" or "The Daughter of an Oath"

HER CHARACTER: Her beauty made her victim to a king's desire. Though it is difficult to discern her true character, she seems to have found the courage to endure tragedy, winning the king's confidence and eventually securing the kingdom for her son Solomon.

HER SORROW: To have been molested by a supposedly godly man, who then murdered her husband. To have suffered the loss of one of her sons.

HER JOY: To have given birth to five sons, one of whom became king of Israel after David's death.

KEY SCRIPTURE: 2 Samuel 11:1–12:25

Monday

HER STORY

*B*athsheba squeezed the sponge, moving it rhythmically across her body as though to calm the restless cadence of her thoughts. Normally, she looked forward to the ritual bath marking the end of her monthly period, but tonight the water soothed her skin without refreshing her spirit.

She should be glad for the cool breeze. For flowers. For a lush harvest. But spring could also yield its crop of sorrows, as she well knew. Spring was the season for armies and battles. Once the rains had ceased and the harvest had been gathered, men marched off to war, leaving their women behind.

Bathsheba shivered as she stood up. Though her husband, Uriah, was a seasoned soldier, she still worried about him, wishing she could fall asleep in his arms. But he was camped with the rest of the king's army beneath the open skies of Rabbah, an Ammonite fortress some forty miles northeast of Jerusalem.

The king rose from his bed, unable to sleep. Pacing across the palace roof, he gazed at the city below. Jerusalem seemed calm, a city at peace with itself though at war with its neighbors. Soon his soldiers would gather a great harvest of Ammonite captives, laborers for his expanding kingdom. The casual observer might have thought David a man at peace with his growing power. Instead, the king could not quiet an increasing sense of discontent.

Then, in the half-light, David noticed the figure of a young woman bathing in the walled garden of a house below him. He leaned against the outer edge of the roof for a closer view. Wet hair curling languidly against skin soft as lamb's wool. Breasts like rounded apples. He reached as though to steal a touch. Unaware of watching eyes, the woman toweled herself dry and stepped into the house. He waited and watched, but even the king could not see through walls.

Over the next few days, David made inquiries and discovered that the vision had a name: She was Bathsheba, the wife of one of his soldiers, Uriah the Hittite. He sent for her. She came to him and became pregnant with his child.

Fearing discovery, the king ordered Uriah home from battle. But the soldier surprised him by refusing to spend the night with his wife: "The ark and Israel and Judah are staying in tents, and my lord's men are camped in the open fields. How could I go to my house to eat and drink and lie with my wife? As surely as you live, I will not do such a thing!"

So David convinced Uriah to spend another day in Jerusalem, managing to get him drunk. Surely the wine would overcome his scruples. But it didn't. So David played his last card, entrusting Bathsheba's husband with a letter to Joab, commander of the army. It read: "Put Uriah in the front line where the fighting is fiercest. Then withdraw from him so he will be struck down and die."

So Uriah died by treachery, and David claimed Bathsheba as his wife, her child as his own.

One day, the prophet Nathan approached David, saying: "There were two men in a certain town, one rich and the other poor. The rich man had a large number of sheep and cattle, but the poor man had nothing except one little ewe lamb he had bought. He raised it, and it grew up with him and his children. It shared his food, drank from his cup, and even slept in his arms. It was like a daughter to him.

"Now a traveler came to the rich man, but the rich man refrained from taking one of his own sheep or cattle to prepare a meal for the traveler who had come to him. Instead, he took the ewe lamb that belonged to the poor man and prepared it for the one who had come to him."

David was incensed: "As surely as the LORD lives, the man who did this deserves to die! He must pay for that lamb four times over, because he did such a thing and had no pity."

Then Nathan said to David, "You are the man! This is what the LORD, the God of Israel, says: 'I anointed you king over Israel, and I delivered you from the hand of Saul. I gave your master's house to you, and your master's wives into your arms. I gave you the house of Israel and Judah. And if all this had been too little, I would have given you even more. Why did you despise the word of the LORD by doing what is evil in his eyes? You struck down Uriah the Hittite with the sword and took his wife to be your own. Now, therefore, the sword will never depart from your house.'"

David's lust for Bathsheba marked the beginning of his long decline. Though God forgave him, he still suffered the consequences of his wrongdoing. His sin was a whirlpool that dragged others into its swirling path. And despite David's prayer and pleading, God allowed the son David had conceived with Bathsheba to die from an illness.

But why did Bathsheba have to suffer along with the man who molested her and murdered her husband? Though the story gives us little insight into her true character, it is hardly likely that Bathsheba was in a position to refuse the king. In Nathan's parable, in fact, she is depicted as an innocent lamb. Why, then, have so many people painted her as a seductress? Perhaps Bathsheba's innocence is too painful to face. That a good person can suffer such tragedies, especially at the hands of a godly person, appalls us. Worse yet, God punishes both David and Bathsheba by taking their son. If we can believe that Bathsheba had an affair with David, we could accept her suffering more easily; her guilt would make David's sin seem less grave and God's punishment less cruel.

Though Bathsheba may not have understood the reasons for her suffering, God gave her favor with King David, making her both a powerful queen and the mother of David's successor, Solomon, who became famous for his great wisdom.

Tuesday

HER LIFE AND TIMES

RITUAL BATHING

A warm tub of water with a fragrance of flowers, soaking, eyes closed. That's the sort of image conjured up in most of our minds when it comes to bathing. But in Bathsheba's day, most bathing took place not for the purpose of physical cleanliness—people of that time had little knowledge of the spread of disease and germs through uncleanness. Most bathing took place in order to become ritually clean after a period of being unclean.

Bathsheba had just completed her monthly period. The flow of blood was finished; the seven days prescribed in Leviticus 15:19 were past, and she now needed to cleanse herself. She probably stood in or near a basin of water, using a sponge or cloth to clean herself, then either squeezing water over herself as a rinse or pouring water from a pitcher over her body.

Scripture mentions cleansing with water hundreds of times, most of them referring to ritual rather than physical cleansing. Cleansing took place after many kinds of skin diseases were healed (Leviticus 14:8), and after men and women had unusual discharges (Leviticus 15:13). Men and women both had to wash themselves after sexual intercourse in order to be ceremonially clean (Leviticus 15:18). Priests cleansed themselves before offering sacrifices (Exodus 29:4; Leviticus 8:6), and the sacrifices themselves were washed before being offered to God (Leviticus 1:9).

Physical cleansing more often took the form of washing one's hands before eating or washing one's feet when entering a house. Dirty, dusty roads and open sandals made foot washing something that needed to be done frequently. Since foot washing was commonly the job of the lowest member or servant of a household, Jesus modeled a splendid humility when he bathed his disciples' feet in the upper room (John 13:5).

The Bible sometimes describes the righteous as those with "clean hands" (Job 17:9; Psalm 24:4). Cleanliness is also used in Scripture as a metaphor for being forgiven: "I am clean and free from guilt" (Job 33:9). "Cleanse me with hyssop, and I will be clean; wash me, and I will be whiter than snow" (Psalm 51:7). In the end times, the bride of Christ will be dressed in "fine linen, bright and clean" (Revelation 19:8).

We live in a culture that glorifies outward cleanliness with our soaps and lotions and toothpastes and disinfectants, our bathing and brushing, our washing and wiping. But how concerned are we with inner cleanliness? Do we have clean hands but spirits filthy with hate? Do we have soft, clean-shaven legs but hearts hardened to the hurts of others? Do we have clean, blemish-free faces that seldom smile? Outward cleanliness is admirable — but only if an inward cleanliness accompanies it.

Wednesday

HER LEGACY IN SCRIPTURE

Read 2 Samuel 11:1–12:25.

1. What part do you think Bathsheba played in the events of 2 Samuel 11:2–4? Totally innocent? Artful seductress? Something in between? Explain why you think so.

2. How do you think Bathsheba felt when she realized she was pregnant with David's child? Why did she immediately tell him?

3. God called David a "man after my own heart" (Acts 13:22; cf. 1 Samuel 13:14). How could God say this, given the awful things he did to Bathsheba and Uriah?

4. What do you think Bathsheba was doing and feeling while her son got sick and died? Why do you think the Bible focuses on David's response rather than hers?

5. Solomon's name from the Lord was actually Jedidiah (2 Samuel 12:24–25), which means "loved by the LORD." What sense of God's restoration for Bathsheba and David does this name give you?

6. What does this story say to you about your own experience as a sinner and/or a victim of others' sin?

Thursday

HER PROMISE

The story of David and Bathsheba outlines in graphic detail the horror of sin and where it leads. David's first step toward sin leads to adultery, lying, deceit, murder, and, finally, the death of a son. The link between sin and restoration comes when David admits his sin and Nathan says the Lord has taken it away (2 Samuel 12:13). How much guilt is Bathsheba's isn't clear; however, when God tells them through the prophet Nathan that he loves their son Solomon and wants him to be called Jedidiah, the restoration is Bathsheba's as well as David's. If God could forgive this terrible sin of David, don't you think he could forgive your sin, whatever it may be?

Promises in Scripture

The LORD, the LORD, the compassionate and gracious God, slow to anger, abounding in love and faithfulness, maintaining love to thousands, and forgiving wickedness, rebellion and sin.

—EXODUS 34:6–7

If my people, who are called by my name, will humble themselves and pray and seek my face and turn from their wicked ways, then will I hear from heaven and will forgive their sin and will heal their land.

—2 CHRONICLES 7:14

For the sake of your name, O LORD,
    forgive my iniquity, though it is great.

—PSALM 25:11

For I [God] will forgive their wickedness
    and will remember their sins no more.

—HEBREWS 8:12

Friday

HER LEGACY OF PRAYER

This is what the LORD, the God of Israel says: "I anointed you king over Israel, and I delivered you from the hand of Saul.... And if all this had been too little, I would have given you even more. Why did you despise the word of the LORD by doing what is evil in his eyes? You struck down Uriah the Hittite with the sword and took his wife to be your own."

—2 SAMUEL 12:7–9

REFLECT ON: 2 Samuel 12:1–25.

PRAISE GOD: That he is quick to note our suffering.

OFFER THANKS: That God calls the powerful to abide by the same moral standards as the weak.

CONFESS: Any unforgiveness you may have toward another.

ASK GOD: To restore your confidence and to free you from any tendency to take on the mind-set of a victim.

Lift Your Heart

*I*f you have suffered abuse—whether sexual, physical, or emotional—don't bury your feelings, absorbing the shame and guilt that belong to the abuser. Instead, share your pain with at least one other person—a trusted friend or counselor. Find other women who have endured similar abuse and gone on to lead fruitful and significant lives. Determine that you will not let someone else's sin ruin your life. Learn the skills of a survivor. Even if you've never been abused, you probably know someone who has—a daughter, a friend, or an acquaintance. Do whatever you can to help that person and pray that God will restore her hope.

Father, forgiveness is so hard sometimes. I want justice, not mercy. Please help me to begin the process of forgiveness by letting go of my desire for revenge. Every time I start wishing something negative on those who've hurt me, help me to pray a blessing on their behalf instead. Only you can give me the desire to forgive. Only you can help me do the impossible.

Tamar
Daughter of King David

HER NAME MEANS
"Date Tree" or "Palm Tree"

HER CHARACTER: Tamar shared her father's, David's, good looks. Young and innocent, she was naive to the danger that threatened from her own family.

HER SORROW: That her half brother saw her only as an object for his lust, destroying her future as a result, and that her father, the king, did nothing to protect her.

KEY SCRIPTURE: 2 Samuel 13:1–22

Monday

HER STORY

David's daughter Tamar was a knockout. No doubt she was destined for a marriage that would strengthen the king's political alliances. Though not under lock and key, she probably lived a rather protected life. But all the precautions in the world couldn't save her from the danger that threatened from David's inner circle.

Amnon was David's heir. As the king's eldest son, he was used to getting his way. But lately he'd grown despondent. Something was bothering him, chasing away his sleep, gnawing at his heart.

One day, Jonadab, Amnon's cousin, asked him: "Why do you, the king's son, look so haggard morning after morning? Won't you tell me?"

Amnon confided in his friend, saying, "I'm in love with Tamar, my brother Absalom's sister."

"Go to bed and pretend to be ill," Jonadab shrewdly advised. "When your father comes to see you, say to him, 'I would like my sister Tamar to come and give me something to eat. Let her prepare the food in my sight, so I may eat from her hand.'"

So David, concerned for his son, unwittingly sent his daughter into a trap that would ruin her life.

After Tamar had prepared a meal for Amnon, he asked her to enter his bedroom and feed him. But as soon as Tamar did, he grabbed her, begging, "Come to bed with me, my sister."

"Don't, my brother!" she said to him. "Don't force me. Such a thing should not be done in Israel! Don't do this wicked thing. What about me? Where could I get rid of my disgrace? And what about you? You would be like one of the wicked fools in Israel. Please speak to the king; he will not keep me from being married to you." But despite her pleas, Amnon forced himself on her.

As soon as the storm of his passion died down, Amnon's infatuation turned to hatred. He threw Tamar out of his house, bolting the door against her, as though she, not he, were the guilty one. Desolate, the young girl tore her robes, throwing ashes on her head and weeping loudly as she wandered the streets. When her brother Absalom found her, he hushed her, saying, "Be quiet now, my sister, he is your brother. Don't take this thing to heart." But Absalom himself took it to heart, hating his half brother Amnon for what he had done.

Though David was furious when he heard the news, he did nothing to punish Amnon. Did he favor his son over his daughter, thinking her hurt a small matter? Or had his moral authority been so compromised by his lust for Bathsheba that he simply could not bring himself to confront his eldest son? Whatever the case, Absalom did not share his father's hesitation. Instead, he bided his time, waiting for an opportunity for vengeance. Two years later he murdered Amnon.

First rape, then murder. David's household was devastated not by barbarians outside the gate but by those inside his own family. After Amnon's death, David must have been haunted by Nathan's earlier prophecy after David's own adultery with Bathsheba: "Now, therefore, the sword will never depart from your house.... Out of your own household I am going to bring calamity upon you" (2 Samuel 12:10–11). The father's lust was mirrored by the son's; the father's violence, by one son's murder of the other.

Tamar, unprotected by her father, betrayed by her own brother, lived in Absalom's house, a desolate woman, without the possibility of marriage or children because she was no longer a virgin. Thus a chain of sin wove its way through David's family, enslaving the innocent along with the guilty.

Tuesday

HER LIFE AND TIMES

RAPE

Tamar's half brother, Amnon, raped her. The stark words don't begin to communicate the humiliation and despair that rape brings to those who experience it. This account in 2 Samuel 13 movingly describes Tamar's pleas to her brother not to do this to her, pleas that echo through hundreds of years of women who have been forced into the sexual act against their will. "Since he was stronger," Amnon could force himself on her, and Tamar had no effective means of resistance.

God's reaction to sexual sin is evident throughout the Bible. He doesn't turn away from the victim, and he doesn't allow the rapist to go unpunished. Deuteronomy 22:25 says that "the man who has done this shall die." Leviticus 18:29 reminds the Israelites that "everyone who does any of these detestable things—such persons must be cut off from their people." In the New Testament, Paul repeatedly reminds believers to pursue sexual purity: "Let us behave decently, as in the daytime, not in orgies and drunkenness, not in sexual immorality and debauchery, not in dissension and jealousy. Rather, clothe yourselves with the Lord Jesus Christ" (Romans 13:13–14). "Flee from sexual immorality" (1 Corinthians 6:18). "Among you there must not be even a hint of sexual immorality" (Ephesians 5:3).

Amnon went unpunished by his father but died when his half brother Absalom took his revenge—he didn't go unpunished forever. And what about Tamar, the beautiful virgin princess in her rich royal robes? She felt too degraded to go back to her own home in David's palace. How could she face her other virgin sisters? Instead, she went to live as "a desolate woman," with her brother Absalom. The effects of rape on its victims is the same today: desolation, grief, misery.

The Bible doesn't gloss over the fact that God's people have participated in these dreadful acts; it describes many instances of rape, incest, homosexuality, and adultery. Why would a holy God think it necessary to include such sordid stories in Scripture? Perhaps because he knows our thoughts and actions, even if the world is blind to them. Through these stories God reminds us that he never forsakes his own, whether victim or criminal. Just as he offers help and comfort to the victims, never forsaking them in their trouble, he also offers healing and forgiveness to the evildoer.

Wednesday

HER LEGACY IN SCRIPTURE

Read 2 Samuel 13:1–22.

1. Do you think Amnon truly loved Tamar? Why or why not?

2. Describe your feelings as a woman when you read Tamar's pleas in 2 Samuel 13:9–14.

3. Why did Tamar say that sending her away was "a greater wrong" than rape (13:16)? What did she want?

4. What should David have done to Amnon? What could he have done for Tamar?

5. Have you ever been betrayed by someone you trusted? If so, how has it affected your life? Where is God in your story?

Thursday

HER PROMISE

The horrifying facts of Tamar's experience—not only the rape itself but the effect it had on her future and her emotional well-being—are not too far from the experiences of many women today. Statistics reveal a staggering number of women who have been violated by family members when they were very young. The effects of those experiences can haunt a woman's existence, influencing her relationships with her husband, with male and female friends, and with her children. Help is available to those who seek it, but the ultimate hope and help can only be found in the love and acceptance God so willingly offers. His forgiving spirit can help recovery begin. His comforting spirit can bring a soothing balm to the hurt of the past. His constant presence can bring healing for the loneliness and detachment many feel.

Promises in Scripture

For the LORD your God is a merciful God; he will not abandon or destroy you.

—DEUTERONOMY 4:31

Be strong and courageous. Do not be afraid or terrified because of them, for the LORD your God goes with you; he will never leave you nor forsake you.

—DEUTERONOMY 31:6

Hear my voice when I call, O LORD;
*   be merciful to me and answer me.*
My heart says of you, "Seek his face!"
*   Your face, LORD, I will seek.*
Do not hide your face from me,
*   do not turn your servant away in anger;*
*   you have been my helper.*
Do not reject me or forsake me,
*   O God my Savior.*
Though my father and mother forsake me,
*   the LORD will receive me.*

—PSALM 27:7–10

Friday

HER LEGACY OF PRAYER

Though [God] slay me, yet will I hope in him.

—JOB 13:15

REFLECT ON: 2 Samuel 13:1–31.

PRAISE GOD: For giving us a hope rooted not in the events of this life, but in eternity.

OFFER THANKS: That God has the power to restore our hope.

CONFESS: Any hopelessness about your life.

ASK GOD: To show you that he really does care about you.

Lift Your Heart

Whether we suffer from sexual abuse, the loss of a loved one, divorce, sickness, or financial reverses, we can sometimes feel hopeless about the future. But anyone who belongs to God will not be consigned to a hopeless end. Even if you have difficulty believing this, pray for the grace to want to believe it. As a small gesture expressing your desire, plant a bulb garden in the fall. This simple act will affirm your belief that even after the harshest winter, spring will come again with its profusion of color and new life. If fall is still far away, buy a colorful bouquet of flowers to grace your bedside table for the week ahead.

Father, plant something new in my life, a sprig of hope that will set me on a new course. Help me to live in the present, spending my emotional energies on this moment rather than squandering them on regrets about the past or anxieties about the future.

The Wise Woman of Abel

HER CHARACTER: Rather than passively waiting for someone else to save her city, she had the wisdom and courage to act quickly and decisively.

HER SORROW: That her city, though faithful to the king, was besieged by his army because it had been infiltrated by a rebellious leader.

HER JOY: That she was able to successfully intercede for the town, thus averting disaster for many innocent people.

KEY SCRIPTURE: 2 Samuel 20:14–22

Monday

HER STORY

Teddy Roosevelt once said that "nine-tenths of wisdom consists in being wise in time." After the dust settles, the storm clears, the action stops, it's often too late for wisdom to work its marvels.

Many women in Scripture stand out for their wisdom. One woman, who lived in a town at Israel's northern border, is identified solely as "a wise woman" (2 Samuel 20:16), acting quickly to save her city.

The sad stories of Bathsheba and Tamar highlighted the decline of David's household. Eventually, Absalom, David's third son, rebelled and was killed in a battle for the throne. In the midst of this political instability, a rabble-rouser by the name of Sheba, from the tribe of Benjamin (Saul's tribe), attempted still another revolt. But Joab, the commander of David's army, chased Sheba all the way to Abel Beth Maacah, in the north.

Joab had constructed siege ramps to assault the walls of Abel and squelch the rebellion. It was evident that the entire city would be destroyed unless someone acted quickly to preserve the peace.

Suddenly, a woman stood on the walls of Abel and shouted: "Listen! Listen! Tell Joab to come here so I can speak to him.

"We are the peaceful and faithful in Israel," she cried out. "You are trying to destroy a city that is a mother in Israel. Why do you want to swallow up the LORD's inheritance?" she challenged Joab.

"Far be it from me to swallow up or destroy!" he replied. "A man named Sheba son of Bicri, from the hill country of Ephraim, has lifted up his hand against the king, against David. Hand over this one man, and I'll withdraw from the city."

"His head will be thrown to you from the wall," she shouted back.

The woman turned to her fellow citizens, urging them to act. In just moments, a man's head came careening over the wall. Disaster was averted.

The men in this story appear to behave only in conventional terms: mobilize the army, build a siege ramp, violently smash the city walls, squelch the rebellion. But the woman looked for another solution. Gruesome as it was, it kept the peace and spared lives on both sides. Through her intercession on behalf of her people, innocent lives on both sides of the city walls were spared.

Tuesday

HER LIFE AND TIMES

SIEGE

When Joab's men gathered outside of Abel Beth Maacah, a wise woman braved the warriors gathered outside and bargained with Joab for the life of Abel's inhabitants. No doubt she and others like her were part of the reason that Abel was known as "a city that is a mother in Israel" (2 Samuel 20:19), a place to go for answers to life's difficult questions. Its inhabitants must have been shrewd as well as wise to gain such notoriety.

War was a regular feature of life for the Israelites, so much so that freedom from war gained special notice in Scripture (Joshua 11:23; 14:15; 2 Chronicles 14:6–7). Battles between opposing armies were often waged in valleys or other wide-open spaces. Inhabitants of embattled areas would flee to the nearest walled and fortified city. In order to gain entrance and control of such a city, armies would gather outside the city walls and prevent anyone from going in or going out. When water and food became scarce or ran out altogether, the city's inhabitants would be forced to surrender.

When a city surrendered, its populace could look forward to one of two consequences: death or slavery. Often the deprivation and horror of a siege were preferable to surrender and its results. Depending on how well the city was prepared, a siege could last anywhere from days to weeks to months. An army of Egypt besieged the Philistine city of Ashdod for an incredible twenty-nine years.

Occupants of fortified cities spent much time in preparation for sieges. Strengthening the walls, gathering and storing extra food, and figuring out a way to gather and store large amounts of water required time and expertise. Some cities built long underground tunnels to allow water to flow freely into the city. Builders of these tunnels took care to disguise the water's source, for armies could then easily cut it off or use it to gain entrance into the city. Sometimes huge cisterns were dug within the city walls to catch and store rain water.

The attacking army outside a city's walls would move vast amounts of earth to build ramps to the upper parts of the city wall. From these ramps they would then use battering rams to attempt to break down the wall in that area, all the while defending themselves against the arrows and rocks and darts of the city's inhabitants. Joab's army built such a ramp and battered the wall of Abel in order to capture it and the rebel Sheba, who had taken refuge within. But rather than throwing down arrows or rocks, the wise woman of Abel shouted words of conciliation, and in so doing, preserved innocent lives.

Wednesday

HER LEGACY IN SCRIPTURE

Read 2 Samuel 20:14–22.

1. What do you think it was like for mothers with small children in Abel when Joab's army surrounded it?

2. Why do you suppose a "wise woman," rather than one of the leading men of the city, called out to Joab? What does this say about her?

3. What do Joab's terse words in verse 17 tell you about his reaction to this woman?

4. What do you think about what the town of Abel did to Sheba? Was the bargain they struck with Joab a good one? Why or why not?

5. The facts of this story are brutal and disturbing, but the facts of life for many today are just as brutal. War, abuse, poverty, illness, or death can besiege families or towns. How can you be a wise woman in your corner of the world?

Thursday

HER PROMISE

*T*he wise woman of Abel saw a need for immediate action, and she acted. She recognized that this was not a time to passively wait for someone else to take the reins of leadership, not a time for quibbling or wavering, just a time to do what needed to be done. Through this woman, God saved the innocent inhabitants of her city. There are times when quick action is required of us as well. We may hesitate, we may wish to go another way, we may dodge and shuffle, but in the end we must act. When we're living in obedience and close relationship with God, we can trust that we don't go alone. God is there, giving us the help and assurance we require.

Promises in Scripture

Do not let this Book of the Law depart from your mouth; meditate on it day and night, so that you may be careful to do everything written in it. Then you will be prosperous and successful. Have I not commanded you? Be strong and courageous. Do not be terrified; do not be discouraged, for the LORD your God will be with you wherever you go.

—JOSHUA 1:8–9

Stop doing wrong,
  learn to do right!
Seek justice,
  encourage the oppressed.
Defend the cause of the fatherless,
  plead the case of the widow.

—ISAIAH 1:16–17

Jesus sent two disciples, saying to them, "Go to the village ahead of you, and at once you will find a donkey tied there, with her colt by her. Untie them and bring them to me. If anyone says anything to you, tell him that the Lord needs them, and he will send them right away."

—MATTHEW 21:1–3

Friday

HER LEGACY OF PRAYER

If you call out for insight
  and cry aloud for understanding,
and if you look for it as for silver
  and search for it as for hidden treasure,
then you will understand the fear of the LORD
  and find the knowledge of God.
For the LORD *gives wisdom,*
  and from his mouth come knowledge and understanding.

—PROVERBS 2:3–6

REFLECT ON: 2 Samuel 20:16–20.

PRAISE GOD: For his wisdom, which far surpasses anything we might imagine.

OFFER THANKS: That true wisdom has nothing to do with intellectual ability but everything to do with humble dependence on God.

CONFESS: Any laziness that keeps you from searching out God's wisdom for your own life.

ASK GOD: To help you treasure his wisdom so that you are willing to actively seek it.

Lift Your Heart

Wisdom has nothing to do with how many "gray cells" you possess. You can be smart as a whip but still full of foolishness. Take a few moments to reflect on this condensed and paraphrased passage from the book of Proverbs (3:13–18): "Blessed is the woman who has found wisdom. She has found something more precious than gold. None of her desires can compare with wisdom. For wisdom brings life, wealth, honor, and peace. Wisdom is a tree of life to be gladly embraced."

Here are a few vital suggestions for cultivating wisdom in your life:

• Pray for it, remembering it is a gift from God.

- Read and meditate regularly on Scripture.
- Surround yourself with wise friends — listen and learn from them. (Consider meeting regularly with a spiritual director.)
- Make quick obedience a hallmark of your spiritual life; it leads to wisdom.

Lord, you are the source of the wisdom that brings life, wealth, honor, and peace. May wisdom be like a growing tree in my life, bearing abundant fruit for your kingdom.

Rizpah

HER NAME MEANS
"A Hot Stone" or "Coal"

HER CHARACTER: Saul's concubine Rizpah was the mother of Armoni and Mephibosheth. Though a woman with few rights and little power, she displayed great courage and loyalty after the death of her sons.

HER SORROW: That her only sons were executed and their bodies dishonored because of their father's crime.

HER JOY: That the bodies of her sons were finally given an honorable burial.

KEY SCRIPTURE: 2 Samuel 21:8–14

Monday

HER STORY

One day a rabbi stood on a hill overlooking a certain city. The rabbi watched in horror as a band of Cossacks on horseback suddenly attacked the town, killing innocent men, women, and children. Some of the slaughtered were his own disciples. Looking up to heaven, the rabbi exclaimed: "Oh, if only I were God." An astonished student, standing nearby, asked, "But, Master, if you were God, what would you do differently?" The rabbi replied: "If I were God I would do nothing differently. If I were God, I would understand."*

---

*As told by Joanna Laufer and Kenneth S. Lewis in *Inspired* (New York: Doubleday, 1998), 5.

One day a woman named Rizpah was standing on a hill in Israel, watching the execution of seven men. Her grief was sharp, for among the dead were her own two sons. Executed for their father's crime, their bodies were left to rot on the hillside, despite a law requiring burial by sunset. Perhaps, like the rabbi, Rizpah wished she were God, even for a moment. Maybe then she would understand the "why" of what she had just witnessed.

It is not hard to imagine Rizpah's suffering. To watch as her body convulses in sorrow. To see her pound a fist against her breast to beat away the grief. *When will she turn away from the gruesome spectacle?* we wonder. But instead of fleeing the scene of her sorrow, she faces it, drawing close to bloodied bodies she once had cradled in her arms. Then she spreads sackcloth on a rock and sits down, refusing to move except to beat off birds of prey by day and jackals by night. Her vigil would last for several months—from mid-April to early October. Rizpah would not bury her grief as long as the bodies of her sons remained unburied.

Joshua had promised to live in peace with the Gibeonites, but Saul had murdered many of them during his reign, attempting to annihilate them. As a result of Saul's oath-breaking, Israel suffered a famine for three years running. In retribution, the Gibeonites had asked David for seven of Saul's male offspring. David surrendered Saul's two sons by Rizpah and five grandsons by Saul's daughter Merab. Blood was spilt for blood.

Scripture doesn't say whether Rizpah's sons shared their father's guilt. But like all mothers whose children have perished by violence—those in Bosnia, Kosovo, Rwanda, Iraq, Afghanistan, our own inner cities, and even our suburbs—Rizpah must have understood the terrible link between sin and death. One person's sin is a cancer that spreads. By refusing to hide her grief, by living out her anguish in public, Rizpah gave meaning to her sons' deaths, making the entire nation face the evil of what had happened.

Finally, the rains came. Finally, the king's heart was touched. Hearing of Rizpah's loyalty and courage, David ordered the remains of the executed to be buried. He even ordered Saul's and his son Jonathan's bones to be reclaimed and buried.

Scripture doesn't say that God ordered David to hand the men over to the Gibeonites in the first place, or even that the famine ended when they were executed. Instead, as Virginia Stem Owens points out in her book *Daughters of Eve*, the Bible indicates that God answered prayers on behalf of the land after the dead were given a decent burial. David's act in honor of the dead may have signaled an end to Israel's divisions. Finally, the land could be healed and the Israelites could reunite under David's leadership.

Rizpah made the people look at the cost of sin. Like many women in ancient cultures, she had few rights and little power. But her persistent courage gave meaning to her sons' deaths and helped a nation deal with the sin of its leader. Her story is tragic; her response, memorable. Perhaps because of her, other mothers in Israel were spared a similar grief, at least for a time.

Tuesday

HER LIFE AND TIMES

BURIAL

*R*izpah's vigil at the side of her dead sons has love as well as ritual or custom as its source. To allow these sons, these beloved though grown children, to be ravaged by the animals in the area was unthinkable to this mother. So Rizpah kept her lonely vigil, warding off the birds that would peck at their flesh and the animals that would try to drag their bodies away.

As it is today, burial in biblical times was an occasion for showing love and respect for someone who had died. Loved ones usually buried the dead the same day as the death took place, or at least within twenty-four hours (John 11:17, 39). Family members washed the body, anointed it with herbs and spices, then wrapped it in a cloth (John 11:44). The burial itself frequently took place in a cave or in a tomb hewn from the rock that is so prevalent in Palestine. The same cave or tomb would be used by many members of one family (Genesis 49:29 – 32).

In New Testament times, official mourning for the dead began with the playing of the flute as soon as the death took place. These mournful flute players not only played throughout the preparation for the burial, they also accompanied the procession to the place of burial and continued to play during the official time of mourning, usually seven days (Matthew 9:23). Professional mourners were often also present, accompanying the family to the grave site and staying with the family afterward, adding their wailing and tears to the family's (Jeremiah 9:17).

Even Jesus, present at the creation of the universe, wept at the death of his friend Lazarus (John 11:1 – 43). In his human nature, Jesus understood the finality of death for those who go on living. He participated in the customs of the day and wept with Lazarus's friends and family. But in his divine nature, Jesus also understood the transitory nature of life and the fact that death is not an appalling conclusion but a glorious beginning.

Wednesday

HER LEGACY IN SCRIPTURE

Read 2 Samuel 21:1–14.

1. The killings pretty much wiped out Saul's male descendants. Why would David order such wholesale executions?

2. Rizpah's vigil probably lasted several months. What do you think she went through during that time? What kept her going?

3. What do you think induced David to gather up these bones and bury them?

4. What hard or risky thing can you imagine yourself doing with the passion and determination of Rizpah?

5. How is God's love for you like Rizpah's love for her children?

Thursday

HER PROMISE

*R*izpah's consistency and tenacity is a lesson for all who are inclined to give up when the going gets tough. Out of love and a need to do what was right, she stuck out bad weather, cold, fatigue, and wild animals to protect her dead sons. Finally, someone in authority took notice and did something. Her faithfulness was rewarded, and she could rest.

God promises the same to us. He asks us only to be faithful and to leave the rest up to him. Whatever the situation—harsh parents, unloving spouses, rebellious children, financial difficulties, sickness, or death—God knows and will uphold and provide in his time.

Promises in Scripture

The LORD has rewarded me according to my righteousness, according to my cleanness in his sight.

—2 SAMUEL 22:25

For the LORD loves the just
   and will not forsake his faithful ones.

—PSALM 37:28

Yet this I call to mind
   and therefore I have hope:
Because of the LORD's great love we are not consumed,
   for his compassions never fail.
They are new every morning;
   great is your faithfulness.

—LAMENTATIONS 3:21–23

Friday

HER LEGACY OF PRAYER

*Rizpah daughter of Aiah took sackcloth and spread it out for herself
on a rock. From the beginning of the harvest till the rain poured down
from the heavens on the bodies, she did not let the birds of the air
touch them by day or the wild animals by night.*

—2 SAMUEL 21:10

REFLECT ON: 2 Samuel 21:8–14.

PRAISE GOD: For giving mothers the power to love their children
so fiercely.

OFFER THANKS: For the way other women have stood by you in
times of difficulty.

CONFESS: Any tendency to back off rather than confront
important moral issues with love and courage.

ASK GOD: To stretch your love beyond your own family circle
so that it becomes a force that shapes the world
around you.

Lift Your Heart

others are often their children's first line of defense. How
tragic when children never experience the power of a
mother's protecting love. So many abused children shuffle through
our social system with devastating results. So many unborn children
perish quietly, with no one to mourn their passing. We cannot save
all the motherless children, but we can reach out one at a time. Pray
about whether you could become a "big sister" to a young girl in
need. Go out of your way to make a neglected child feel welcome in
your home. Speak out against the forces in our culture that devalue
human life. Lend your voices to those that clamor for peace in our
world. Do what you can where you can. Let your love be fierce and
strong. Don't back off.

*Father, thank you for my mother's protecting, persistent love. I know
your own love better because of how she loved me. Help me become a
spiritual mother to those you bring into my life.*

The Queen of Sheba

HER CHARACTER: Though a pagan queen like Jezebel, she prized wisdom above power. She appears to have been intellectually gifted, with a good head for business and diplomacy.

HER JOY: That her quest for wisdom was rewarded beyond her expectations.

KEY SCRIPTURES: 1 Kings 10:1–13; Matthew 12:42

Monday

HER STORY

Sheba was a fragrant land, famous for its perfumes and spices. Located on the southwestern tip of Arabia, bordering the Red Sea, it traded precious commodities like gold, frankincense, and myrrh to kingdoms in Africa, India, and the Mediterranean. Little wonder that passing caravans brought news of the wide world to Sheba's queen.

Lately, the queen had heard marvelous stories of Solomon, the son of Bathsheba and David, now Israel's third king. At his birth, a prophet had named him "Beloved of the Lord." Some said he was the wisest man alive.

The queen smiled as she recalled the tale of the two prostitutes. Both had claimed to be mother to the same infant. How could the king possibly know who was telling the truth and who a lie? But Solomon merely ordered the baby cut in half, to be divided equally between the two women. He knew the real mother would relinquish her rights rather than let her child perish. Indeed, the king's cleverness had quickly revealed the truth, reuniting the heartbroken mother and her child.

The queen had also heard of the fabulous temple and palace Solomon had built in Jerusalem. Such a ruler, she realized, would have little trouble controlling the international trade routes crisscrossing his kingdom.

Though Jerusalem lay fifteen hundred miles to the north, the queen was determined to see for herself whether Solomon measured up to even half the tales told of him. Hoping to establish a trade agreement with Israel, she assembled a caravan of camels and loaded them with precious spices, gems, and four and a half tons of gold. Her entrance into Jerusalem would have created an unforgettable spectacle, adding to Solomon's growing fame.

Day after day, the queen pounded Solomon with hard questions. But nothing was too difficult for the king to explain. Overawed, the queen exclaimed: "The report I heard in my own country about your achievements and your wisdom is true. But I did not believe these things until I came and saw with my own eyes. Indeed, not even half was told me; in wisdom and wealth you have far exceeded the report I heard. How happy your men must be! How happy your officials, who continually stand before you and hear your wisdom! Praise be to the LORD your God, who has delighted in you and placed you on the throne of Israel. Because of the LORD's eternal love for Israel, he has made you king, to maintain justice and righteousness."

Then the queen gave Solomon all the gold and spices she had brought with her, perhaps foreshadowing the Magi's gift of gold, frankincense, and myrrh to the Christ child nearly a thousand years later. In fact, Jesus himself referred to the Queen of Sheba when he replied to the Pharisees who had demanded from him a miraculous sign: "The Queen of the South will rise at the judgment with this generation and condemn it; for she came from the ends of the earth to listen to Solomon's wisdom, and now one greater than Solomon is here" (Matthew 12:42).

Though ruler of a pagan nation, the Queen of Sheba was so drawn to the wisdom of God that she made an arduous and dangerous journey, traveling three thousand miles round-trip in order to meet the world's wisest man.

Tuesday

HER LIFE AND TIMES

GIFT GIVING

*F*our and a half tons of gold—and that was just part of the gift the Queen of Sheba gave to Solomon when she visited him in Jerusalem. She had probably heard of his riches as well as his wisdom and knew that no puny gift would do; something magnificent was in order. Imagine a caravan of camel after camel entering Jerusalem, bearing gifts for Solomon. A camel could carry about two hundred pounds when traveling through the desert (a staggering four hundred pounds plus its rider on shorter, less strenuous journeys). That means forty-five camels were required to carry just the gold!

Most personal meetings in ancient cultures included gift giving. A visit to someone's home required bringing along a gift for the host or hostess. Even chance encounters in the desert included gift exchanges (Genesis 14:18–20). Gift giving in ancient cultures was also a way of expressing submission to someone who was in a superior position, whether in government, in the military, or in religious life. At times, a gift might be given to gain favor or even to bribe someone.

Some of the gifts mentioned in the Old Testament are staggering in scope. Check out the gifts of gold, silver, and clothing that Abraham's servant gave to Rebekah and her family (Genesis 24:53). These sorts of gifts—the bride price, or the dowry—given by the groom's family to the bride's family formed a significant part of the traditions surrounding marriage. One of Solomon's wives received an entire town from her father as a wedding gift (1 Kings 9:16). Jacob's reconciliation gift to Esau consisted of a herd of 550 animals (Genesis 32:13–15). Besides the thousands of animals the Israelites gave as gifts to God after their victory over the Midianites, they gave gold and silver jewelry, which weighed a total of 420 pounds (Numbers 31:51–52).

The Queen of Sheba wasn't the only one who brought gifts to Solomon; so many brought gifts of "silver and gold, robes, weapons and spices, and horses and mules" that in Solomon's time silver was "as common in Jerusalem as stones" (1 Kings 10:23–27). But the most famous gifts in the Bible were those given by the Magi to the child Jesus (Matthew 2:11).

The New Testament writers often talked about the gifts we give not to each other but to God. No gift, no matter how small, is displeasing to God if it is given with a generous and cheerful heart. In fact, Jesus praised the widow who gave only two small coins because she gave all she had out of a heart of love for God, contrasting her with others who gave a small amount of their wealth, often grudgingly (Luke 21:1–4). More important to God than the size of our gifts is the condition of our hearts when we give (2 Corinthians 9:7).

Greater and finer and more thrilling than any gift we can give to each other or to God are the gifts he gives to us. Solomon, in the midst of all his wealth and wisdom, thanked God for the gift of a good and simple life: satisfying work to do, peaceful rest at night, a bit of happiness (Ecclesiastes 3:13; 5:19). Matthew quotes Jesus telling his followers of God's wonderful care of us and his willingness to give us good things: "If you, then, though you are evil, know how to give good gifts to your children, how much more will your Father in heaven give good gifts to those who ask him!" (Matthew 7:11).

But the crowning touch, the gift worth more than all the gold in the world, is the gift God so lovingly and willingly gave us of eternal life through his Son (Romans 6:23). No thank-you note required; just a life of gratitude to God. In the words of Paul, "Thanks be to God for his indescribable gift!" (2 Corinthians 9:15).

Wednesday

HER LEGACY IN SCRIPTURE

Read 1 Kings 10:1–13.

1. What do you think it meant that Solomon was famous because of "his relation to the name of the LORD"?

2. What questions do you think the Queen of Sheba might have asked him?

3. From everything you observe in this passage, how would you describe the queen?

4. What is wisdom? Describe someone who is truly wise. Do you know anyone who you think is truly wise? Name that person.

5. How important is wisdom to you? Why is that?

Thursday

HER PROMISE

The Queen of Sheba was a wealthy and influential ruler whose nation dominated commercial trading in the Middle East at that time. She must have had a certain measure of wisdom, or at least intelligence, to rule such a country. Still, she had questions, many of them, and she sought out the region's famed King Solomon, depending on his wisdom for answers. Solomon didn't disappoint her; she went away satisfied.

Do you have any questions that need answers? Questions about yourself? About things that have happened in your life? About the will of God? About God's love for you? If you do, go to the source of all wisdom, God himself, for answers. When you diligently seek him, he doesn't always give clear answers, but he will give peace. And you will go away satisfied. He promises.

Promises in Scripture

And I—in righteousness I will see your face;
   when I awake, I will be satisfied with seeing your likeness.

—PSALM 17:15

O God, you are my God,
   earnestly I seek you....
My soul clings to you;
   your right hand upholds me.

—PSALM 63:1, 8

Teach us to number our days aright,
   that we may gain a heart of wisdom....
Satisfy us in the morning with your unfailing love,
   that we may sing for joy and be glad all our days.

—PSALM 90:12, 14

Ask and it will be given to you; seek and you will find; knock and the door will be opened to you. For everyone who asks receives; those who seek find; and to those who knock, the door will be opened.

—MATTHEW 7:7–8

Friday

HER LEGACY OF PRAYER

How happy your men must be! How happy your officials, who continually stand before you and hear your wisdom! Praise be to the LORD your God, who has delighted in you and placed you on the throne of Israel! Because of the LORD's eternal love for Israel, he has made you king, to maintain justice and righteousness.

— 1 KINGS 10:8–9

REFLECT ON: 1 Kings 10:1–13.

PRAISE GOD: For his generosity.

OFFER THANKS: For God's wisdom working through others.

CONFESS: Any tendency to trust too much in your own wisdom without seeking godly counsel.

ASK GOD: To pour out wisdom on leaders in the church and in the government so that his ways are honored in your family, community, and nation.

Lift Your Heart

Think about the gifts the Queen of Sheba lavished on Solomon — the perfume, spices, precious stones, and gold — as tangible acknowledgments of his greatness. Yet Solomon was only a man. What can you lavish on the One who is far greater than he? You can be generous with your praise, telling God everything you love about him. You can be generous with your time, going out of your way to help those in need. You can be generous with your trust, acting and praying in a way that shows your confidence in God's goodness and power. You can be generous with your money, giving what you can from your small hoard. This week, don't be stingy. Think of at least one extravagant way to express your awe and your affection for God.

Jesus, everything I've heard about you is true, but I didn't believe it until you showed yourself to me. Then I realized I hadn't been told the half of it. Your wisdom, mercy, power, and kindness exceed everything I've ever heard. How happy are the women who belong to you! I praise the Father for delighting in you and placing you above everything and everyone. Because of the Lord's eternal love, he has made you our King.

Jezebel

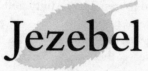

HER NAME MEANS
"Where Is the Prince?"

HER CHARACTER: A religious woman, she spread idolatry throughout Israel. Powerful, cunning, and arrogant, she actively opposed God, even in the face of indisputable proofs of his sovereignty.

HER TRIUMPH: To have enhanced her own power at the expense of others.

HER TRAGEDY: Her arrogance led to a shameless death.

KEY SCRIPTURES: 1 Kings 16:29–33; 18:1–19:2; 21:1–25; 2 Kings 9

Monday

HER STORY

*J*ezebel was a Phoenician princess, daughter of the priest-king of Sidon. Married to King Ahab, she reigned as queen in northern Israel one hundred years after David's death and sixty years after Israel split into northern and southern kingdoms just after Solomon's death.

A woman of great conviction and unwavering devotion, Jezebel's ardent worship was directed not to the God of Israel but to the pagan fertility god Baal, thought to control the rain and hence the harvest. So determined was she to convert Israel to her own religion that she hunted down and killed all the prophets she could lay hands on, replacing them with 850 of her own.

Despite Jezebel's efforts, one prophet had escaped her, and he was the most annoying of all. His name was Elijah, which meant "My God Is Yahweh." By contrast, Jezebel meant "Where Is the Prince (Baal)?" or "The Prince (Baal) Exists." Inevitably, the two squared off.

By pushing Baal worship, Jezebel was spreading idolatry across Israel, but her brand of worship wasn't producing the desired results for the fields remained barren. The fertility gods, it seemed, had gone AWOL or else they were impotent.

Elijah, meanwhile, warned King Ahab: "As the LORD, the God of Israel, lives, whom I serve, there will be neither dew nor rain in the next few years except at my word."

After three-and-a-half years of drought and famine, Elijah challenged the king to assemble the prophets of Baal and Asherah to compete in a lopsided contest—850 to 1. Two bulls were prepared for sacrifice, but the fire for sacrifice was not lit. Instead, the true God would prove himself by sending fire from heaven.

From morning until noon Baal's prophets danced and shouted, "O Baal, answer us!" But the god of the storm was silent.

Relishing the spectacle, Elijah couldn't resist a few well-aimed taunts: "Shout louder! Surely he is a god! Perhaps he is deep in thought, or busy, or traveling. Maybe he is sleeping and must be awakened." Elijah's sarcasm spurred the prophets of Baal to more frenzied efforts, but that day Baal, the god of fire, couldn't even light a match.

Then Elijah's turn came. To dramatize the difficulty of his task, he drenched the sacrifice with water not once but three times, praying: "O LORD, God of Abraham, Isaac, and Israel, let it be known today that you are God in Israel and that I am your servant and have done all these things at your command."

Immediately, fire burned up the sacrifice. Rallying the people, Elijah then slaughtered Jezebel's 850 prophets.

Enraged at the news, the queen sent a messenger to Elijah, vowing to kill him. But he fled south, beyond her grasp.

Still, Jezebel kept busy, managing to find other targets for her schemes. One day she discovered her husband, Ahab, in a childish rage. Pouting, Ahab confided his troubles to her. Naboth, his near neighbor, had a lovely vineyard that the king desired. It would make such a nice vegetable garden. Yet his stingy subject refused to sell it.

"Is this how you act as king over Israel?" Jezebel challenged. "Get up and eat! Cheer up. I'll get you the vineyard."

Jezebel wrote a letter in Ahab's name and sent it to the elders of the town instructing them to produce witnesses to testify falsely that Naboth had cursed both God and the king, offenses punishable by death.

Ahab felt better when he heard the news that Naboth had been stoned to death as a traitor. Now his table would be laden with delicious vegetables straight from the garden. But then who should show up but Elijah, interrupting the king's leisurely stroll through his new garden.

"So you have found me, my enemy," the king greeted him.

"I have found you," Elijah replied, "because you have sold yourself to do evil in the eyes of the LORD. I am going to bring disaster on you. I will consume your descendants and cut off from Ahab every last male in Israel—slave or free. And also, concerning Jezebel, the LORD says: 'Dogs will devour Jezebel by the wall of Jezreel.'"

Elijah's words came true. Ahab eventually died in battle, the dogs licking the blood from his chariot. Jezebel, however, survived him by at least ten years. Then one day, a man called Jehu came riding into Jezreel to carry out the last half of Elijah's prophecy.

Tough as nails, Jezebel stood proudly at the window of her palace. Never one to back away from a challenge, Jezebel seized the initiative, shouting at Jehu: "Have you come in peace, Zimri (the name of a traitor), you murderer of your master?"

But Jehu simply ignored her, challenging those who stood near her. "Who is on my side? Throw her down!" Quickly, Jezebel's servants shoved her through the window. The palace walls were splattered a bloody red as horses trampled her body and the palace dogs finished the job. A powerful figure while she lived, hardly anything of her remained just shortly after her death.

Paired with Israel's worst king, Jezebel was the nation's worst queen and one of the Bible's most infamous women. How different her story would have been had she harnessed her power, her drive, and her devotion. A strong character, Jezebel could have been a female apostle Paul, whose misguided zeal was redirected toward the kingdom of God. Instead, unlike many biblical figures who are depicted with a mixture of good and bad traits, she stands out as someone purely evil, whose moral character is one-dimensional. Totally devoted to her gods, she reflected their image completely. Despite obvious miracles and repeated warnings, she was a woman who chose to harden her heart and suffer the consequences.

Tuesday

HER LIFE AND TIMES

BAAL WORSHIP

*J*ezebel. Her name is synonymous with wickedness. Of all the beautiful biblical names used for children today, you won't find one Jezebel.

The daughter of Ethbaal, king of Sidon, Jezebel was raised and trained in Baal worship. She spent the years of her reign not only worshiping Baal but forcing Baal worship on her subjects. Statues of Baal showed him standing straight and tall wearing a helmet topped with bull's horns, a sign of power and fertility. In one hand he held a spear entwined with leaves, possibly symbolizing lightning and plant growth. His other hand held a club, which may have symbolized strength or thunder.

Baal worship involved the use of incense and sacrifice so common in the forms of worship of that day. The sacrifice at times involved innocent humans (Jeremiah 19:5). Also, since the main function of the god Baal was to make the land and animals and people fertile, fertility rites formed the chief part of Baal worship. Male and female attendants performed sexual acts in order to induce Baal to lavish fertility on the land.

When the Israelites wandered from their faith in the one true God, they often became attracted to worshiping the false god Baal. They worshiped this god during the time of Barak and Balaam (Numbers 22:41) as well as during the time of the judges (Judges 2:13; 6:28–32). Even after Elijah's triumph over Baal on Mount Carmel and the death of 450 priests of Baal that day (1 Kings 18:16–40), Baal worship continued off and on all during the reigns of the kings of Israel and Judah.

The worship of any false god is, of course, hateful to the true God. We know that. To us, Baal worship seems like a disgusting and foolish practice. We are far too sophisticated to understand its appeal. But aren't false gods just as prevalent today as in Jezebel's day? Consider the way we worship sports heroes, movie stars, and multimillionaires. Ours is a society that often bows to gods of money, sex, and power. We would do well to remember that anything, no matter how good, that supplants God's place in our lives can become an idol if we let it.

Wednesday

HER LEGACY IN SCRIPTURE

Read 1 Kings 21:1–29 and 2 Kings 9:30–37.

1. How did Jezebel relate to her husband?

2. How did she relate to other people?

3. What is significant about the fact that Jezebel "painted her eyes" and "arranged her hair" (2 Kings 9:30)? Why did she do this? What does it say about her?

4. How do you feel about the fact that Jezebel got what she deserved? In general, do you like to see people get what they deserve? Why or why not?

5. Take a minute to imagine yourself as strong and evil as Jezebel. Then imagine yourself as strong as Jezebel but good. Let your mind go with the picture. What would you do if you were that strong but good?

Thursday

HER PROMISE

*J*ezebel's end (2 Kings 9:33–37) is exactly what Elijah had earlier prophesied for her (1 Kings 21:23). No doubt judgment for her wicked life was swift and sure. It's hard to reconcile this aspect of our God with our image of him as loving and compassionate, yet he is a God who hates evil and will surely punish it. If, however, we come to him for forgiveness and reconciliation, he is also a God who loves to show mercy.

Promises in Scripture

Those who cling to worthless idols forfeit the grace that could be theirs.

—JONAH 2:8

Where sin increased, grace increased all the more.

—ROMANS 5:20

We implore you on Christ's behalf: Be reconciled to God. God made him who had no sin to be sin for us, so that in him we might become the righteousness of God.

—2 CORINTHIANS 5:20–21

Mercy triumphs over judgment!

—JAMES 2:13

Friday

HER LEGACY OF PRAYER

Who knows the power of your anger?
  For your wrath is as great as the fear that is due you.
Teach us to number our days aright,
  that we may gain a heart of wisdom.

—PSALM 90:11–12

REFLECT ON: 2 Kings 9.

PRAISE GOD: That he does not allow evil to go unpunished.

OFFER THANKS: For justice, even when it seems delayed.

CONFESS: Any tendency to take God's mercy for granted.

ASK GOD: To give you a healthy fear of offending him.

Lift Your Heart

Had Jezebel thought more about her inevitable end, her story may have been remarkably different. As much as we like to pretend we're never going to die, it's healthy to consider our own demise from time to time. Doing so humbles us, strips away our illusions, reminds us we are creatures answerable to a creator. Take thirty minutes to imagine your last day on earth. With whom do you want to spend it? What kind of memories do you want to leave behind? Do you have any lingering regrets, any unfinished business, any unfulfilled dreams? Ask God to guide you through this exercise. Let him show you what in your life can be affirmed and celebrated and what still needs to be transformed by his grace. Then tell him you're willing to do whatever it takes to become the woman he wants you to be.

Lord, I don't want to fear you for the wrong reasons, but for the right ones—to stand in awe because of who you are. Gracious God, let me never make light of your justice or your power. Instead, let me live in a way that honors you. For you are Wonderful Counselor, Mighty God, Everlasting Father, Prince of Peace.

The Widow of Zarephath

HER CHARACTER: A Phoenician woman, she showed extraordinary hospitality to one of God's prophets, providing a safe harbor for him during a period of famine.

HER SORROW: To suffer extreme poverty, famine, and the loss of husband and son.

HER JOY: To experience repeated miracles of God's provision.

KEY SCRIPTURES: 1 Kings 17:8–24; Luke 4:25–26

Monday

HER STORY

*H*er arms were spindly and rough, like the dry twigs she had gathered for kindling. Her body shook as she stood over the fire, greedily sipping and sucking the steam from the pan, as though the smell of frying bread could fill her belly and soothe her fears. She had lived her life a stone's throw from the Mediterranean, at Zarephath, seven miles south of Sidon, in a territory ruled by Jezebel's father. She had always loved the sea, but now its watery abundance seemed only to mock her, reminding her of all she lacked.

Tears escaped her eyes, try as she might to blink them back. How hard it was to suffer her fears alone, to wake in the night with no one to warm her, no one to whisper sweet lies about tomorrow. If only her husband were alive to squeeze a harvest from the fields. But he had died before the drought, leaving her with a small son, a house, and little else. Every night she hoped for rain, but every morning she woke to a brilliant sky.

Though she starved herself to feed her child, his distended belly accused her. His need condemned her. She had failed in the most basic ways a mother could, unable to protect, nurture, and provide. These days she stood with shoulders hunched as though to hide her breasts. Today she had scraped the last bit of flour from the barrel and poured the last drop of oil from the jug. She began to prepare for a final supper for herself and her child.

But then a stranger had called to her: "Woman, would you bring me a little water in a jar so I may have a drink?"

Graciously, she had gone to fetch it, only to have him call after her, "And bring me, please, a piece of bread."

Is the man mad? she wondered. *He might as well ask me to snap my fingers and produce a cow to feast on.*

She turned on her heel and replied, "As surely as the LORD your God lives, I don't have any bread—only a handful of flour in a jar and a little oil in a jug. I am gathering a few sticks to take home and make a meal for myself and my son, that we may eat it—and die."

But the man had persisted. "Don't be afraid. Go home and do as you have said. But first make a small cake of bread for me from what you have and bring it to me and then make something for yourself and your son. For this is what the LORD, the God of Israel, says: 'The jar of flour will not be used up and the jug of oil will not run dry until the day the LORD gives rain on the land.'"

Instead of cursing the stranger for his callousness, as we might expect, the woman did exactly as he had requested, feeding him the food she had reserved for herself and her son.

The woman from Zarephath wasn't a Jew, but a Phoenician. She had no idea that the stranger was Elijah, a prophet who had the gall to inform King Ahab that God was withholding rain to punish Israel's idolatry. She would have been astonished to learn that this same God had instructed Elijah to "go at once to Zarephath of Sidon and stay there. I have commanded a widow in that place to supply you with food."

The widow of Zarephath had felt utterly alone, not knowing God had his eye on her. Yet for some reason she believed Elijah and acted accordingly, giving him everything she had.

After that, every time she dipped her hand into the flour, every time she poured oil from the jug, the widow saw another miracle unfold, another sign of favor, additional evidence of God's provision. Just as Elijah had promised, the supply of flour and oil lasted day after day, month after month, never failing until at last the rains came and revived the land.

How like God to construct a parable of grace during a time of judgment, to display his mercy and power in the midst of weakness and need. The widow's faith saved not only her son and herself but actually provided a refuge for Elijah, who may have wondered why God chose such flimsy protection—a destitute woman who lived in the territory of his worst enemy, Jezebel.

Later, the widow's faith would again be tested when her young son died. But she would also be the first woman to witness God's power to raise the dead, which he did in response to Elijah's repeated prayers on behalf of her child. As a woman who endured extreme difficulties, her story reveals God's power to provide what we need the most—a commodity of the heart called faith.

Tuesday

HER LIFE AND TIMES

WIDOWS

The widow of Zarephath lived in a country that treated widows as second-class citizens, ignored them, and allowed them to go hungry. When Elijah came and asked the widow for bread, it appeared as though he was asking her to give up the last food she had for herself and her son. Actually, he was providing her with sustenance that would last until the famine was over.

Since a woman alone seldom had any way to provide financially for herself, she was dependent on her sons if she had any, and on the community around her if she didn't. The Bible tells how God himself has a special love and care for women who have lost their husbands (Psalm 68:5; 146:9). He commanded the Israelites to treat widows with compassion and to provide for them. When the prophets declared the Israelites to be disobedient, they often proved it by exposing their lack of concern for the widows around them (Isaiah 1:23; 10:1–2; Ezekiel 22:6–7; Malachi 3:5). When someone cared for the widowed, it was worthy of note (Job 29:13).

In the New Testament, Paul gave instructions to widows, telling them that if they were young, they should remarry. The church had to take care of a widow only if she was over sixty and had no other family members to provide for her (1 Timothy 5:3–16). The touching story of Dorcas in Acts 9:36–42 shows how much a simple act, done for a widow who is truly in need, can mean.

Today's church is also responsible for caring for the widows in their communities. Often, insurance payments, Social Security, and the like may take care of a widow's financial requirements, but her needs go far beyond having enough money in a checking account. Fellow believers can show their love by freely giving emotional support to the woman, by helping out physically with child care or household chores, or by providing friendship.

Wednesday

HER LEGACY IN SCRIPTURE

Read 1 Kings 17:7–24.

1. Why do you suppose the God of Israel sent the prophet of Israel to get help from a pagan widow?

2. The woman is searingly honest with Elijah in 1 Kings 17:12. What is she telling him here?

3. Why do you think she does what Elijah asks her?

4. In 1 Kings 17:17–18, where does she place blame for her son's death? If her reaction surprises you in any way, tell how.

5. What do you think you're meant to take away from this story? What does it say about God?

Thursday

HER PROMISE

$\mathcal{G}$od doesn't ignore the needs of those who cannot help themselves. He doesn't urge them to pick themselves up and get going when they have no resources to do so. He doesn't pat them on the back and say he's sorry life is so tough. Instead, he sometimes intervenes by miraculous understatement, in this case by making sure that a little bit of oil and flour—just enough for a small loaf—didn't run out.

An unexpected check comes just when you need it. Another mother gives you her kids' outgrown clothing so you can clothe your own children. God uses something or someone to change your husband's heart just when you thought he didn't love you anymore. Our God is still a miraculous provider, granting what we need sometimes in the most unexpected ways.

Promises in Scripture

From your bounty, O God, you provided for the poor.

—PSALM 68:10

I will bless her with abundant provisions;
*   her poor will I satisfy with food.*

—PSALM 132:15

But if a widow has children or grandchildren, these should learn first of all to put their religion into practice by caring for their own family and so repaying their parents and grandparents, for this is pleasing to God. The widow who is really in need and left all alone puts her hope in God and continues night and day to pray and to ask God for help.

—1 TIMOTHY 5:4–5

Friday

HER LEGACY OF PRAYER

Then the woman said to Elijah, "Now I know that you are a man of God and that the word of the LORD from your mouth is the truth."

— 1 KINGS 17:24

REFLECT ON: 1 Kings 17:8–24.

PRAISE GOD: For his constant attentiveness.

OFFER THANKS: For all the ways God has already provided for you and for the ways he will provide in the future.

CONFESS: Any tendency to act as though God really doesn't care about what's happening to you.

ASK GOD: To make you a woman who relies on him daily for her physical, emotional, and spiritual needs.

Lift Your Heart

Whenever we spin anxious scenarios about the future, we waste precious emotional energy. This kind of worrying represents a negative use of the power of our imagination. As such, it can be a misguided attempt to control the future. But instead of controlling the future, we soon discover that anxiety controls us. Jesus said, "Do not worry about tomorrow, for tomorrow will worry about itself. Each day has enough trouble of its own" (Matthew 6:34).

Begin to form habits that will help you break the power of worry in your life. Start by thanking God each morning for some small sign of his goodness: a loving friend, a beautiful garden, a child's smile. Gratitude will increase your sense of God's presence in your life. Then, set aside some time to think about ways God has taken care of you in the past. Write them down and make them part of your faith arsenal, so that when you are tempted by anxious thoughts you can remind yourself with concrete examples of how God has already provided for you.

Father, how easy it is to let anxiety snuff out my gratitude. Help me to linger thankfully in your presence rather than simply rushing on to my next desperate request. Use my weakness and need as a showcase for your strength.

The Shunammite Woman

HER CHARACTER: Generous and hospitable, she was a wealthy and capable woman who showed great kindness to one of God's prophets.

HER SORROW: To lose the son that had been promised her.

HER JOY: To experience just how deep God's faithfulness goes.

KEY SCRIPTURES: 2 Kings 4:8–37; 8:1–6

Monday

HER STORY

*J*ust a few miles north of Jezreel, where Jezebel's story had drawn to its grim conclusion, lived a wealthy Israelite woman whose sharp eye kept track of travelers from Nazareth to Jerusalem. One of the more colorful characters who frequented the road outside her house was Elisha, the prophet who succeeded Elijah.

One day the Shunammite woman invited Elisha to linger for a meal. Afterward, she said to her husband, "Let's make a small room on the roof and put in it a bed and a table, a chair and a lamp for him. Then he can stay there whenever he comes to us."

Moved by her kindness, Elisha inquired, through his servant, Gehazi, whether he could use his influence with Israel's king on her behalf. But the woman wasn't looking for favors at court, so Elisha pressed his servant, saying, "What, then, can be done for her?"

Gehazi merely pointed out the obvious: the woman and her aging husband were childless, without an heir to carry on the family name.

So Elisha summoned the woman and made an incredible promise: "About this time next year you will hold a son in your arms."

"No, my lord," she objected. "Don't mislead your servant, O man of God!"

Yet, a year later, just as Elisha had foretold, the woman held a squalling infant in her arms, laughing as she told others the story of God's surprising gift. Unlike so many of her female forebears — Sarah, Rebekah, Rachel, Tamar, Hannah — the Shunammite woman seemed content without children. Elisha's promise, however, was an arrow homing straight to its target, fulfilling the unspoken desire of her heart.

One morning, a few years later, a servant entered the house with the little boy in his arms, explaining that the child had complained of a headache while visiting his father in the fields. Perhaps he had lingered too long in the sun.

The boy's face was flushed, his forehead hot as his mother caressed it, hushing him with soothing sounds and songs. But despite murmured words of reassurance, she felt her own fear spreading. The tighter she held him, the more his spirit seemed to retreat. His breathing was labored, his eyes listless. At about noon he died.

Without a word, she carried his small body to the prophet's room, laying it tenderly on Elisha's bed. Closing the door, she summoned a servant and left immediately for Mount Carmel, where she hoped to find Elisha.

Spotting her in the distance, the prophet wondered aloud what could prompt her to make the twenty-five-mile journey north. "Run to meet her," he urged Gehazi, "and ask, 'Are you all right? Is your husband all right? Is your child all right?'"

But the woman merely brushed Gehazi aside with polite words and rushed straight to Elisha, exclaiming: "Did I ask you for a son, my lord? Didn't I tell you, 'Don't raise my hopes'?"

Immediately the prophet instructed Gehazi: "Tuck your cloak into your belt, take my staff in your hand, and run. If you meet anyone, do not greet him, and if anyone greets you, do not answer. Lay my staff on the boy's face."

The woman, however, wasn't about to settle for a stand-in. So the prophet hurried to Shunem just behind Gehazi, who had gone on ahead to carry out his master's orders. When Elisha arrived, he found the boy lying quiet and cold on his couch. Elisha closed the door behind him. Praying, he stretched his body across the boy's so that hands, mouth, and eyes touched. As he lay there, he could feel the chilled body warming beneath him. He got up and paced the room for a while. At last he stretched himself across the lifeless body again and prayed. The boy's chest lifted. Then he sneezed! Then sneezed again.

The Shunammite woman may, in fact, have heard the story of how Elijah had raised the son of the widow of Zarephath in similar circumstances. If so, that miracle would certainly have fueled her hope, giving her the courage to seek her own miracle rather than collapse under so great a weight of grief. Now, as she saw for herself the irrefutable sign of God's loving-kindness, she fell at Elisha's feet and bowed to the ground. God had been true to his word, fulfilling his promise to her and then preserving it in the face of impossible circumstances.

Tuesday

HER LIFE AND TIMES

HOSPITALITY

*E*lisha stayed for a meal at the Shunammite woman's house after she "urged" him to do so. He felt so well taken care of, so comfortable, and so at home that he made a habit of coming to her home whenever he was in the area—often enough that the woman asked her husband to have a special room added just for Elisha.

Hospitality played an important role in the lives of the people of the Middle East. Desert travel was strenuous, and Holiday Inns hadn't yet been invented. When travelers came to a town at the end of the day, they would stop in the town's center or near the town gates and wait for an invitation for the night. If no invitation came, they would spend the night outside.

Hosts were responsible not only to feed and provide sleeping arrangements for their guests but also were expected to ensure the safety of the guests, protecting them from robbery and harm (Genesis 19:8). When meals were served, the host acted as a servant, serving the guests and watching over their needs. If one guest was particularly favored over another, he or she would be served an extra large or extra special portion of the food (Genesis 43:34).

Examples of hospitality are plentiful in the Scriptures. Abraham made a sumptuous meal for the three strangers who visited him (Genesis 18), preparing bread, a tender calf, curds, and milk. Rebekah practiced a basic form of hospitality when she offered water to Abraham's servant and his animals (Genesis 24:15–21). Solomon fed everyone in his palace, plus aliens and visitors to the region. His list of daily provisions in 1 Kings 4:22 provides a picture of what was required to feed a staggering number of people. Nehemiah not only refused to demand "the food allotted to the governor," he also generously fed at least 150 people each day (Nehemiah 5:17–18).

Six times the New Testament exhorts believers to be hospitable. There's no talk of fatted calves or extravagant dinners in these passages, just a simple exhortation to make sure you care for those around you. As Romans 12:13 puts it, "Share with God's people who are in need. Practice hospitality." You never know, you just might entertain angels without knowing it (Hebrews 13:2)!

Wednesday

HER LEGACY IN SCRIPTURE

Read 2 Kings 4:8–37.

1. Why do you think stopping at this woman's house became a habit for Elisha?

2. Why do you think the woman responded to the promise of a son as she did in verse 16? Compare verse 28.

3. Why did she tell both her husband and Gehazi that everything was "all right" when it wasn't? What was her goal?

4. Hundreds of mothers lost sons in this period when God saved one boy through Elijah and now this one through Elisha. What do you make of these stories? What do they tell you about God?

5. What do you admire about the Shunammite woman that you would like to imitate?

Thursday

HER PROMISE

*T*he Shunammite woman knew there was hope even in the most devastating of circumstances. She had been promised a son when she was barren, and now she tenaciously held on to that promise even though her little son lay dead on Elisha's couch. "It's all right," she said to her husband, knowing full well that their boy was gone. The God who had given her the promise wasn't gone. She knew he wouldn't forsake her.

"It's all right." Can you express that sentiment even when your world is crashing in on you? Perhaps not. Remember, however, that even in the most agonizing of circumstances, even when you feel abandoned, even when tragedy strikes—God is there. Trust his word and gain assurance from the Shunammite woman who, in the midst of appalling circumstances, could say, "It's all right."

Promises in Scripture

God is not a man, that he should lie, nor a son of man, that he should change his mind. Does he speak and then not act? Does he promise and not fulfill?

—NUMBERS 23:19

Praise be to the God and Father of our Lord Jesus Christ, the Father of compassion and the God of all comfort, who comforts us in all our troubles.

—2 CORINTHIANS 1:3–4

For no matter how many promises God has made, they are "Yes" in Christ.

—2 CORINTHIANS 1:20

Let us hold unswervingly to the hope we profess, for he who promised is faithful.

—HEBREWS 10:23

Friday

HER LEGACY OF PRAYER

"About this time next year," Elisha said, "you will hold a son in your arms."

—2 KINGS 4:16

REFLECT ON: 2 Kings 4:8–37.

PRAISE GOD: That he never overlooks even a small kindness performed out of love for him.

OFFER THANKS: For the kindness you have experienced at the hands of others.

CONFESS: Your tendency to overlook others' needs because you are so focused on your own.

ASK GOD: To make you jealous for opportunities to care for others in basic and practical ways.

Lift Your Heart

The Shunammite woman is a wonderful example of someone who anticipated Jesus' words to his disciples to "seek first his [the Father's] kingdom and his righteousness, and all these things will be given to you as well" (Matthew 6:33). Like the lilies of the field, she didn't worry about God's provision and so experienced it abundantly. Ask for an opportunity this week to perform an act of practical kindness or hospitality for someone else. Consider lending your prayers, your gifts, and your energy on a regular basis to a group or ministry working to bring justice to those most in need of it.

Father, show me someone's need today. Then help me break out of my own small world and find a way to show your love to that person.

Athaliah

"The Lord Is Great"

HER CHARACTER: Granddaughter of Omri, one of Israel's most idolatrous and evil kings, she was the daughter of Ahab and most likely of Jezebel as well. She was the only woman to rule over Judah. While Ahab and Jezebel spread Baal worship in the northern kingdom of Israel, Athaliah was busy promoting it a few years later in the southern kingdom of Judah. Controlled by her need for power, she murdered her own family members to secure it.

HER JOY: That her ruthlessness paid off, at least for a time, making her the ruler of Judah.

HER SORROW: That her attempt to destroy the royal line of Judah failed.

KEY SCRIPTURES: 2 Kings 11; 2 Chronicles 22; 23:11–21

Jehosheba

HER NAME MEANS
"Swear by His Name"

HER CHARACTER: A princess and the wife of the high priest, she was a courageous woman whose actions preserved the line of Judah, from which the Messiah would come.

HER JOY: To have preserved the life of her brother's youngest son, Joash, so that he could become the rightful king of Judah.

HER SORROW: To have endured Athaliah's reign in Judah and to have suffered the loss of many of her nephews at the queen's hand.

KEY SCRIPTURES: 2 Kings 11:2; 2 Chronicles 22:11

Monday

THEIR STORY

*W*icked queens are the stuff of fairy tales. Remember the snow queen in the tales of Hans Christian Andersen, or the evil queen in *The Lion, the Witch and the Wardrobe*? Athaliah was at least as bad as her fairy-tale counterparts, a queen who chilled the hearts of God's people by murdering her own grandsons and promoting Baal worship in the southern kingdom of Judah, just as her parents, Ahab and Jezebel, had promoted it in the north.

Athaliah married the king of Judah, thereby cementing an alliance between the northern and southern kingdoms. But after a few years he died and was succeeded by Athaliah's son, Ahaziah. In just a few months, Jehu, Jezebel's nemesis, slaughtered the new king.

After Queen Athaliah's husband and son were killed, she must have felt vulnerable and isolated, doubly so since her father Ahab's line had also been destroyed in Israel. Her paranoia and lust for power formed a toxic mixture, moving her to murder her own son's children to secure Judah's throne for herself. Indeed she may even have gloated that she, Baal's emissary, had snuffed out Judah's royal heirs, making it impossible for God to fulfill his promise of a future Messiah from David's line in the tribe of Judah.

For a few years, from about 841–835 BC, Athaliah reigned in Judah, promoting Baal worship and leading the people further and further from God. But right under her nose a conspiracy was brewing. Unknown to her, one of her grandsons still lived. Her own stepdaughter, Jehosheba, had hidden the infant, Joash, before the queen could murder him along with Ahaziah's other sons. Married to the high priest, Jehosheba risked her life by tucking the royal heir away in the temple for six years. Then, when the boy turned seven, her husband arranged a coup, crowning young Joash king.

As soon as Athaliah caught wind of the plot, she rushed to the temple, tearing her robes and screaming, "Treason! Treason!" But like her mother, Jezebel, before her, no one paid the slightest attention. Instead, Queen Athaliah was promptly seized and executed just outside the temple. As soon as the queen was dispatched, the people of Judah celebrated by destroying the temple of Baal along with its chief priest.

While the comparisons between Athaliah and Jezebel are all too obvious, their story reminds us of another that took place seven hundred years before. Egypt's Pharaoh, determined to destroy God's people, had ordered every male baby drowned in the Nile River. Like Pharaoh, hoodwinked by one of his own children (his daughter saved Moses and raised him as her own), Athaliah was fooled by her stepdaughter, Jehosheba. Once again a woman's courage and compassion helped to subvert evil and keep the promise alive.

Tuesday

THEIR LIFE AND TIMES

THE TEMPLE

Smart Jehosheba! She hid little Joash away in the place Baal-worshiping Athaliah was least likely to stumble on him: in the temple of the Lord. Though at times the people of Israel misused the temple to worship idols, it remained primarily a place for worship of the true God.

King David had been the one to begin making plans for a great temple to replace the tabernacle as a place for worship. The tabernacle was not a permanent building, and David thought it only fitting that God should have as magnificent a house as his own (2 Samuel 7:2). David gathered great stores of stone and iron and bronze and "more cedar logs than could be counted" (1 Chronicles 22:4) in preparation for building the temple. He also obtained "a hundred thousand talents of gold, a million talents of silver." Believe it or not, that's about 3,750 tons of gold and an astonishing 37,500 tons of silver!

David's son Solomon actually built the temple in Jerusalem. The building began during the fourth year of his reign (966 BC) and wasn't completed until the eleventh year. The structure was built of stone cut and dressed at quarries and transported to the temple site. The stone was then covered with cedar wood, carved with cherubim and palm trees and flowers, then covered with gold. A reading of 1 Kings 5–8 gives a marvelous picture of the lavish structure Solomon dedicated to the Lord.

Jehosheba and her husband, the high priest, hid the heir to the throne in that same structure. The temple now housed not only the presence of the true God, but also the ancestor of God's Son, Jesus the Messiah. Through the brave actions of one woman, the lineage of David was protected and our salvation through the Messiah was assured.

Wednesday

THEIR LEGACY IN SCRIPTURE

Read 2 Kings 11:1–21.

1. Athaliah grew up as the daughter of Jezebel. How do you suppose that upbringing affected the person she became?

2. Athaliah's mother and brothers (Jezebel and her sons) were murdered in Israel. Athaliah's son was murdered in Judah. She then ordered the murders of her son's children so that she could reign. How do you think she justified her actions in her own mind?

3. What do you think went through Jehosheba's mind when she saved the baby Joash while his brothers and sisters were slaughtered (verse 2)? Describe how you imagine these events from her point of view.

4. Joash was the last of King David's line. Jehosheba probably didn't know she was playing a role in assuring the eventual birth of the Messiah, Jesus, the promised descendent of David. What does this say about the way God works in the world?

5. Athaliah was brave in a way—she took action in her own interests, with horrible results. Jehosheba was brave in a more admirable way. When has your life called for courage? In what ways do you need courage now?

Thursday

THEIR PROMISE

God always wins. That's a pretty simplistic way of saying it, but it's true nonetheless. Even when people like Athaliah try to stomp out an entire family and put an end to God's plan for redemption, when people like the priests of Baal lead others to worship idols instead of the true God, God will always triumph in the end. The negative forces of our culture make us wonder where we're headed as a people. Many of our leaders show little integrity or morality, and dishonesty is overlooked in the workplace. Kindness is often the exception rather than the rule. But don't despair. This is not a battle God plans to lose. In the end, he will prevail!

PROMISES IN SCRIPTURE

No one whose hope is in you will ever be put to shame.

—PSALM 25:3

Many are the plans in a human heart,
*   but it is the LORD's purpose that prevails.*

—PROVERBS 19:21

But thanks be to God, who always leads us in triumphal procession in Christ.

—2 CORINTHIANS 2:14

Friday

THEIR LEGACY OF PRAYER

But Jehosheba, the daughter of King Jehoram, took Joash son of Ahaziah and stole him away from among the royal princes who were about to be murdered and put him and his nurse in a bedroom. Because Jehosheba, the daughter of King Jehoram and wife of the priest Jehoiada, was Ahaziah's sister, she hid the child from Athaliah so she could not kill him.

—2 CHRONICLES 22:11

REFLECT ON: 2 Chronicles 22:10–12; 23.

PRAISE GOD: For his power, which is far greater than the power of evil.

OFFER THANKS: That God always does what he says he will no matter the odds against him.

CONFESS: Any tendency to allow difficult circumstances to suffocate your faith.

ASK GOD: For courage to act on behalf of the innocent regardless of consequences.

Lift Your Heart

*S*cripture often yields its richest insights once you learn to slow down and pray through what you have just read. Use the story of Jehosheba to teach yourself how to pray the Scriptures. Though a minor character, overlooked by most readers, she played a decisive role in the life of God's people.

Put yourself in her shoes for just fifteen minutes. Imagine what she must have felt like, not for a moment, but for several years as she defied an evil and powerful queen. Where did she find the strength? What were her temptations and fears? Let your imagination help you envision what her life might have been like. Ask God to speak to you through her story. Then ask for the grace to be like her—to be a woman who always cherishes, protects, and nurtures life.

After you've done that, take a moment to think about Jehosheba's joy the moment she learned of Athaliah's final defeat, realizing that the boy whose life she saved was now her king. Let another woman's story encourage you to do what is right regardless of the risks involved.

Lord, when I am faced with evil, whether it is in government, in the church, or in my neighborhood or family, help me to do whatever is in my power to resist. Give me wisdom to know what to do, courage to act well, and grace to trust you for the outcome.

Huldah

HER NAME MEANS

"Weasel"

HER CHARACTER: Trusted by the king with a matter of great importance, she was a prophetess whose word ignited a significant religious reform.

HER SORROW: That God's people refused to respond to him with loving obedience, ignoring repeated warnings about the consequences of their unfaithfulness.

HER JOY: As a prophetess, she was privileged to be a messenger of God.

KEY SCRIPTURES: 2 Kings 22:14–20; 2 Chronicles 34:22–33

Monday

HER STORY

She pressed the leather scroll against her breast, as though cradling a living being. The high priest, Hilkiah, and several other men of Jerusalem stood before her. King Josiah wanted to know—would the words of the Book of the Law, which Hilkiah had just discovered in the temple, come to pass?

Holding the scroll by its wooden handles, she unrolled it carefully and began reading:

"Hear, O Israel: The LORD our God, the LORD is one. Love the LORD your God with all your heart and with all your soul and with all your strength.... Fear the LORD your God, serve him only, and take your oaths in his name. Do not follow other gods, the gods of the peoples around you; for the LORD your God, who is among you, is a jealous God and his anger will burn against you, and he will destroy you from the face of the land" (Deuteronomy 6:4–5, 13–15).

"Cursed in the city and cursed in the country ... sudden ruin because of what you have done ... wasting disease ... madness, blindness and confusion ... an object of scorn and ridicule to all the nations ... because you did not obey the LORD your God" (cf. Deuteronomy 28:15–68).

Though her voice was steady, Huldah's throat felt sore from the effort of speaking such words aloud, terrible threats that made her eyes well over, warnings that spawned vision upon vision from the past. In her mind, she watched as Judah's kings Ahaz and Manasseh sacrificed their sons to pagan deities. She saw the smoke of incense rising before pagan idols in the temple. She looked on as prophets were murdered, as diviners and sorcerers were honored, as kings bowed down to the stars and the people followed suit, prostituting themselves to false gods and spurning the advances of the Almighty. She saw the children of Israel marching in chains from the land of milk and honey. Her face flushed as a burning sensation rushed through her body and searing words spilled from her lips:

"This is what the LORD says: 'I am going to bring disaster on this place and its people, according to everything written in the book the king of Judah has read. Because they have forsaken me and burned incense to other gods and provoked me to anger by all the idols their hands have made, my anger will burn against this place and will not be quenched.' Tell the king of Judah, who sent you to inquire of the LORD: 'Because your heart was responsive and you humbled yourself before the LORD when you heard what I have spoken against this place and its people, that they would become accursed and laid waste, and because you tore your robes and wept in my presence, I have heard you, declares the LORD. Therefore I will gather you to your fathers, and you will be buried in peace. Your eyes will not see all the disaster I am going to bring on this place.'"

Huldah is one of only four women with an authentic prophetic ministry mentioned in the Old Testament (along with Miriam, Deborah, and Isaiah's wife). Though prophets like Jeremiah and Zephaniah were also active at the time, King Josiah consulted Huldah about the amazing discovery of the Book of the Law (material that probably forms the core of the book of Deuteronomy).

Beyond the brief scene imaginatively retold above, we know little of her story — only that God entrusted her with his word in a time of national crisis. A hundred years earlier, Judah had witnessed God's punishment of the northern kingdom. Faithless Israel had been led captive to Assyria, just as the prophets had warned. Huldah surely knew the sordid details. She could not have missed its frightening significance for Judah. She may also have endured part of Manasseh's fifty-five-year reign, the longest and worst of any king in Judah. Certainly, she would have been heartened by the recent reforms of King Josiah—his attempts to restore the temple though the people had all but forgotten God.

But her words of prophecy confirmed the king's fear. Judah was standing on a precipice. God was a jealous lover who blessed those who loved and obeyed him and cursed those who did not. Across the centuries, his slow anger was building to a fiery crescendo. Judah's infidelities had not gone unnoticed.

After Huldah's prophecy, Josiah led one of the greatest religious reforms in history, purging Judah and even parts of Israel of paganism. But the kings who followed him soon reversed course, leading the people astray once again. Thirty-five years after Huldah's prophecy, Judah was taken in chains to Babylon and all of its cities were destroyed.

The magnificent kingdom of David and Solomon had come to an end. But though every other nation captured by Assyria and Babylon ceased to exist, Israel still had a future. Chastened, it was never destroyed. Disciplined, it was never forsaken. All because God still loved his people.

The words of Isaiah, a prophet who preceded Huldah by a few decades, proclaimed a future day of restoration: "They will rebuild the ancient ruins and restore the places long devastated; they will renew the ruined cities.... Instead of their shame my people will receive a double portion, and instead of disgrace they will rejoice in their inheritance" (Isaiah 61:4, 7).

Judgment and mercy, law and grace, punishment and salvation—these are the tensions that characterize the story of God's love affair with his people. Huldah was a woman who understood the paradox and who was not afraid to proclaim the truth, even to a king. Her words must have cost her, but she spoke them anyway. She cherished God's word in a time of spiritual crisis.

Tuesday

HER LIFE AND TIMES

BOOKS AND SCROLLS

*A*ncient writers recorded their thoughts and information on clay tablets. Literally hundreds of thousands of these tablets have been found, many of which have yet to be read. And it is estimated that 99 percent of the ancient tablets still in existence have yet to be found.

Later, writers wrote on scrolls. The paper for the scrolls was made from processed papyrus reeds, which grew along the Nile River. The separate pieces were glued together into one long sheet and then rolled onto wooden dowels, with the beginning of the scroll on the right and the end on the left. Readers of Hebrew, usually men and sometimes boys—girls were seldom taught to read—read the columns of letters from top to bottom, right to left. The reader would roll up the read portion of the scroll while unrolling the unread portion.

After some time the Israelites began to form another sort of paper, called parchment, from the skins of animals. They were careful to use only skins from clean animals for the paper to be used to record the Scriptures. The animal skins were treated until they were supple and very light in color, and then several of these prepared skins would be sewn together to form one scroll. For instance, an old copy of the book of Isaiah found as part of the Dead Sea Scrolls in 1947 is a scroll made of seventeen pieces of skin of varying sizes sewn together. The scroll is about ten inches in height and an amazing twenty-four feet long when unrolled.

Books as we know them today, with page after page bound together between two covers, did not develop until the second century AD The fact that the writing still had to be done by one person, laboriously by hand, limited the number of these books until the 1400s, when Johannes Gutenberg invented the printing press. His first book? The Bible, now known as the famous Gutenberg Bible. As few as ten full copies of this first printing are still in existence today.

Original documents of the Old and New Testaments, called autographs, no longer exist. Parchment and papyrus both decay over time and when exposed to dampness. Also, New Testament books and letters may literally have been read to pieces or may have been destroyed during times of persecution.

The Book of the Law discovered in the temple during Josiah's day was probably made from papyrus. Historians are uncertain exactly how much of the law was contained in this scroll. Some think it contained the entire Pentateuch (Genesis through Deuteronomy), while others believe it only contained the book of Deuteronomy. Josiah's reaction, however, would cause one to believe that at least the curses of Leviticus 26 or Deuteronomy 28 were included. Huldah, the faithful prophetess during a time of national unfaithfulness, bravely spoke God's judgment. She emphasized the words of judgment Josiah had already read in the Book of the Law, and then went on to pronounce a reprieve for Josiah because of his sorrow over the sins of his people. Once again, God had faithfully and wonderfully demonstrated his divine judgment as well as his divine willingness to forgive.

Wednesday

HER LEGACY IN SCRIPTURE

Read 2 Kings 22:8–20.

1. The nation had been following false gods for so long that the Book of the Law (probably part of Deuteronomy) had been laid aside and forgotten. How would you describe the king's emotional reaction when he heard God's law? Why do you think he responded as he did?

2. Describe what you think Huldah might have been like: her person, her character, her relationship with God.

3. What does God's message to the nation and to the king say about him: his character and the way he deals with people?

4. What would it be like for you to have to deliver to your people the message that Huldah delivered to hers?

5. When God lets you know you've done wrong, how do you typically respond?

Thursday

HER PROMISE

*T*he story of Huldah and her words to the king illustrate the contrast between God's judgment and his mercy. He judges those who deserve his punishment, but he quickly forgives those who repent. In fact, he is eager to forgive, waiting only for us to come to him in repentance.

Promises in Scripture

> *For the sake of your name, O LORD,*
> *forgive my iniquity, though it is great.*

—PSALM 25:11

> *Who is a God like you,*
> *who pardons sin and forgives the transgression*
> *of the remnant of his inheritance?*
> *You do not stay angry forever*
> *but delight to show mercy.*
> *You will again have compassion on us;*
> *you will tread our sins underfoot*
> *and hurl all our iniquities into the depths of the sea.*

—MICAH 7:18–19

> *If we confess our sins, he is faithful and just and will forgive us our sins and purify us from all unrighteousness.*

—I JOHN 1:9

Friday

HER LEGACY OF PRAYER

When the king heard the words of the Law, he tore his robes.... "Go and inquire of the LORD for me and for the remnant in Israel and Judah about what is written in this book that has been found."

—2 CHRONICLES 34:19, 21

REFLECT ON: 2 Chronicles 34:14–33.

PRAISE GOD: For speaking clearly about what he expects from us.

OFFER THANKS: That he gave us his Word in the Bible.

CONFESS: Any complacency in the face of God's commandments.

ASK GOD: For the grace to take his Word seriously so that you understand the connection between love and obedience.

Lift Your Heart

*E*very woman knows the pleasure of a clean house, where floors are thoroughly scrubbed and waxed, windows shined, and cobwebs routed from every nook and cranny. Our hearts can become sullied by daily wear and tear, by disobedience and disregard for doing things God's way. Set aside a day to conduct a little spring cleaning of your soul. How well have you been doing on the basics—the Ten Commandments?

Check Deuteronomy 5:6–21 for a review in case you've forgotten the commandments or are unfamiliar with them. Don't be so literal in your reading of them that you forget that idolatry can take the form of cherishing money, power, or even a person whom you love more than God. Have you ever murdered someone with hateful words? Have you ever stolen someone's reputation because of envy? As you become conscious of your failings, don't wallow in them. Simply admit your sin, asking God's forgiveness and the grace to change. Ask him to make your heart an attractive place for his indwelling presence. Then enjoy his forgiveness and take hold of his grace.

Father, may I have ears to hear your Word and a heart to obey it. Cleanse me from my sin and wash me until I am whiter than snow. Make my soul clean and pure, a broad and spacious place for your indwelling Spirit.

Esther

HER NAME MAY DERIVE FROM
"Ishtar," the Babylonian Goddess of Love,
or from the Persian Word for "Star"
Her Hebrew Name, "Hadassah," Means "Myrtle"

HER CHARACTER: An orphan in a foreign land, she was willing to conceal her Jewish identity in a bid for a pagan king's affection. Esther seemed willing to made moral compromises by sleeping with the king and then taking part in a wedding that would necessarily have required her to pay homage to foreign gods. Even so, she displayed great courage in the midst of a crisis. Prior to risking her life for her people, she humbled herself by fasting and then put her considerable beauty, social grace, and wisdom in the service of God's plan.

HER SORROW: To learn that her husband, the king, had unwittingly placed her life and the life of her people in jeopardy.

HER JOY: To watch mourning turn to celebration once the Jews enjoyed relief from their enemies.

KEY SCRIPTURE: Esther 1–10

Monday

HER STORY

Vashti, queen of Persia, was the most powerful woman in the Middle East, yet her power was as fragile as a candle in a storm. Her husband, Xerxes, had just summoned her to appear before a festive gathering of his nobles. Vashti, however, having no intention of parading herself like a prized cow in front of a herd of drunken men, refused.

What should be done to punish her insolence? One of the king's counselors spoke for all: "Queen Vashti has done wrong, not only against the king but also against all the nobles and the peoples of all the provinces of King Xerxes. For the queen's conduct will become known to all the women, and so they will despise their husbands and say, 'King Xerxes commanded Queen Vashti to be brought before him, but she would not come.' There will be no end of disrespect and discord."

So poor Vashti bore the brunt of every man's fears. She who had refused the royal summons was forever banished from the royal presence, and a great domestic uprising was squelched before it even began.

After a while, a search was conducted for a new queen to replace Vashti. It so happened that many Jews were living in Persia at the time. Exiled from Judah a hundred years earlier (after Jerusalem's fall in 587 BC), they had been deported to Babylon, which in turn was conquered by Persia. Mordecai and his orphaned cousin Esther were among those living in exile, 650 miles northeast of Jerusalem.

Like many other young virgins, the beautiful Esther was gathered into the king's harem. To refuse the privilege may well have meant her death. Counseled by Mordecai to keep her Jewish origins a secret, because being a Jew would probably have disqualified her from becoming queen, she spent the next twelve months awaiting her tryst with the king. When the moment came, Esther so pleased Xerxes that she became queen in Vashti's place.

Some time later, an Amalekite named Haman rose to power in Persia. Haman was so highly placed that other officials knelt before him as a sign of respect. One man, however, the Jew Mordecai, refused to kneel. Haman became so angry that he decided to eliminate every Jew in the kingdom.

To ascertain the most favorable moment for destroying them, Haman piously consulted his gods by casting lots (or *pur*). A date eleven months into the future was revealed—March 7 by our reckoning. Haman immediately persuaded Xerxes to issue a decree that all the Jews in his realm were to be slaughtered on that day. By way of incentive, the decree proclaimed that anyone who killed a Jew could plunder his possessions.

Mordecai reacted immediately by contacting his cousin Esther and asking her to beg Xerxes for mercy. But Esther was afraid and replied, "For any man or woman who approaches the king in the inner court without being summoned the king has but one law: that they be put to death unless the king extends the gold scepter to them and spare their lives. But thirty days have passed since I was called to go to the king."

Mordecai replied, "Do not think that because you are in the king's house you alone of all the Jews will escape. For if you remain silent at this time, relief and deliverance for the Jews will arise from another place, but you and your father's family will perish. And who knows but that you have come to royal position for such a time as this?"

So Esther instructed Mordecai, "Go, gather together all the Jews who are in Susa, and fast for me. Do not eat or drink for three days, night or day. I and my maids will fast as you do. When this is done, I will go to the king, even though it is against the law. And if I perish, I perish."

On the third day, Esther approached the king. As soon as Xerxes saw her, he held out the golden scepter. "What is it, Queen Esther?" he asked. "What is your request? Even up to half the kingdom, it will be given to you."

But Esther merely invited the king and Haman to join her that evening for a banquet she had prepared especially for them. That evening the king again pressed her to ask for whatever she desired, but Esther simply invited the king and Haman to another banquet, to be held the following night.

That evening, on his way home, Haman caught sight of Mordecai, sitting smugly rather than kneeling as he passed by. Haman was outraged, but his wife consoled him by proposing an evil scheme—he need merely build a gallows and then ask the king to hang Mordecai on it the next morning.

While Haman was happily constructing a gallows for his enemy, the king was pacing the royal bedroom. Unable to sleep, he ordered one of his servants to read from the annals of the kingdom. That evening's reading just happened to be about how Mordecai had once saved the king's life by warning of a plot against him. It struck the king that Mordecai had never been properly rewarded for his loyalty.

So the next morning the king asked Haman: "What should be done for the man the king delights to honor?"

Assuming the king intended to reward him in some new and marvelous way, the foolish Haman replied with a grandiose suggestion: "For the man the king delights to honor, have them bring a royal robe the king has worn and a horse the king has ridden. Then let one of the king's most noble princes robe the man and lead him on the horse through the city streets, proclaiming before him, 'This is what is done for the man the king delights to honor!'"

"Go at once," the king commanded him. "Get the robe and the horse and do just as you have suggested for Mordecai the Jew."

Haman was dumbstruck. The man who had planned to bury his enemy was suddenly forced to exalt him that very day!

That night, as the king and Haman were once again drinking wine at the queen's banquet, the king implored Esther to ask for whatever her heart desired. This time she spoke her mind: "If I have found favor with you, O king, and if it pleases your majesty, grant me my life—this is my petition. And spare my people—this is my request. For I and my people have been sold for destruction and slaughter and annihilation."

"Where is the man who has dared to do such a thing?" the king demanded.

"The adversary and enemy is this vile Haman."

And so Haman's star, which had risen to so great a height, fell suddenly, like a bolt of lightning crashing from the sky. He was hanged on the very same gallows he had built for the Jew Mordecai, and all his property was given to Esther. Furthermore, the king, because he could not revoke one of his own edicts, issued another to counteract the first one. It gave Jews throughout the empire the right to protect themselves, to destroy and plunder every enemy who might raise a hand against them on the seventh of March.

As news of the king's edict spread, many people from various nationalities became so terrified that they claimed to be Jews themselves. The very day Haman's gods had revealed as a day of reckoning for the Jews became a day of reckoning for their enemies. Ever after, the Jews commemorated these events with the Feast of Purim. As the book of Esther says, these days were celebrated "as the time when the Jews got relief from their enemies, and as the month when their sorrow was turned into joy and their mourning into a day of celebration."

Subject to foreign powers after the exile, God's people must have felt among the weakest elements of society. But weaker even than a Jewish man exiled to a foreign land was a Jewish woman. And weakest of all would have been a young orphan of Jewish descent. God had once again employed one of his favorite methods for accomplishing his purposes: He had raised an imperfect woman, the weakest of the weak, placing her in a position of immense strategic importance.

But it had been up to Esther to decide whether she would play the part God offered. Like Moses, she chose to identify with God's people even if it meant risking her life to do so. And even though exile was a punishment for Israel's long unfaithfulness, God showed that he was still with his people, delivering and protecting them in surprising ways, turning the table on their enemies through a series of stunning reversals. Earthly powers were at work to kill and destroy, but a heavenly power, far greater in scope, was at work to save and preserve.

Tuesday

HER LIFE AND TIMES

THE FESTIVAL OF PURIM

When Haman threw the lot or the *pur* to discover what day would be the best day to annihilate the Jews in Xerxes' kingdom, he unwittingly established a festival called Purim, when, instead of annihilation, the Jews celebrated their deliverance. Esther and her cousin Mordecai jointly worked to overturn Haman's plot, and when they were successful, they sent out a proclamation to all the Jews living in Xerxes' kingdom to "celebrate annually the fourteenth and fifteenth days of the month of Adar as the time when the Jews got relief from their enemies, and as the month when their sorrow was turned into joy and their mourning into a day of celebration" (Esther 9:21–22).

Adar 14 and 15. Adar was the last month in the Jewish calendar — our February/March. Josephus, the first-century Jewish general and historian, claimed that Jews all over the world celebrated the festival of Purim in his day, and it continues to be a popular festival for Jews today.

Worship and fasting typically make up the first day of the festival. The entire book of Esther is read aloud, and the congregation responds with "Let his name be blotted out" each time Haman's name is read. The children in the group respond to Haman's name with noisemakers and rattles. On the second day of the feast, rejoicing and celebration break out. Food, music, dramas and plays, special songs, and recitals all add to the festive mood. People give gifts to each other and also make sure they don't forget to give gifts and food to the poor, as that was a special wish of Mordecai (Esther 9:22).

Like the Passover, the Feast of Purim celebrates divine deliverance. Saved from Pharaoh's rule and slavery in Egypt and delivered from the destruction planned by Haman, the Jews celebrated a deliverance that only God could have orchestrated. Previously doomed, they were now delivered. As believers, we too have something to celebrate. Instead of a Moses or an Esther, God sent his own Son to deliver us, saving us from the terrible destruction of sin and death. Surely, that's reason enough to celebrate!

Wednesday

HER LEGACY IN SCRIPTURE

Read Esther 3:12—4:17.

1. By concealing her Jewishness and being willing to become a member of King Xerxes' harem, Esther seemed to be caving in to the pagan culture in which she lived. What do you think of her actions in this regard?

2. From other ancient sources we know that Esther's husband, the king, was legendary for his irrational temper and fits of cruelty. Describe Esther's dilemma. What will happen if she does nothing? What might happen if she does what Mordecai asks?

3. Look at 4:12–14. What do you see in Mordecai's words that might have motivated Esther to take the risk?

4. Why does Esther ask all the city's Jews to fast (4:15–16)?

5. God is never named in the original Hebrew version of this story, nor does the writer mention prayer. Where, if anywhere, do you see God in this story?

6. Esther's position was no accident, and neither is yours. Think about the time and people among whom God has placed you. What might God have for you to do right where you are now?

Thursday

HER PROMISE

*G*od often uses the most unlikely characters to fulfill his purposes. He elevates a Jewish orphan to become queen of a great empire. Esther begins as a nobody and becomes a somebody, a woman who somewhat reluctantly risks her life to make a stand.

Again, God reveals his penchant for using the most unlikely, ordinary people to accomplish his divine purposes. But, you may wonder, could God ever use you to accomplish his purposes, with all your foibles and imperfections, your lack of talent or influence? Yes, he can! He isn't looking for people who are perfect or talented or influential. He is only looking for people who are willing.

Promises in Scripture

Who knows but that you have come to royal position for such a time as this?

—ESTHER 4:14

For if the willingness is there, the gift is acceptable according to what one has, not according to what he does not have.

—2 CORINTHIANS 8:12

Let us throw off everything that hinders and the sin that so easily entangles, and let us run with perseverance the race marked out for us. Let us fix our eyes on Jesus.

—HEBREWS 12:1–2

Friday

HER LEGACY OF PRAYER

For if you remain silent at this time, relief and deliverance for the Jews will arise from another place, but you and your father's family will perish. And who knows but that you have come to royal position for such a time as this?

—ESTHER 4:14

REFLECT ON: Esther 5–8.

PRAISE GOD: That he turns the wisdom and the power of the world on its head, often using the most surprising tactics to accomplish his plan.

OFFER THANKS: That God has an important purpose for your life.

CONFESS: Any tendency to view your life in isolation from God's people, to shrink back from some step of faith God may be calling you to take.

ASK GOD: For the grace to act courageously and wisely.

Lift Your Heart

*M*any Jewish girls celebrate the Feast of Purim by dressing up as Queen Esther. One way we can emulate her today is by fasting. Before Esther took action, she employed a time-honored spiritual discipline to expose her need before God. Fasting was a visible sign of her dependency and weakness, an eloquent form of begging God's help. This week, do a little eloquent begging yourself by choosing a day to fast from breakfast and lunch—dinner, too, if you're brave! Drink only water or fruit juice. Perhaps you have a particular need or problem you would like to surrender to God. Tell God that you need him more than you need food. Don't try to manipulate him by your self-sacrifice, but simply allow your weakness to emerge in his presence.

Lord, I need you so much more than food or water. Without your presence, your protection, your wisdom, your gift of faith, I would be lost. I'm hungry for you alone. Hear my prayer and give me everything I need to do your will. Use me in the church and in the world around me to accomplish your purposes.

The Woman of Proverbs 31

HER CHARACTER: She represents the fulfillment of a life lived in wisdom.

HER JOY: To be praised by her husband and children as a woman who surpasses all others.

KEY SCRIPTURE: Proverbs 31:10–31

Monday
HER STORY

*P*roverbs brims with less-than-glowing descriptions of women. There are wayward wives, prostitutes, women with smoother-than-oil lips, strange women, loud women, defiant women, wives who are like a continual drip on a rainy day or decay in their husbands' bones, women whose feet never stay home, brazen-faced women, and even a woman so repulsive she is likened to a gold ring in a pig's snout!

Any woman reading Proverbs may be tempted to conclude that its authors tended to blame women for weaknesses actually rooted in the male psyche, especially when it comes to sexual sin. But to balance things out there are also some odious descriptions of men, including scoundrels, villains, chattering fools, and sluggards. And Proverbs actually opens and closes with positive portrayals of women: first as wisdom personified and then as a woman who can do no wrong.

Just who was this woman on a pedestal described in Proverbs 31? Was she, as many think, the ideal wife and mother? In traditional Jewish homes, husbands and children recited the poem in Proverbs 31 at the Sabbath table. Written as an acrostic, each line begins with a Hebrew letter in alphabetical sequence, making it easy to memorize. The poem describes a wealthy, aristocratic woman with a large household to direct. She was hardworking, enterprising, capable, strong, wise, skilled, generous, thoughtful of others, dignified, God-fearing, serene — a tremendous credit to her husband. She arose while it was still dark to feed her family. She looked at a field, considered its merits, and purchased it. She wove cloth and made linen garments, which she then sold. "Her children arise and call her blessed; her husband also, and he praises her: 'Many women do noble things, but you surpass them all'" (verses 28–29).

The description of the woman in Proverbs 31 offers a refreshing contrast to other ancient depictions of women, which tend to portray them in more frivolous and decorative terms, emphasizing only their charm or beauty. Still, the perfect woman of Proverbs 31 hasn't always been a friend to ordinary women. In fact, she has sometimes been rubbed into the faces of lesser women by critical husbands and preachers unable to resist the temptation. What woman could ever measure up to her? And is a woman's worth to be measured only by what she can accomplish in the domestic sphere? Or is the woman in Proverbs 31 a symbol of all the contributions a woman could make within the culture of her day? Regardless of how you answer these questions, there is more to her story than simply being the ideal wife and mother.

Before we can discover more about her true identity, it is worth posing a broader question: Are there really all that many women running around in the pages of Proverbs? Perhaps, in fact, there are only two main women in Proverbs: the wise woman and the woman of folly (as some have called her). The latter encompasses the adulteress and her many wicked counterparts; the former encompasses wisdom in the abstract and wisdom made concrete in the woman of Proverbs 31.

In Proverbs 3:13–16 a young man is instructed: "Blessed is the man who finds wisdom, the man who gains understanding, for she is more profitable than silver and yields better returns than gold. She is more precious than rubies; nothing you desire can compare with her. Long life is in her right hand; in her left hand are riches and honor." Here is wisdom in the abstract, personified as a woman.

Proverbs 31 echoes this praise: "A wife of noble character who can find? She is worth far more than rubies.... She brings him good, not harm, all the days of her life. She selects wool and flax and works with eager hands. She is like the merchant ships, bringing her food from afar. She gets up while it is still dark; she provides food for her family and portions for her servant girls. She considers a field and buys it; out of her earnings she plants a vineyard" (verses 10, 12–16). Here is a concrete example of what wisdom looks like in a person's life.

By contrast, the man who welcomes the brazen-faced woman, the prostitute, the adulteress is nothing but a fool. He has fallen prey to the woman of folly, who offers deceitful pleasures that will lead to his death.

From beginning to end, Proverbs is a practical handbook for leading a life based on wisdom. In the end, there are only two choices for both men and women: to embrace wisdom or to love folly. The woman of Proverbs 31 may well be meant to inspire both men and women with a picture of what a virtuous life, male or female, is capable of producing: shelter for others, serenity, honor, prosperity, generosity, confidence about the future—true blessedness. Who wouldn't want to be like such a woman? Who wouldn't sing her praises?

Tuesday

SPINNING AND WEAVING

The woman of Proverbs 31 was a real pro at working with fabrics. She started by selecting the wool and flax (verse 13), then spinning it into threads (verse 19). She wove the woolen threads into rich scarlet clothing to keep her family warm in snowy weather (verse 21). She wove the flax threads into linen for bed coverings, for fine clothing for herself, and for clothing and sashes to sell (verses 22, 24).

Traditionally women's work, the spinning and weaving of cloth for clothing, bedding, rugs, and other needs occupied a tremendous amount of the time and talents of Hebrew women. Fibers from plants like cotton and flax or wool from sheep were spun and twisted in order to produce a long thread. That thread could then be used to sew fabrics together with needles made of bone or it could be used to weave new fabric. Weaving, an art that the Hebrews probably perfected while they were in Egypt, was done on a rudimentary loom.

Old Testament families used fabrics for a variety of purposes. The oldest and most common fabric in biblical times was wool. Woolen fabrics were woven from the hair of lambs and sheep and were made into the everyday clothing worn by the common person, even in hot weather. Linen, which was woven from the flax plant, formed the fabrics from which inner clothing was made. Some linen was so finely woven that it formed a silky, translucent cloth from which the rich made their garments. Heavy cloth woven from goat or camel hair formed waterproof tents and outer clothing.

Sound like a lot of work? It was. The women of a household spent virtually every spare moment on one part or another of the task of making fabrics. The "wife of noble character" in Proverbs 31 works "with eager hands" (verse 13), and it seems as if the spindle and distaff never leave her fingers (verse 19). That's why "she has no fear for her household" (verse 21). Spinning and weaving have kept her busy all the time, but she and her family are ready for the cold weather.

Does just reading about the Proverbs 31 woman make you tired? Do you wish she would just sit down and rest a moment? Whatever your response to this larger-than-life woman, you can't help but notice that she never wasted the time given her. In our convenient culture of store-bought clothing and fast-food restaurants, you may not need to weave your own cloth or cook your own meals—but that's not the issue. The issue is what you are doing with the time that's been given to you.

Wednesday

HER LEGACY IN SCRIPTURE

Read Proverbs 31:10–31.

1. Does this passage seem out of touch with reality to you? Why? What would make it seem more of a reality for today's woman?

2. How does this woman's husband view and treat her? Why?

3. List some of the different tasks that keep this woman busy. Now list *how* she goes about her work.

4. Look at Proverbs 31:25. Imagine someone saying these words about you. What thoughts and feelings leap to your mind?

5. What does it mean to fear the Lord (Proverbs 31:30)? Why is that more important than being beautiful or good at home decorating or crafts or business?

6. What would it take for you to become more of a woman who fears the Lord, one who can laugh at the days to come?

Thursday

HER PROMISE

*M*any women find Proverbs 31 discouraging. Don't let that happen to you. Remember, this very capable woman is ultimately praised not so much for all she accomplishes as for one thing: She fears the Lord. The woman who is worthy of praise is not necessarily the one who does all her own sewing or is a great cook or is a natural beauty—the woman who gets the praise is the woman who fears the Lord. That's the target to aim for. Not outward beauty. Not a perfectly decorated home. Not even more intellectual knowledge or business acumen. Instead, aim for a bold, all-consuming love for God. Then you too will be worthy of praise.

Promises in Scripture

> *The fear of the LORD—that is wisdom,*
> *and to shun evil is understanding.*

> —JOB 28:28

> *Charm is deceptive, and beauty is fleeting;*
> *but a woman who fears the Lo r d is to be praised.*

> —PROVERBS 31:30

> *"Love the LORD your God with all your heart and with all your soul and with all your strength and with all your mind"; and, "Love your neighbor as yourself."*

> —LUKE 10:27

Friday

HER LEGACY OF PRAYER

For wisdom is more precious than rubies,
and nothing you desire can compare with her.

—PROVERBS 8:11

REFLECT ON: Proverbs 8:11–36.

PRAISE GOD: For the gift of wisdom, which preserves, blesses, and
                even prolongs our life.

OFFER THANKS: For the benefits of wisdom you have already tasted
                in your daily life.

CONFESS: Any tendency to choose the wisdom of the world
                over the wisdom of God.

ASK GOD: Every day to make you a woman who longs for wis-
                dom, who prefers it to silver and gold.

Lift Your Heart

Proverbs is full of pithy statements that contain profound wisdom for daily life. Look through this book of Scripture and select a few favorites, then commit them to memory. Here's a few to get you started:

A cheerful heart is good medicine,
    but a crushed spirit dries up the bones.

—Proverbs 17:22

Fools find no pleasure in understanding
    but delight in airing their own opinions.

—Proverbs 18:2

Those who get wisdom love their own lives;
    those who cherish understanding will soon prosper.

—Proverbs 19:8

Lord, you know better than I the kind of heart in which wisdom grows best—one in which patience, faith, and humility are there to nourish it. Help me cultivate a heart in which wisdom can quickly take root and flourish. Let wisdom be so much a part of my life that it produces a shelter for others.

The Shulammite Woman

HER CHARACTER: Hers is the only female voice that speaks directly and extensively to us in Scripture. Ruth's, Esther's, Hannah's, and Mary's voices, for instance, are all mediated through narration. The Shulammite woman boldly declares her longing and desire to be united to her lover in marriage.

HER SORROW: To have been separated from her beloved at times.

HER JOY: To enjoy so passionate a love.

KEY SCRIPTURE: Song of Songs 1–8

Monday

HER STORY

*S*he was young, beautiful, and desirable. He was handsome, strong, and agile, a shepherd or a king who lavished strange praise upon his beloved: He compared the Shulamite woman's hair to a flock of goats running down a mountain slope, her nose to the tower of Lebanon, and her teeth ("each with its twin"!) to sheep that have just bathed. We smile at such images. But we are fascinated by this beautifully written collection of love songs. And though we know it is not merely some ancient Valentine's Day card, we are not quite certain what to make of it.

Unlike any other book in the Bible, the Song of Songs is full of erotic imagery. The Shulammite woman was as passionate as her lover, initiating contact with him, openly declaring her feelings. She yearned for kisses from his mouth, so in love that even his name smelled sweet to her. She wandered the city at night (or dreamt of wandering it) searching for him. She wished she could pass him off as her brother so that she could kiss him publicly without creating a scandal. Each declaration from her elicited a passionate response from her lover, who sang of her,

> Your stature is like that of the palm,
>   and your breasts like clusters of fruit.
> I said, "I will climb the palm tree;
>   I will take hold of its fruit."
> May your breasts be like the clusters of the vine,
>   the fragrance of your breath like apples,
>   and your mouth like the best wine.
> —Song of Songs 7:7–9

Despite the ancient imagery, we get the message.

The story of the Shulammite woman and her lover isn't properly a story, one with a clear narrative line, but a poetic expression of love in all its emotional ups and downs. The songs capture the desire, the anguish, the tension, and the ecstasy of love. But speakers and scenes shift so quickly that it can be difficult to understand. No wonder there have been so many different interpretations of the Song of Songs, more than any other book of the Hebrew Scriptures.

What makes this portion of Scripture even more enigmatic is that it never once mentions God. But if God has nothing to do with these love songs, how did this material ever make it into the canon of Scripture in the first place?

The Jews believed the book was not primarily about individual lovers but about God's love for his people Israel. Christians initially read it as a parable of Christ's love for the church and later as a parable of his love for the individual soul. Modern commentators tend to view it more literally, as an expression of the sacredness of married life, the fullest expression of love between a man and a woman. They praise its inclusion in the Bible because it celebrates marital love and the sexual expression of that love. Anyone inclined to believe the Bible teaches a negative view of sex should read this book of Scripture before drawing such a conclusion.

But who wrote these eloquent love songs? Some say various poets, while others say they were written by Solomon in praise of one of his many wives. Yet others have suggested they were written by a woman. Whatever the case, most admit that the poetry of the Song of Songs can be understood in more than one way. The story of the Shulammite, mysterious as it is, touches our longing to love and be loved.

Tuesday

HER LIFE AND TIMES

ROMANTIC LOVE

The erotic poetry of Song of Songs is not merely an expression of sexual desire but of the romantic love between a young man and a young woman. The love between the lover and the beloved is not merely one of physical pleasure and intimacy but one of a depth of feeling and commitment. True love doesn't fade with the changes brought about by time but is stronger even than death. Neither the waters of time nor the rivers of disappointment or tragedy can wash it away (Song of Songs 8:6–7).

Most marriages in biblical times were arranged. When children were very young, their parents formed alliances to provide wives and husbands for their children. Many of these marriages took place when the participants were young, so young that the rabbis eventually established the minimum age for marriage at twelve for girls and thirteen for boys. Mere children even then, romantic and committed love developed over the years of marriage.

Although not all marriages were love matches in the beginning, many arranged marriages were eventually characterized by love. Isaac loved the wife his father's servant had gotten for him (Genesis 24:67). Elkanah loved Hannah, a wife he probably received by arrangement with her family (1 Samuel 1:8). A beautiful example of the sacrificial love of a husband for his wife is given in Exodus 21:2–5, where a husband willingly goes into servitude for life rather than leave the wife he loves.

A man could, however, choose his own bride, even against the desires or arrangements of his parents. Jacob wanted to marry Rachel because he loved her (Genesis 29:18) and got her sister, Leah, also as part of the bargain. Samson begged his father to get a young Philistine woman for him, certain she was the right one for him (Judges 14:3).

The Old Testament seems to assume that husbands will love their wives, whether chosen by or for them. The Teacher in Ecclesiastes tells husbands to be sure to "enjoy life with your wife, whom you

THE SHULAMMITE WOMAN   271

love" (Ecclesiastes 9:9), as though a husband's love for his wife is a given. The New Testament, however, urges husbands to love their wives. Four separate and clear times (Ephesians 5:25, 28, 33; Colossians 3:19) Paul mentions that husbands should love their wives, once even comparing that love to the love Christ has for his church.

If you have been so fortunate in your own marriage to experience a love even half as passionate as the one described in the Song of Songs, read it in light of your story, thanking God for his blessing. But even if you haven't, you can be glad that married love and its sexual expression was God's idea to begin with. You can also read the Song of Songs as a dialogue between God and your own soul. God's love, after all, is more passionate than any human love you could ever experience. He is the true Lover of your soul, ready to sing with you the greatest and most beautiful song of all.

Wednesday

HER LEGACY IN SCRIPTURE

Read Song of Songs 4:9–5:1.

1. What picture of married love do you get from this passage?

2. When you think about your own marriage or singleness in light of this passage, what thoughts and feelings arise in you?

3. Imagine God having such passion for you. How do you respond?

Read Song of Songs 8:6–7.

4. How do these verses express the commitment between the lover and the beloved? What does it take to sustain such a commitment?

5. Throughout history, intimate love relationships have been shamefully distorted and profaned. Song of Songs gives God's vision of what love relationships were meant to be. What can you do to pursue such a relationship with your husband or with God?

Thursday

HER PROMISE

*G*od doesn't promise the Song of Songs kind of erotic, intimate, earthly love to everyone. He blesses many marriages with it, but it is not something everyone enjoys. However, he does promise to love his people with the same depth of love described here. That includes you. You are his treasured one, his beloved, and he delights in you just as these lovers delight in each other.

Promises in Scripture

> For you are a people holy to the LORD your God. The LORD your God has chosen you out of all the peoples on the face of the earth to be his people, his treasured possession.

—DEUTERONOMY 7:6

> Praise be to the LORD,
>   for he showed his wonderful love to me.

—PSALM 31:21

> For the LORD takes delight in his people;
>   he crowns the humble with salvation.

—PSALM 149:4

> I have loved you with an everlasting love.

—JEREMIAH 31:3

> The LORD your God is with you,
>   he is mighty to save.
> He will take great delight in you,
>   he will quiet you with his love,
>   he will rejoice over you with singing.

—ZEPHANIAH 3:17

Friday

HER LEGACY OF PRAYER

Place me like a seal over your heart,
   like a seal on your arm;
for love is as strong as death,
   its jealousy unyielding as the grave.
It burns like blazing fire,
   like a mighty flame.
Many waters cannot quench love;
   rivers cannot wash it away.
If one were to give
   all the wealth of his house for love,
   it would be utterly scorned.

—Song of Songs 8:6–8

REFLECT ON: Songs of Songs 1:2–4; 2:10–13; 8:6–8.

PRAISE GOD: That nothing can separate us from his love.

OFFER THANKS: That Christ's passion has rendered us beautiful in the eyes of God.

CONFESS: Any failure to believe God truly is the Lover of your soul.

ASK GOD: To help you enter into this dialogue of love with him.

Lift Your Heart

The Shulammite woman was so captivated by her lover that his name was like perfume that made everything in her world smell good. In biblical times, names actually revealed the person. Knowing someone's name was equivalent to knowing that person's essence. This week, light a fragrant candle as you take time to reflect on one or more of God's names. Look up relevant Scripture passages and ask God to reveal himself more deeply to you.

Creator of Heaven and Earth (Genesis 14:19)
My Song (Exodus 15:2)
Prince of Peace (Isaiah 9:6)
Good Shepherd (John 10:14)
Counselor (John 14:26)
Father of Compassion (2 Corinthians 1:3)
Savior (1 Timothy 4:10)
Light (1 John 1:5)

————————————

Lord, I have placed you as a seal over my heart. Neither death nor life, neither angels nor demons, neither the present nor the future, nor any powers, neither height nor depth, nor anything else in all creation will be able to separate me from your love.

Gomer

HER NAME MEANS
"Completion"

HER CHARACTER:	Though a married woman, she carried on numerous love affairs, crediting her lovers for the gifts her husband had given her.
HER SORROW:	To have become the symbol of spiritual adultery—a picture of Israel's unfaithfulness to God.
HER JOY:	That her husband continued to love her despite her unfaithfulness.
KEY SCRIPTURE:	Hosea 1–3

Monday

HER STORY

The man stood at the door, craning his neck and peering through the half-light. His limbs felt stiff and cold, despite the desert heat that still warmed the narrow street. Other than a stray dog curled in a knot against the wall of a neighboring house, he saw nothing. It was too late for a woman to be walking the streets alone. But, then, she wouldn't be alone, would she?

He didn't want to go inside yet, to listen to the absence of her chatter, to lie down on the empty bed. By noon tomorrow, the news of her betrayal would fill every gossip-hungry soul in town like swill in a pig's belly. Hosea, the man who would steer the nation with his prophecies, couldn't even control his own wife.

He felt grief and fury like a storm breaking inside him. He had meant to guard his heart; he had never intended to give himself so completely. His pain was the worse for loving her so well. For Gomer had squandered his gifts, mocked his tenderness, and allowed herself to be seduced by other lovers.

Hadn't God warned him and instructed him to "go, take to yourself an adulterous wife and children of unfaithfulness, because the land is guilty of the vilest adultery in departing from the Lord"? He had named his children "Jezreel" (God Scatters), "Lo-Ruhamah" (Not Loved), and "Lo-Ammi" (Not My People). Each successive child measured the growing rift between husband and wife. Hosea wondered whether he had even fathered the last two.

The word of the Lord that had filled Hosea's mouth now troubled his soul, rushing back with appalling force. So this was how God felt about his own people—bitterly betrayed, cut to the heart, disgusted, outraged. His tender love, his every gift meant nothing to a people enamored with Canaanite gods. Israel's leading men were the worst whores of all—virtuosos when it came to playing the harlot, cheating the poor and imploring idols to bless them with peace and riches.

But peace was elusive. Six kings had ruled the northern kingdom during a period of just twenty-five years. Four were murdered by their successors and one was captured in battle. All the while, Assyria perched like a vulture at its borders.

If only Israel would learn its lesson and turn back to the Lord before it was too late—if only Gomer would turn back. Hosea wanted to shout in her face, shake her awake to her sin. Enough of patience. Enough of tenderness. She had ignored his threats, shrugging them off as so many flies on a donkey. What choice had he now? He would strip and shame her, punishing her unfaithfulness.

In the midst of his bitter grief, he heard the voice of God, strong and clear: "Go, show your love to your wife again, though she is loved by another and is an adulteress. Love her as the LORD loves the Israelites, though they turn to other gods."

So Hosea took back the wife he couldn't stop loving. And the word of the Lord transformed Lo-Ruhamah into Ruhamah (Loved) and Lo-Ammi into Ammi (My People).

The story of Gomer and Hosea portrays God's jealousy for his people. For the first time, a prophet dared to speak of God as husband and Israel as his bride. But this is a tangled love story, one in which God's heart is repeatedly broken. Despite his pleas, regardless of his threats, Israel would not turn back to him until after the northern kingdom was destroyed by Assyria a few years later.

Still, the knit-together lives of Hosea and Gomer were a living reminder to the Israelites of both God's judgment and his love. Hosea's beautiful words still move us as we think about the church today, about our own unfaithfulness and God's forgiveness: "I will betroth you to me forever; I will betroth you in righteousness and justice, in love and compassion. Let us acknowledge the LORD; let us press on to acknowledge him. As surely as the sun rises, he will appear; he will come to us like the winter rains, like the spring rains that water the earth."

No longer Lo-Ruhamah, we are Ruhamah (Loved), and no longer Lo-Ammi but Ammi (My People). For our Maker has become our Husband, the one who hates our sin but loves us still.

Tuesday

HER LIFE AND TIMES

PROPHETS

Gomer's husband, Hosea, appeared on the scene as the last of the prophets who spoke the "word of the LORD" (Hosea 1:1) to the doomed northern kingdom of Israel. Before long, the Assyrians would conquer the capital of Samaria and take thousands of Israelites captive. When the book of Hosea begins with "the word of the LORD," it asserts Hosea's authority as a prophet, that God has spoken to him, and that he must relay the message to the people.

The Israelites in Palestine had the law God had given to Moses and the people at Sinai. This consisted of the Ten Commandments as well as the other rules for living included in the books of Moses (Genesis through Deuteronomy). However, those laws didn't cover many of life's situations and decisions. God instituted the office of the prophet for the many times when a specific revelation of God was needed for the people to know what direction they should follow.

We don't always know how prophets received their messages from God. At times they had visions and dreams. Ezekiel and Daniel both record visions that contained a definite message from God. Other times, as in Hosea, the prophets simply declared that their words were from the Lord. The emphasis of God's prophets was never on the method of receiving his word—whether mysterious or obvious—but on the message itself and on the people's need to follow. God made it clear that if the people would only listen and obediently follow the words of the prophets, he would give them all they needed to face an unknown future.

Just as God provided for his people in the Promised Land, he has provided for us. He may not miraculously reveal the path or supernaturally tell us his will, as he did with the Israelites, but he has revealed himself and his plans for us through the Bible, and his messengers today underscore and explain what Scripture tells us. We can be assured that God will go with us, just as he went with the Israelites, holding our hands as we face whatever our futures hold.

Wednesday

Read Hosea 1:2–2:7; 3:1–5.

1. In what ways does Hosea 2:2–7 reflect Hosea's feelings about Gomer? In what ways do these verses reflect God's feelings about his people?

2. Why is adultery a fitting symbol for the way humans treat God?

3. Put God's promises for his people in Hosea 1:10–2:1 into your own words.

4. In Hosea 3:2, Hosea has to pay money and goods to buy Gomer back from whatever situation she's landed herself in. She has apparently run off and ended up selling herself into prostitution to survive. What would it take for a man to do what Hosea does in 3:1–3?

5. How are you like Gomer? How has God pursued you and bought you back?

Thursday

HER PROMISE

A tempestuous marriage. A wife who will not remain faithful to the husband who loves her. A husband who not only remains faithful, but loving. Children whose paternity is in doubt. All these are the elements not of a soap opera but of a wonderful picture of God's love and faithfulness to his often unloving and unfaithful people. The promises portrayed in the life of Gomer apply not only to the people of Israel but to the people of today. God loves us and remains faithful to us. Even when we abandon him and turn away, he waits with arms open. He only asks our repentance and his blessings will again overflow.

Promises in Scripture

I will give them a heart to know me, that I am the LORD. They will be my people, and I will be their God, for they will return to me with all their heart.

—JEREMIAH 24:7

Let us acknowledge the LORD;
*   let us press on to acknowledge him.*
As surely as the sun rises,
*   he will appear;*
he will come to us like the winter rains,
*   like the spring rains that water the earth.*

—HOSEA 6:3

Repent, then, and turn to God, so that your sins may be wiped out, that times of refreshing may come from the Lord.

—ACTS 3:19

Friday

HER LEGACY OF PRAYER

"In that day," declares the LORD,
"you will call me 'my husband';
you will no longer call me 'my master.'"

—HOSEA 2:16

REFLECT ON: Hosea 1–3.

PRAISE GOD: For his mercy.

OFFER THANKS: That God loved you before you ever thought of
loving him.

CONFESS: Any tendency to love money, pleasure, children, husband, or career more than you love him.

ASK GOD: To increase your hunger to know him more intimately.

Lift Your Heart

Sometimes couples grow apart not because either have been unfaithful, but because of sheer busyness. If your relationship with God is bogging down in life's details, why not plan an intimate evening or weekend with him? Let it be a time of quieting your soul in his presence, of hushing life's everyday demands. Spend the day walking a solitary beach, or hidden away at a retreat center or a friend's cottage or cabin. Take your Bible and a book of poetry by Christina Rossetti, or Mark Buchanan's *The Rest of God*, or C. S. Lewis's *The Lion, the Witch and the Wardrobe*, or Kathleen Norris's *The Cloister Walk*.

If you're artistic, bring paint and art paper and commune with God through the pictures you create. Let it be a time of praising him, of telling him how much you love him, of thanking him for all the ways he has loved you. Don't try to have a great spiritual experience, just relax and let God know you want to be with him.

Lord, how can I begin to understand how faithfully you've loved me?
Draw me into your presence and hold me close. Quiet my noisy heart
and speak to me.

Elizabeth

"God Is My Oath"

HER CHARACTER: A descendant of Aaron, Elizabeth was a woman the Bible calls "upright in the sight of God." Like few others, male or female, she is praised for observing all the Lord's commandments and regulations without blame. She is the first to acknowledge Jesus as Lord.

HER SORROW: To be barren for most of her life.

HER JOY: To give birth to John, later known as John the Baptist, the Messiah's forerunner. His name, divinely assigned, means, "The Lord Is Gracious."

KEY SCRIPTURE: Luke 1:5–80

Monday

HER STORY

Her eyes were a golden brown. Like currants set in pastry, they winked out at the world from cheeks that had baked too long in the sun. Snowy strands of hair straggled from beneath a woolen shawl, tickling her wrinkled face. Small hands rested tenderly on her rounded belly, softly probing for any hint of movement. But all was still. From her vantage point on the roof of the house, she noticed a figure walking up the pathway and wondered who her visitor might be.

She and Zechariah had been content enough in their quiet house these last few months, secluded in their joy. Each morning she had opened her eyes as though waking to a fantastic dream. Sometimes she shook with laughter as she thought about how God had rearranged her life, planting a child in her shriveled-up, old-woman's womb.

Six months ago, Zechariah had been chosen by lot to burn incense before the Most Holy Place, a once-in-a-lifetime privilege. But during his week of priestly service in the temple, he had been frightened half to death by a figure who appeared suddenly next to the altar of incense. "Your wife Elizabeth will bear you a son," the angel told him, "and you are to give him the name John. He will be a joy and delight to you, and many will rejoice because of his birth, for he will be great in the sight of the Lord." It was Sarah and Abraham all over, Rebekah and Isaac, Rachel and Jacob. God was once again kindling a fire with two dry sticks.

For the life of her, Elizabeth couldn't understand her husband's response to the messenger that had so terrified him. Once you'd laid eyes on an angel, how could you fail to believe that anything was possible? But Zechariah had blurted out his skepticism and suffered the consequences. His voice had been snatched away and would not be given back until the angel's words came to pass. These days he communicated by scribbling on a wax tablet.

Elizabeth looked down again at the figure advancing up the path, a green sprig of a girl. The older woman stepped carefully down the stairs and into the house to welcome her guest. But with the young woman's words of greeting came something that felt like a gale force wind, shaking the beams and rafters of the house. Steadying herself, the older woman felt suddenly invigorated. Her unborn baby leapt inside her as she shouted out a welcoming response: "Blessed are you among women, and blessed is the child you will bear! But why am I so favored, that the mother of my Lord should come to me? As soon as the sound of your greeting reached my ears, the baby in my womb leaped for joy. Blessed is she who has believed that what the Lord has said to her will be accomplished!"

Mary had made the journey all the way from Nazareth to visit her relative Elizabeth. The same angel who had spoken to Zechariah in the temple had whispered the secret of the older woman's pregnancy to the virgin, who was also with child. The magnificent song of praise that burst from Mary's lips during their meeting may have

taken shape during the course of her sixty-mile journey south, to the
hill country of Judea where Elizabeth lived:

> My soul glorifies the Lord
>   and my spirit rejoices in God my Savior,
> for he has been mindful
>   of the humble state of his servant.
> From now on all generations will call me blessed,
>   for the Mighty One has done great things for me—
>   holy is his name.
> His mercy extends to those who fear him,
>   from generation to generation.
> He has performed mighty deeds with his arm;
>   he has scattered those who are proud in their inmost
>   thoughts.
> He has brought down rulers from their thrones
>   but has lifted up the humble.
> He has filled the hungry with good things
>   but has sent the rich away empty.
> He has helped his servant Israel,
>   remembering to be merciful
> to Abraham and his descendants forever,
>   even as he said to our fathers.

Luke 1:46–55

The two women held each other, their bonds of kinship now
stronger than what mere flesh and blood could forge. For Israel's
God—the God of Sarah, Rebekah, Rachel, Leah, Miriam, Deborah, Naomi, Ruth, Abigail, and Hannah—was on the move again,
bringing the long-ago promise to fulfillment. And blessed was she
who did not doubt that what the Lord had said to her would be
accomplished.

Tuesday

HER LIFE AND TIMES

INCENSE

*E*lizabeth's husband, Zechariah, had been given a special, serious privilege. When it was his priestly division's turn to serve in the temple, he was chosen by lot—which was God's way of making the choice—to burn incense in the temple. Each morning and evening he took fire from the altar of burnt offering and placed it on the golden altar of incense that stood before the curtain separating the Holy Place from the Most Holy Place. He then poured the dusty incense from a golden urn onto the fire. While Zechariah performed this duty, all the worshipers who were at the temple that day stood outside and prayed. The smoke and aroma of the incense symbolized their prayers rising up to God. The fragrance also served to fumigate air tainted with the odor of the blood of animals killed for the sacrifices.

The earliest historical records about worship include information on the burning of incense. All the nations surrounding Palestine appreciated the sweet smell of incense permeating not only their places of worship but also their homes. The incense Zechariah burned in the temple was made according to a special "recipe" (Exodus 30:34–38) of spices and salt that had been ground to a powder. This holy incense could be used only in the temple in worship, never for ordinary, everyday purposes.

The prophet Jeremiah often condemned the Israelites for burning incense to false gods. But he could be even more scathing in his denunciation when they burned incense when their hearts weren't in their worship (Jeremiah 6:20). God made it clear that the mere burning of incense didn't please him; it was only a symbol. He was looking for hearts that were turned toward him with faithfulness and trust.

Isn't that application obvious for us today as well? In all our forms of worship—our hymns and praise songs, our liturgies and dramas and readings—what is important to God is our hearts. Are they turned toward him in faithfulness and trust?

Wednesday

HER LEGACY IN SCRIPTURE

Read Luke 1:5–25, 39–45.

1. What do you learn about Elizabeth and Zechariah from Luke 1:5–7? Does Luke 1:6 imply that they were perfect? If not, what do these words mean?

2. Imagine an angel coming to you with some unexpected and unbelievable announcement. How do you think you would react?

3. When Elizabeth saw Mary, she was filled with the Holy Spirit and loudly exclaimed a blessing (Luke 1:42–44). Have you ever been moved to praise God like that? If so, when? If not, what would have to happen to move you to do that?

4. Elizabeth was going to be the mother of a prophet, yet she praised God for what he was doing in *Mary's* life. What does this say about Elizabeth?

5. Reread Luke 1:45. What does the Lord want you to believe?

Thursday

HER PROMISE

God always keeps his promises! For hundreds of years, God had been telling the people of Israel that he would send a Messiah. One who would provide a direct bridge to God himself. One whose sacrifice would provide redemption for all time. The events in this first chapter of Luke are just the beginning of the fulfillment of God's greatest promise to his people. With Mary we can say: "My soul glorifies the Lord and my spirit rejoices in God my Savior!"

Promises in Scripture

But for you who revere my name, the sun of righteousness will rise with healing in its wings. And you will go out and leap like calves released from the stall.

—MALACHI 4:2

John saw Jesus coming toward him and said, "Look, the Lamb of God, who takes away the sin of the world!"

—JOHN 1:29

Here is a trustworthy saying that deserves full acceptance: Christ Jesus came into the world to save sinners.

—1 TIMOTHY 1:15

Friday

HER LEGACY OF PRAYER

Blessed is she who has believed that what the Lord has said to her will be accomplished!

—LUKE 1:45

REFLECT ON: Luke 1:5–80.

PRAISE GOD: That he is the Creator who shapes every child in the womb.

OFFER THANKS: For the gift of children.

CONFESS: Any tendency to cheapen the value of human life, including unborn life.

ASK GOD: To restore our appreciation for the miracle of human life.

Lift Your Heart

person's a person, no matter how small!

—FROM *Horton Hears a Who* BY DR. SEUSS

Mary's visit to Elizabeth probably occurred when Elizabeth was in her sixth month of pregnancy. The younger woman may have stayed long enough to help the older one with her delivery. In any case, Mary would have been in the first trimester of her pregnancy and Elizabeth in her third. Here's what would have been happening to the children growing in their wombs:

Jesus:

18 days—his nervous system appeared.
4 weeks—his heart began beating.
30 days—most of his major organ systems had begun to form.
7 weeks—his facial features would have been visible.
8th week—all his major body structures and organs were present.
10th week—tiny teeth were forming in his gums.

12th week—his brain was fully formed and he could feel pain.
He may have even sucked his thumb.

John:

6th month—he could grasp his hands, kick, do somersaults, and
hear voices and sounds outside the womb.

Take a few moments to praise your Creator with the beautiful
words of Psalm 139:13–16:

For you created my inmost being;
   you knit me together in my mother's womb.
I praise you because I am fearfully and wonderfully made;
   your works are wonderful,
   I know that full well.
My frame was not hidden from you
   when I was made in the secret place.
When I was woven together in the depths of the earth,
   your eyes saw my unformed body.
All the days ordained for me were written in your book
   before one of them came to be.

---

*Dear God, you are the Lord and Giver of life. Help me to respect,
protect, and nurture it no matter what color, no matter what age, no
matter what gender of human being I encounter. I ask this in the
name of Jesus, the bread and water of life. Amen.*

Mary
Mother of Jesus

HER NAME MAY MEAN
"Bitterness"

HER CHARACTER: She was a virgin from a poor family in an obscure village in Galilee. Her response to Gabriel reveals a young woman of unusual faith and humility. Her unqualified yes to God's plan for her life entailed great personal risk and suffering. She must have endured seasons of confusion, fear, and darkness as the events of her life unfolded. She is honored, not only as the mother of Jesus, but as his first disciple.

HER SORROW: To see the son she loved shamed and tortured, left to die like the worst kind of criminal.

HER JOY: To see her child raised from the dead; to have received the Holy Spirit along with Christ's other disciples.

KEY SCRIPTURES: Matthew 1:18–25; 2; Luke 1:26–80; 2:1–52; John 19:25–27

Monday

HER STORY

*S*he sat down on the bench and closed her eyes, an old woman silhouetted against the blue Jerusalem sky. Even the wood beneath her conjured images. Though she could no longer recall the exact curl of his smile or the shape of his sleeping face resting next to hers, she could still see the rough brown hands, expertly molding the wood to his purposes. Joseph had been a good carpenter and an even better husband.

These days the memories came unbidden, like a gusty wind carrying her away to other times and places. Some said drowning people see their lives unfold in incredible detail just before they die. Age had a similar effect, she thought, except that you could relive your memories with a great deal more leisure ...

A cool breeze teased at her skirts as she balanced the jug on her head, making her way toward the well. A stranger, she noticed, was approaching from the opposite direction. Even in the dusky light, his clothes shone, as though bleached bright by the strongest of fuller's soap.

"Greetings," he shouted, "you who are highly favored! The Lord is with you."

No Nazarene, she was sure, would ever dare greet a maiden like that. But with each step his words grew bolder, not softer, rushing toward her like water cascading over a cliff:

"Do not be afraid, Mary....

You have found favor with God....

You will give birth to a son....

He will be called the Son of the Most High....

The Holy Spirit will come upon you....

Elizabeth your relative is going to have a child in her old age."

Wave after wave broke over her as she listened to the angel's words—first confusion and fear, then awe and gratitude, and finally a rush of joy and peace. Her whole being drenched in light. Then she heard more words, this time cascading from her lips, not his:

"I am the Lord's servant.

May it be to me as you have said."

Though the angel departed, Mary's peace remained. The Most High had visited the lowliest of his servants and spoken the promise every Jewish woman longed to hear: "You will be with child and give birth to a son, and you are to give him the name Jesus. The Lord God will give him the throne of his father David, and he will reign over the house of Jacob forever; his kingdom will never end."

The moon hung like a smile in the night sky as Mary lifted the brimming buckets and began walking across the fields. As the water swayed and splashed to the rhythm of her movements, she realized that she too felt full and satisfied—as though she had just finished a favorite meal. Questions, she knew, would come with the morning. For now, it was enough to look up at the stars and know that God was at work shaping her future.

"Mama, Mama," he yelled, running toward her, chubby arms flung out beseechingly.

"Jesus, what is it now, child?" she smiled, scooping the chunky boy into her arms before he could topple over in the usual tangle of arms and legs. But he was all kisses, squealing and nuzzling his curly head against her breast, as though to bury himself in her soft, warm flesh. She sighed contentedly. How many mothers had she known? But none had adequately described the sheer wonder of a child—the laughter, the constant surprise, the tenderness. Not to mention the fear and worry that were also part of the bargain.

But this was no time to entertain such thoughts. The men from the East had recently left. How strange these Magi seemed, with their tales of a star that had led them all the way to Bethlehem in search of a new king. They had bowed before her dark-eyed child, laying out their treasures of gold, incense, and myrrh—as though paying homage to royalty. One morning, however, they had packed in haste, saying only that a dream had warned them to return home without reporting news of their successful search to King Herod. Even the mention of that king's name had filled her with dread. Bethlehem lay just six miles south of Jerusalem—dangerously close to the man who had murdered his own children out of jealousy for his throne. How would such a ruler respond to rumors of a child-king in Bethlehem?

Two nights ago Joseph had shaken her awake, shushing her with details of the dream he had just had: "Mary, an angel appeared to me. We must leave before sunrise. Herod plans to search for our child and kill him!"

Now they were on their way to Egypt, reversing the steps of Moses, Aaron, and Miriam, who had led her ancestors to freedom so long ago. Mary wondered, as they rested, if they would ever see their homeland again.

"Woman," he breathed the word softly, painfully, through lips encrusted with blood, his lean arms flung out on either side of him, as though imploringly. The palms of his hands were pinned with spikes. He looked at her first and then at the young man standing beside her. "Here is your son." The words came haltingly.

Then to the man, he sighed: "Here is your mother."

She wanted to reach for him with all the might of her love, to bury his sorrow in her breasts, to tell him he was the son she needed most. Would not the God who pitied Abraham also pity her? Would he allow her to suffer what even the patriarch had been spared—the sacrifice of a child? All her life she had loved the God whose angel had spoken to her, calling her "highly favored." But how could a woman whose son was dying on a Roman cross ever consider herself "favored"?

Suddenly her own words came back to her, as though a younger version of herself was whispering them in her ear: "I am the Lord's servant. May it be to me as you have said."

The midday sky had blackened, but she could still see her son's twisted form on the cross, his eyes searching hers. Thorns circled his forehead in the shape of a crown, a crude reminder of the sign the Roman governor had fastened to the wood: "Jesus of Nazareth, King of the Jews."

She thought of the Magi and their priceless gifts. The gold and incense, royal treasures that had helped them survive their stay in Egypt. She had always wondered about the myrrh. Now she knew—it was embalming oil for the king the wise men had come to worship.

"My God, my God, why have you forsaken me?" His cry pierced her. The earth shook violently and she fell to her knees, barely able to complete the words of the psalm for the man who hung dead on the cross:

O my God, I cry out by day, but you do not answer,
   by night, and am not silent....
But I am a worm and not a man,
   scorned by men and despised by the people.
All who see me mock me;
   they hurl insults, shaking their heads....
Yet you brought me out of the womb;
   you made me trust in you
   even at my mother's breast.
From birth I was cast upon you;
   from my mother's womb you have been my God....
   They have pierced my hands and my feet.
I can count all my bones;
   people stare and gloat over me.
They divide my garments among them
   and cast lots for my clothing.
But you, O LORD, be not far off;
   O my Strength, come quickly to help me....
You who fear the LORD, praise him!
   All you descendants of Jacob, honor him!...
   Future generations will be told about the Lord.
They will proclaim his righteousness
   to a people yet unborn—
   for he has done it.

—Psalm 22

By the time Mary opened her eyes, the setting sun had turned the city into a golden land. She smiled, wiping the tears from her wrinkled face. How true the angel's words had been. No woman from Eve onward had ever been blessed as she, the mother of the Messiah, had been. Yes, the past was alive inside her, but it was the future that filled her with joy. Soon, she would see her son again and this time it would be *his* hands that would wipe away the last of her tears.

Tuesday

HER LIFE AND TIMES

ANGELS

*M*ary cowered in fear when the angel Gabriel appeared to her—not an uncommon reaction. Most often in Scripture, when an angel appeared to a human being, the reaction was one of fright. While we're not told exactly what angels look like or how they appear, one description in Matthew's gospel says the angel's "appearance was like lightning, and his clothes were white as snow" (Matthew 28:3). Certainly it's obvious from the reactions of those who saw them that angels are supernatural beings and therefore frightening.

The 291 references to angels in Scripture give us a varied picture of their duties. Angels in heaven stand before God's throne and worship him (Revelation 5:11–12). An angel helped Hagar and Ishmael when they were in trouble in the desert (Genesis 21:17). An angel freed the apostles from prison (Acts 5:19). An angel directed Philip to the desert road where he met and witnessed to the Ethiopian eunuch (Acts 8:26). An angel appeared to Paul to comfort him (Acts 27:23–24), to Elijah when he was worn out and discouraged in the desert (1 Kings 19:3–9), and to Daniel and his friends in places of danger (Daniel 3:28; 6:22). Sometimes God uses angels to punish his enemies (Genesis 19:1; 2 Kings 19:35).

Angels played an important role in the life of Jesus. After first appearing to Zechariah, Mary, and Joseph, angels announced Jesus' birth to the shepherds (Luke 2:9). Angels came and ministered to Jesus after he was tempted in the desert (Matthew 4:11) and when he was in the garden just before his crucifixion (Luke 22:43). A violent earthquake accompanied the angel that came to earth and rolled back the stone over Jesus' tomb (Matthew 28:2). When Jesus ascended into heaven, two angels, "men dressed in white" (Acts 1:10), told the disciples he would be coming back in the same way.

In the book of Revelation, John describes a glorious scene: "Then I looked and heard the voice of many angels, numbering thousands upon thousands, and ten thousand times ten thousand. They encircled the throne and the living creatures and the elders. In a loud voice they sang: 'Worthy is the Lamb, who was slain, to receive power and wealth and wisdom and strength and honor and glory and praise!'" (Revelation 5:11 – 12).

Imagine the sight: hundreds of thousands of beings—purest white, like lightning—all moving in concert around God's throne. Listen: Can you imagine their loud, supernatural voices praising Jesus? *Worthy is the Lamb!* Then "every creature in heaven and on earth and under the earth and on the sea, and all that is in them" (Revelation 5:13) will join in with them, singing the same song of praise. What a sight! What a sound! Mary will be there praising her son. Will you be there praising your Savior?

Wednesday

HER LEGACY IN SCRIPTURE

Read Luke 1:26–38.

1. Imagine yourself in Mary's place. What thoughts and feelings go through your mind when you hear what Gabriel says in verse 28? Verse 31? Verses 32–33? Verse 35?

2. Which part of this would be hardest for you to accept with the calm and humility Mary expresses in verse 38? Why?

Read Luke 1:46–55.

3. What does Mary's song tell you about her character and the things that are important to her?

Read John 19:25–30.

4. Imagine Mary watching her son die and remembering her song from Luke 1:46–55. How would that song sound to her now?

5. In what circumstance do you need to say to God, "I am the Lord's servant. May it be to me as you have said"? What makes that hard or easy for you to say?

Thursday

HER PROMISE

When God says nothing is impossible (Luke 1:37), he means it. He is all-powerful, omnipotent, the Savior of the world. No matter what he has promised, no matter how hard or impossible that promise seems to fulfill, he can and will do it.

Promises in Scripture

> *For the LORD your God dried up the Jordan before you until you had crossed over.... He did this so that all the peoples of the earth might know that the hand of the LORD is powerful and so that you might always fear the LORD your God.*
>
> —JOSHUA 4:23–24

> *With people this is impossible, but with God all things are possible.*
>
> —MATTHEW 19:26

> *For the foolishness of God is wiser than human wisdom, and the weakness of God is stronger than human strength.*
>
> —1 CORINTHIANS 1:25

Friday

HER LEGACY OF PRAYER

Greetings, you who are highly favored! The Lord is with you.

—LUKE 1:28

REFLECT ON: Luke 1:26–38.

PRAISE GOD: That nothing is impossible with him.

OFFER THANKS: That a woman's body became the dwelling place of divinity.

CONFESS: Any tendency to devalue yourself as a woman.

ASK GOD: To make you a woman, like Mary, who brings Jesus into the world by expressing his character, power, forgiveness, and grace.

Lift Your Heart

Choose one episode in the life of Mary—her encounter with Gabriel, the birth of her child, the scene with the shepherds, the presentation in the temple, the Magi's visit, the escape to Egypt, her son's agony on the cross, or her presence with the disciples in the upper room. Imagine yourself in her place. What are your struggles, your joys? What thoughts run through your mind? Does anything or anyone take you by surprise?

Ask the Holy Spirit to guide your reflections, to help you imagine the sounds, sights, and smells that will bring each scene to life. Let the Scriptures feed your soul with a deeper understanding of God's intention for your life. Pray for the grace to be like the woman who said: "I am the Lord's servant. May it be to me as you have said."

My soul is full of you, my God, and I cannot hold back my gladness. Everyone who sees me will call me blessed because you have noticed me. You saw my lowliness and my need and filled my emptiness with your presence. Form your likeness in me so that, like Mary, I can bring you into a world that desperately needs your love. In the name of Mary's son I pray. Amen.

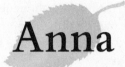

Anna

HER CHARACTER: Married for only seven years, she spent the long years of her widowhood fasting and praying in the temple, abandoning herself entirely to God. A prophetess, she was one of the first to bear witness to Jesus.

HER SORROW: As a widow, she would probably have been among the most vulnerable members of society, with no one to provide for her financially or to take care of her if her health failed.

HER JOY: That her own eyes beheld the Messiah she had longed to see.

KEY SCRIPTURE: Luke 2:22–38

Monday

HER STORY

A small bird darted past the Court of the Gentiles, flew up to the Women's Court, and then on to the Court of Israel (one of the inner courts of the temple, accessible only to Jewish men). Anna blinked as she watched the beating wings swerve into the sunlight and vanish. She wondered into which privileged corner of the temple the little bird had disappeared.

For most of her eighty-four years, she had been a widow who spent her days praying and fasting in the temple. Though Anna had walked past the outer court thousands of times, she never failed to notice the warning inscribed in its walls in both Greek and Latin: "No stranger is to enter within the balustrade round the temple and enclosure. Whoever is caught will be responsible to himself for his death, which will ensue." It was an awesome thing to come into the presence of the Holy One.

Though she could not echo the prayer of Jewish men, who praised God for creating them neither Gentiles nor women, she could at least be grateful for the privilege of ascending beyond the Court of the Gentiles to the Women's Court, where she would be that much closer to the Most Holy Place. Having done so, she bowed her head, rocking back and forth to the rhythm of her prayers (Psalm 84:1–3):

> How lovely is your dwelling place,
>   O Lord Almighty!
> My soul yearns, even faints,
>   for the courts of the Lord;
> my heart and my flesh cry out
>   for the living God.
> Even the sparrow has found a home,
>   and the swallow a nest for herself,
>   where she may have her young—
> a place near your altar,
>   O Lord Almighty, my King and my God.

Suddenly a voice interrupted her recitation of the familiar psalm. Old Simeon, she saw, was holding a baby to his breast, pronouncing words that thrilled her soul: "Sovereign Lord, as you have promised, you now dismiss your servant in peace. For my eyes have seen your salvation, which you have prepared in the sight of all people, a light for revelation to the Gentiles and for glory to your people Israel."

Like her, Simeon had lived for nothing but Israel's consolation. Though he had not seen, yet he had believed. Anna watched as the child's parents hung on the old man's words. Then he handed the infant back to his mother, this time speaking more softly: "This child is destined to cause the falling and rising of many in Israel, and to be a sign that will be spoken against, so that the thoughts of many hearts will be revealed. And a sword will pierce your own soul too."

Anna placed her arms gently around the young mother's shoulders and gazed at the sleeping infant. Words of thanksgiving spilled from her lips. Her heart felt buoyant, her hope unsinkable. More vividly than Jacob, who had dreamed of a ladder full of angels, or Moses, who had beheld a bush burning in the desert, she, Anna, a widow and prophetess from the tribe of Asher, had experienced the very presence of God. Her eyes had seen the promised child, whose brilliance would scatter the darkness and bring deliverance for all God's people.

Now she too felt like a sparrow soaring freely in the house of God. It no longer mattered that she was forbidden entry into the innermost courts of the temple. God himself was breaking down the dividing walls between Jew and Gentile, male and female, revealing himself to all who hungered for his presence. That day a child had transformed the Women's Court into the holiest place of all.

Scripture doesn't tell us whether Anna ever actually wished she were allowed to enter the innermost courts of the temple in Jerusalem. But her longing for God is obvious. Clearly, she was a woman with a great spiritual appetite, who abandoned her life to God and was rewarded by meeting Jesus and his parents just forty days after his birth, during the presentation in the temple.

Tuesday

HER LIFE AND TIMES

THE TEMPLE COURTS

*T*he old woman Anna had probably spent upwards of sixty years in the temple. In fact, she never left it, "but worshiped night and day, fasting and praying" (Luke 2:37). The evidence of her devotion is not just in the fact that she spent all those years in prayer, but that she recognized the Christ. (He was, after all, only about six weeks old.) Yet even though Anna had relinquished a normal lifestyle, spent hours of every day in prayer, and gone without food as a sign of devotion, she was still not allowed access to the actual temple. Despite being relegated to the outer court for women, however, she never let that restriction squeeze her heart or strangle her love for God.

Solomon had built the first temple, an elaborate, white limestone structure, inlaid with gold. Zerubbabel built the second temple when the Jews returned from their captivity in Babylon. Herod the Great built the third temple, where Anna worshiped. He was a tireless builder, and the temple in Jerusalem was only one of his projects.

Herod's temple had four successive courts, each more exclusive than the one before it. The outer court was known as the Court of the Gentiles. This was the only place where non-Jews were allowed. This court was also the place where Jesus later cleared the temple of those buying and selling. The inner court was divided into two sections: the Women's Court, where Anna worshiped, and the Court of Israel. Both Jewish women and men could enter the Women's Court, but only Jewish men were allowed into the Court of Israel. The Court of the Priests surrounded the actual temple building itself and was accessible only to those of the Levitical priesthood.

The customs of her time may have restricted the physical location of Anna's worship, but no earthly regulation could bind her actual worship or devotion. Be an Anna! Don't let anything limit your devotion to God! No earthly rules or restrictions. No past mistakes or sins. No life situations that you can't overcome. Let nothing get in the way of worshiping your God and recognizing your Savior.

Wednesday

HER LEGACY IN SCRIPTURE

Read Luke 2:22–38.

1. Simeon "was waiting for the consolation of Israel" (verse 25). Anna knew there were others in the temple "who were looking forward to the redemption of Jerusalem" (verse 38). These are references to the coming of the Messiah. What would it feel like to wait and hope like that for years and years?

2. What do Simeon's words tell you about Jesus' mission?

3. Why do you think so many people were hoping and praying for the Messiah? What does that say about how they viewed their lives?

4. Describe Anna's lifestyle (verse 37). What aspects of it seem attractive or foreign to you?

5. What do you long for God to accomplish before you die? Or if you don't long for anything, why do you suppose that's the case?

Thursday

HER PROMISE

*A*nna's life revolved around prayer and fasting in the temple. She evidently had no family, no home, no job. Instead, God was her family, the temple her home, and prayer her occupation. Though you may not have the freedom to spend every moment in prayer, as she did, you can be sure the time you do spend is never wasted. If you long to see your Savior, to experience his presence in your life, let Anna's devotion encourage you.

Promises in Scripture

Obey me, and I will be your God and you will be my people. Walk in all the ways I command you, that it may go well with you.

—JEREMIAH 7:23

He has shown all you people what is good.
    And what does the Lord require of you?
To act justly and to love mercy
    and to walk humbly with your God.

—MICAH 6:8

Never be lacking in zeal, but keep your spiritual fervor, serving the Lord.

—ROMANS 12:10

Friday

HER LEGACY OF PRAYER

She never left the temple but worshiped night and day, fasting and praying.

—LUKE 2:37

REFLECT ON: Luke 2:36–38.

PRAISE GOD: That Jesus is the true Bread from heaven, who satisfies the hungry heart.

OFFER THANKS: For men and women who hunger and thirst for God's kingdom.

CONFESS: Any tendency to be so locked into your own concerns that you fail to pray for others in need.

ASK GOD: To increase your hunger for his kingdom.

Lift Your Heart

Anna did more than merely long for the coming Messiah; she prayed and fasted daily for the coming of God's kingdom. Even though Christianity has spread across the globe, there are still many people who suffer from war and injustice, many who have little or nothing to eat, and many more who live in spiritual darkness. This week stretch yourself beyond your immediate concerns. Look at an atlas, a map, or a globe, and choose a country for which to pray. Read newspaper reports and magazine articles that will help you understand what is going on in that nation. Fast and pray for peace, for daily bread, for freedom, for justice, and for Christ's light to shine upon that people.

Jesus, I long for your light to spread across the whole earth so that peoples from every land will know you. Today, give me a burden for another nation or ethnic group that knows little of you. Show me how to pray in a way that builds your kingdom.

The Woman of Samaria

HER CHARACTER: Looked down upon by the Jews because she was a Samaritan and disdained because of her many romantic liaisons, she would not have been most people's first choice to advance the gospel in a region where it had not yet been heard.

HER SORROW: To have lived in a way that relegated her to the margins of her society.

HER JOY: That Jesus broke through barriers of culture, race, and religion in order to reveal himself to her.

KEY SCRIPTURE: John 4:1–42

Monday

HER STORY

*E*very day, the woman carried her water jug to Jacob's well just outside Sychar, a town midway between Jerusalem and Nazareth. Even though it was the hottest time of the day, she preferred it to the evening hours, when the other women gathered. How tired she was of their wagging tongues. Better the scorching heat than their sharp remarks.

She was surprised, however, to see that today someone had already arrived at the well—a Jew from Galilee by the looks of him. At least she had nothing to fear from his tongue, for Jews did their best to avoid Samaritans, despising them as half-breeds who worshiped not in the temple at Jerusalem but at their shrine on Mount Gerizim.

For once she was glad to be ignored, grateful, too, that men did not address women in public.

But as she approached the well, the man startled her, breaking the rules she had counted on to protect her. "Will you give me a drink?" he asked.

What kind of a Jew was this? she wondered. *Certainly not a Pharisee, or he would have taken the long way around Samaria to get to Galilee.* With a toss of her head, she replied, "You are a Jew and I am a Samaritan woman. How can you ask me for a drink?"

But he wouldn't be put off. "If you knew the gift of God and who it is that asks you for a drink, you would have asked him and he would have given you living water."

"Sir," she replied, "you have nothing to draw with and the well is deep. Where can you get this living water? Are you greater than our father Jacob, who gave us this well and drank from it himself, as did also his sons and his flocks and herds?" *That should take him down a notch or two.*

But the man kept pressing. "Go," he told her, "call your husband and come back."

This last request took the wind out of her. Her quick tongue was barely able to reply, "I have no husband."

"You are right when you say you have no husband," Jesus said. "The fact is, you have had five husbands, and the man you now have is not your husband. What you have just said is quite true."

His words cut her. Shaking off the hurt, she tried changing the subject, diverting him by stirring up the old controversy between Jews and Samaritans. "Sir, I can see that you are a prophet. Our fathers worshiped on this mountain, but you Jews claim that the place where we must worship is in Jerusalem."

Jesus declared, "Believe me, woman, a time is coming when you will worship the Father neither on this mountain nor in Jerusalem. You Samaritans worship what you do not know; we worship what we do know, for salvation is from the Jews. Yet a time is coming and has now come when the true worshipers will worship the Father in spirit and truth, for they are the kind of worshipers the Father seeks."

The woman said, "I know that Messiah is coming. When he comes, he will explain everything to us."

310 THE WOMAN OF SAMARIA

Then Jesus declared, "I who speak to you am he."

Leaving her water jar, the woman went back to the town and said to the people, "Come see a man who told me everything I ever did. Could this be the Christ?"

Meanwhile, his disciples, who had gone into the town to look for food, returned and urged him, "Rabbi, eat something."

But Jesus replied, "I have food to eat that you know nothing about."

Dodge, counterdodge—nothing the woman said would keep Jesus at bay. He kept pressing beneath the surface, inviting her to a deeper understanding, hemming her in by revealing his knowledge of the most intimate details of her life. Overwhelmed, she finally admitted the truth. And when she did, Jesus startled her with a revelation about himself: He admitted, for the first time, that he was the Messiah. Though she hadn't known it, she had been conversing with her Savior.

Jesus had arrived at the well thirsty, hungry, and tired from the journey north to Galilee. But by the time his disciples returned from their shopping trip in Sychar, he seemed refreshed and restored by his encounter with the woman.

She, in turn, was so deeply affected by him that she exclaimed to whoever would listen: "He told me everything I ever did." At the Samaritans' urging, Jesus stayed on for two days and many came to believe, saying to the woman: "We no longer believe just because of what you said; now we have heard for ourselves and we know that this man really is the Savior of the world."

Tuesday

HER LIFE AND TIMES

WATER

*C*ool, clear water. A commodity most of us today take for granted. We turn on a faucet, and fresh, clean water is readily available. In Palestine, however, water is scarce and highly valued.

The long, mostly rainless summers cause most of the rivers in Palestine to dry up completely. Even the Jordan River becomes shallow, narrow, and muddy in the summer months. The early peoples of Palestine depended on rain during the spring and fall months for their water supply. Though scarce at other times during the year, the rain during these seasons kept the springs and wells flowing and the cisterns full.

The Jews became adept at gathering every bit of rainwater, storing it up for future use during the dry seasons. Cisterns, covered pools dug out of rock specifically for storing rainwater, were numerous. In Jerusalem, the temple area alone had thirty-seven cisterns, one of them large enough to hold over two million gallons of water. Gutters, pipes, and waterways directed the rainwater from the surface to the underground cisterns, which would provide a constant supply of water, even during dry spells.

Heavy dew provided a good share of the moisture required by crops growing in the summer months. The warm, cloudless nights of Palestinian summers provide prime conditions for dew to form. Where ample water was readily available, farmers irrigated crops and vineyards to maximize the produce received from a field.

Drinking water was stored and carried in goatskins. Many towns and cities had drinking water for sale in their markets and on the streets. Only a small amount of water was used for washing, simply because it was so scarce. However, good hospitality required that a guest in someone's home receive a basin of water to wash at least his or her feet and hands after walking on the dusty roads (Genesis 18:4; John 13:5).

Getting daily water from the neighborhood well or cistern was the duty of the younger women of a household. They would usually go to the well in the evening, when the air was cooler. It's interesting to note that the Samaritan woman went to the well at noon ("the sixth hour"), probably in order to avoid the other women, who may have looked down on her.

Water is used in symbolic ways throughout Scripture. David compared his troubles to "deep waters" (Psalm 69:1–2, 14; 124:5). The book of Proverbs compares people's words to deep waters and wise words to a "bubbling brook" of water (Proverbs 18:4). Good news is like fresh water (Proverbs 25:25). Several passages refer to our sins being washed away (Psalm 51:7; Ephesians 5:26; Hebrews 10:22). Jesus told the Samaritan woman that he had water that would take away her thirst forever. The water he was speaking of was not, of course, two parts hydrogen and one part oxygen, but spiritual water—a water that will fill us so full of himself that all our needs will be met, all our wants satisfied, and all our thirsts fulfilled.

Wednesday

HER LEGACY IN SCRIPTURE

Read John 4:4–42.

1. Trace the Samaritan woman's emotional responses as her encounter with Jesus progressed. What do you think she was feeling in verses 7–9? Verses 10–12? Verses 13–15? Verse 16? Verses 17–20? Verses 21–26?

2. Looking at her life, what do you think this woman was really thirsty for?

3. What have you used to try to satisfy your spiritual thirst apart from Christ? Family? Career? Shopping? Entertainment?

4. Verses 25–26 are the first time Jesus acknowledged exactly who he is. Why do you think he would choose to tell this woman, an outcast of society in a town of Samaria, instead of the leaders of Jewish religion and culture or even his own disciples? What sort of reaction do you have to his choice?

5. What do you think convinced the Samaritan woman that Jesus was who he said he was?

6. If Jesus really is the Savior who knows everything you ever did, what can the Samaritan woman teach you about how to respond to him today?

Thursday

HER PROMISE

*A*re you thirsty? Is there a longing in you that you just can't seem to meet? Do you hunger for something to fill some void, some emptiness you can't even explain? Look everywhere, try everything—you'll find nothing in this world that will satisfy. Only Jesus can provide the living water that will fill you to overflowing, that will satisfy your longing, that will soothe your thirst so completely you'll never be thirsty again.

Promises in Scripture

Satisfy us in the morning with your unfailing love,
that we may sing for joy and be glad all our days.

—PSALM 90:14

Blessed are those who hunger and thirst for righteousness, for they will be filled.

—MATTHEW 5:6

Blessed are you who hunger now, for you will be satisfied.

—LUKE 6:21

Jesus answered, "Everyone who drinks this water will be thirsty again, but those who drink the water I give them will never thirst. Indeed, the water I give them will become in them a spring of water welling up to eternal life."

—JOHN 4:13

Friday

HER LEGACY OF PRAYER

Then, leaving her water jar, the woman went back to the town and said to the people, "Come, see a man who told me everything I ever did. Could this be the Christ?" They came out of the town and made their way toward him.

—JOHN 4:28–30

REFLECT ON: John 4:4–42.

PRAISE GOD: Because in his kingdom, the last shall be first.

OFFER THANKS: For the way he has uncovered your need for him.

CONFESS: Any tendency to act as though God cannot use your neediness but only your strength.

ASK GOD: To give you the humility to face the depth of your need for grace.

Lift Your Heart

It is always difficult to admit our sins, particularly if we think God will love us only if we behave well. Though we might never articulate such a thought, it shapes our theology more than we like to admit. This week, make a list of everything God knows about you that you wish he didn't. Thank him for loving you despite your sins. Then tear up the list, remembering the words of Psalm 103:11–12:

> For as high as the heavens are above the earth,
>   so great is his love for those who fear him;
> as far as the east is from the west,
>   so far has he removed our transgressions from us.

Lord, you know everything about me, even the things I'm hiding from myself. Give me the grace to admit my sin, believing that though you see me, you still love me. Help me to let go of anything that keeps me from experiencing the living water of your Holy Spirit welling up inside me.

The Woman Who Lived a Sinful Life

HER CHARACTER: She was a notorious sinner, possibly a prostitute or adulteress. Rather than trying to defend what was indefensible in her life, she admitted her sin and made a spectacle of herself in a passionate display of love and gratitude.

HER SORROW: That she had offended God so grievously.

HER JOY: That Jesus forgave her sins and commended her for her great faith and love.

KEY SCRIPTURE: Luke 7:36–50

Monday

HER STORY

The woman felt as though the world had unraveled in a moment's time. Doors had opened, walls had crumbled, thoughts of the future no longer frightened but thrilled her. She felt clean and whole, innocent as a girl still living in her father's house. Her heart was a wild confusion of sorrow and joy as she followed the rabbi through the doorway.

Ignoring the stares of the men, she walked over to the place where Jesus was reclining at a table. In her hands she held an alabaster jar of perfume. Her body trembled as she approached. She hardly knew what she was doing as she covered his feet with her kisses and then anointed them with the precious perfume, wiping his feet with her hair. How else could she express her heart to the man who had loved her so well?

Like any good Pharisee, Simon loved the law, measuring his days by the steady rhythm of the regulations by which he lived. They were a fence safeguarding his purity, protecting his sense of settled security. How good of the holy God to provide a map for the righteous, a way of life to set him apart from ordinary Jews—like the woman who had just walked through the door, hoping to glean a few scraps from his table.

Simon was surprised that a sinful woman, even a hungry one, would enter his house. But his surprise grew as he noticed she was not eating but weeping so profusely that her tears were spilling onto the feet of one of his guests. Everything about the scene repelled him, offending his sense of order—a notorious harlot kissing the man's feet, wiping them with her hair, and then pouring perfume over them. It was an astonishing performance.

Even more astonishing was the fact that his guest seemed to enjoy the attention. "If this man were a prophet," Simon thought, "he would know who is touching him and what kind of woman she is—that she is a sinner." All of his questions about Jesus were put to rest by the scene he had just witnessed. His ordered way of looking at the world was safe enough, bolstered by the judgment he had just made.

As though he had overheard Simon's secret thoughts, Jesus turned and spoke to him. "Simon, I have something to tell you.

"Two men owed money to a certain moneylender. One owed him five hundred denarii, and the other fifty. Neither of them had the money to pay him back, so he canceled the debts of both. Now which of them will love him more?"

Simon replied, "I suppose the one who had the bigger debt canceled."

"You have judged correctly," Jesus said.

Then he turned toward the woman and said to Simon, "Do you see this woman? I came into your house. You did not give me any water for my feet, but she wet my feet with her tears and wiped them with her hair. You did not give me a kiss, but this woman, from the time I entered, has not stopped kissing my feet. You did not put oil on my head, but she has poured perfume on my feet. Therefore, I tell you, her many sins have been forgiven—for she loved much. But he who has been forgiven little loves little."

The other guests began to say among themselves, "Who is this who even forgives sins?"

Jesus said to the woman, "Your faith has saved you; go in peace."

Though this woman was a notorious sinner, she recognized her great need for grace. Repentance turned her world on its head, opening up an entirely new view of things. Simon, by contrast, was a religious man who, no doubt, had done his best to live a respectable life. His sin was tucked away, hidden even from himself. His habit of judging others had formed a fence around his one-dimensional view of the universe, shielding his neat and orderly life from the unpredictable power of grace.

But Simon and the woman both owed a debt they could not possibly repay. Though Simon's sin was less obvious, it was the more dangerous. He was like a man who was following a map he was certain would lead to heaven—but when heaven came down and walked into his house, he didn't even know it. The woman, on the other hand, realized just how lost she had been. Forgiven much, she loved much. She found heaven at the feet of Jesus.

Tuesday

HER LIFE AND TIMES

WASHING FEET

he scene in this story is one of about thirteen instances in which Scripture talks about washing one's feet. The sinful woman in this story did the act reserved for the lowest, most inexperienced servant of the household.

Most people in Palestine wore sandals or went barefoot, so their feet were constantly dirty from the dust of the roads and fields. When they went into a house, they removed their sandals at the door. A good host or hostess made sure guests' feet were washed as soon as they entered the home. A basin of cool water and a towel were the only equipment required. After walking on hot dusty roads, the foot washing provided not only clean feet for entering a home but also a refreshing start to a visit.

When the three visitors came to Abraham when he was living "near the great trees of Mamre" (doesn't that sound like a wonderful place to live?), Abraham provided water for them to wash their feet (Genesis 18:1–5). Lot revealed the basic rules of Eastern hospitality when he invited the two angels into his home, telling them to "wash your feet and spend the night" (Genesis 19:1–3). Laban provided water for all of those with Abraham's servant to wash their feet (Genesis 24:32). In Egypt, Joseph made sure his brothers had water to wash their feet after their long journey from Palestine (Genesis 43:24). The priests were told they must always wash their feet and hands before going into the temple (Exodus 30:19–21). Not surprisingly, the list of good deeds that New Testament widows should be known for included, along with raising children and showing hospitality, "washing the feet of the saints" (1 Timothy 5:10).

The fact that foot washing was a task reserved for the lowest servant in the household makes Jesus' act of washing the disciples' feet (John 13) all the more poignant. His simple act shocked them and showed them in the clearest way possible how to be a servant leader. Washing. Touching feet fouled by dust and grime. Kneeling before those who by rights should kneel before him!

Not always so easy, is it? Those unpleasant, humble tasks that require little expertise and gain little notice. Scrubbing the kitchen floor at church. Washing the greasy hair of an elderly man who cannot do it for himself. Folding laundry. Tending sick children. What menial chore is on your list of things to do today? It's not the task itself that's important, it's what's in your heart while doing it. Will you accomplish it with thoughts that you were meant to do greater things? Or with a simple love for the one you serve?

Wednesday

HER LEGACY IN SCRIPTURE

Read Luke 7:36–50.

1. What did it cost this woman to do what she did?

2. What would need to happen for you to be this open in expressing your love for Jesus?

3. What do you think the woman was thinking while Jesus talked to Simon (verses 40–47)? What about when he talked to her (verses 48–50)?

4. How would you respond if a prostitute entered your church or home Bible study and made a display like this?

5. In what ways can you be understanding and loving toward those whose lives have been shattered by sin, like this woman? Toward those whose lives are characterized by judging others, like the Pharisee? Who needs forgiveness more?

6. Take some time to think about the debt Jesus has cancelled for you. Think of specific sins for which he has forgiven you. How can you express your gratitude?

Thursday

HER PROMISE

*L*et's be honest. Many of us would respond to this sinful woman just as the Pharisee did. It's so easy to look more with judgment than love at people whose lives have been devastated by sin. But Jesus looked at her and at Simon and saw the same thing: their need for forgiveness. And he gave it freely. We don't know what Simon's response to Jesus was, but the woman's response is evident in her tears and kisses.

This story isn't included in Scripture just so we can see the forgiveness given to one sinful woman; it's included so we can know that no matter how sinful, how broken, how entrenched in error we might be, forgiveness is available if only we seek it in faith—he's promised.

Promises in Scripture

For the sake of your name, O Lord,
*   forgive my iniquity, though it is great.*

—Psalm 25:11

When we were overwhelmed by sins,
*   you forgave our transgressions.*

—Psalm 65:3

Everyone who believes in him receives forgiveness of sins through his name.

—Acts 10:43

In him we have redemption through his blood, the forgiveness of sins, in accordance with the riches of God's grace that he lavished on us.

—Ephesians 1:7–8

He has rescued us from the dominion of darkness and brought us into the kingdom of the Son he loves, in whom we have redemption, the forgiveness of sins.

—Colossians 1:13–14

Friday

HER LEGACY OF PRAYER

Therefore I tell you, her many sins have been forgiven—for she loved much. But he who has been forgiven little loves little.

—LUKE 7:47

REFLECT ON: Luke 7:36–50.

PRAISE GOD: For the power of forgiveness in your own life.

OFFER THANKS: That God is still ready to forgive you, no matter how frequently or how seriously you have sinned.

CONFESS: Any self-righteousness that has crept into your life.

ASK GOD: To protect you against pride, to enable you to see your sins and believe in his desire and power to forgive you.

Lift Your Heart

How long has it been since tears of repentance have washed your soul? Do you find it easier to linger over others' failings than your own? Harsh attitudes toward the notorious sins of others—even the sins of unprincipled politicians or insensitive husbands—will only dry up your love for God.

No matter how long it's been since you committed your life to God, pride has a way of creeping back in, locking you into a black-and-white vision of the universe. Remember that the Pharisee was forgiven little, not because his sin was inconsequential but because his repentance was so small. This week, search your heart for any judgments, large or small, you have made against others. Make a list of people who you feel have wronged you. Release your judgments against them and ask God to bless them. Then tear up the sheet as a sign that you are repenting of the judgments you made. The next time you are tempted to judge someone, quickly repeat this exercise in your mind.

Lord, when others rejected me, you embraced me. What was untouchable in me you touched. Make me a woman who loves much, a woman who is not afraid to fall at your feet, bathing them with tears.

The Woman with the Issue of Blood

HER CHARACTER: So desperate for healing, she ignored the conventions of the day for the chance to touch Jesus.

HER SORROW: To have suffered a chronic illness that isolated her from others.

HER JOY: That after long years of suffering, she finally found peace and freedom.

KEY SCRIPTURES: Matthew 9:20–22; Mark 5:25–34; Luke 8:43–48

Monday

HER STORY

The woman hovered at the edge of the crowd. Nobody watched as she melted into the throng of bodies—just one more bee entering the hive. Her shame faded, replaced by a rush of relief. No one had prevented her from joining in. No one had recoiled at her touch.

She pressed closer, but a noisy swarm of men still blocked her view. She could hear Jairus, a ruler of the synagogue, raising his voice above the others, pleading with Jesus to come and heal his daughter before it was too late.

Suddenly the group in front of her shifted, parting like the waters of the Jordan before the children of promise. It was all she needed. Her arm darted through the opening, fingers brushing the hem of his garment. Instantly, she felt a warmth spread through her, flushing out the pain, clearing out the decay. Her skin prickled and shivered. She felt strong and able, like a young girl coming into her own—so glad and giddy, in fact, that her feet wanted to rush her away before she created a spectacle by laughing out loud at her quiet miracle.

But Jesus blocked her escape and silenced the crowd with a curious question: "Who touched me?"

"Who touched him? He must be joking!" voices murmured. "People are pushing and shoving just to get near him!"

Shaking now, the woman fell at his feet: "For twelve years, I have been hemorrhaging and have spent all my money on doctors but only grown worse. Today, I knew that if I could just touch your garment, I would be healed." But touching, she knew, meant spreading her defilement—even to the rabbi.

Twelve years of loneliness. Twelve years in which physicians had bled her of all her money. Her private affliction becoming a matter of public record. Every cup she handled, every chair she sat on could transmit defilement to others. Even though her impurity was considered a ritual matter rather than an ethical one, it had rendered her an outcast, making it impossible for her to live with a husband, bear a child, or enjoy the intimacy of friends and family. Surely the rabbi would censure her.

But instead of scolding and shaming her, Jesus praised her: "Daughter, your faith has healed you. Go in peace and be freed from your suffering."

His words must have been like water breaching a dam, breaking through her isolation and setting her free. He had addressed her not harshly, but tenderly—not as "woman" or "sinner," but rather as "daughter." She was no longer alone, but part of his family by virtue of her faith.

That day, countless men and women had brushed against Jesus, but only one had truly touched him. And instead of being defiled by contact with her, his own touch had proven the more contagious, rendering her pure and whole again.

Tuesday

HER LIFE AND TIMES

MENSTRUAL BLEEDING

*A*ny woman who has suffered through "an issue of blood" knows the difficulties and the debilitating effects of the disease. When blood flows freely and frequently instead of in its regular monthly pattern, women endure not only the untidiness of the condition but can also experience a loss of strength and weight.

The woman in this story suffered from such a hemorrhage for twelve long years. She was probably weak and thin. Because of the ritual uncleanness that surrounded such a condition, she most likely didn't often go out in public. Imagine twelve years of this:

> *When a woman has a discharge of blood for many days at a time other than her monthly period or has a discharge that continues beyond her period, she will be unclean as long as she has the discharge, just as in the days of her period. Any bed she lies on while her discharge continues will be unclean, as is her bed during her monthly period, and anything she sits on will be unclean, as during her period. Whoever touches them will be unclean; they must wash their clothes and bathe with water, and they will be unclean till evening.*

> —LEVITICUS 15:25–27

A woman was considered unclean for a mere seven days when she had her regular period (Leviticus 15:19). This woman, however, bore not only the inconvenience but also the curse of being unclean for twelve years. Anyone and anything she touched became unclean. Imagine: She gives her husband a plate of food and their hands touch—he's unclean. She gives her neighbor a hand with her laundry and their hands touch—she's unclean. Anything she sits on at home becomes unclean, as does anything she sits on at a neighbor's home or in public. Before long, everyone is aware of her uncleanness and no one wants to be around her.

Many different conditions could have caused this woman's ailment: fibroid tumors, an infection, a hormone imbalance. Whatever the cause, the doctors she had seen over the years had taken all of her money but given no relief. With the forthrightness and compassion that are characteristic of the gospel writer Mark, he says this woman "had suffered a great deal under the care of many doctors." In fact, at times their cures were probably worse than her sickness. Still, no matter how much money she spent or how much agony she endured, her sickness seemed impossible to cure. Until she met the God of the impossible.

What doctors couldn't do, Jesus could. No repulsive or painful remedies. No visits to doctors more interested in financial gain than in her cure. With just a soft, loving touch of his coat, she was cured. Healed. Freed. Immediately!

The glory of Christ is that he succeeds where others fail. He brings healing when doctors say none is possible. He offers forgiveness when the heart says it can never be forgiven. He extends comfort when the agony is too great to carry, and peace when all is chaos. He presents the possible after twelve years of impossibility.

328   THE WOMAN WITH THE ISSUE OF BLOOD

Wednesday

HER LEGACY IN SCRIPTURE

Read Mark 5:24–34.

1. Choose three words to describe the suffering this woman had experienced for twelve years.

2. She probably touched others in the crowd accidentally while trying to get to Jesus. As an unclean woman, what was she risking by doing this? What did it take to accept such a risk?

3. Why do you think she was afraid to admit she was the one who had touched Jesus?

4. Is there anything about this woman—her suffering, her actions, her healing—that reminds you of yourself? If so, what is it?

5. If you have pursued Jesus for healing and haven't yet received it, what do you do with this story?

Thursday

HER PROMISE

*G*od promises to heal us. That statement may seem to fly in the face of the many who have suffered from illness and disability for years on end, but we need to remember that our concept of healing is not necessarily the same as God's. For some, healing may not take place here on earth. True healing—the healing that will cure even those who don't suffer from any particular physical ailment here on earth—will take place not here but in heaven. There, God promises the ultimate healing from our sickness, our disabilities, our inclination to sin.

Promises in Scripture

I am the LORD, who heals you.

—EXODUS 15:26

O LORD my God, I called to you for help
and you healed me.

—PSALM 30:2

Praise the LORD, O my soul;
all my inmost being, praise his holy name.
Praise the LORD, O my soul,
and forget not all his benefits—
who forgives all your sins
and heals all your diseases,
who redeems your life from the pit
and crowns you with love and compassion.

—PSALM 103:1–4

They will be his people, and God himself will be with them and be their God. He will wipe every tear from their eyes. There will be no more death or mourning or crying or pain, for the old order of things has passed away.

—REVELATION 21:3–4

Friday

HER LEGACY OF PRAYER

When she heard about Jesus, she came up behind him in the crowd and touched his cloak, because she thought, "If I just touch his clothes, I will be healed."

—MARK 5:27–28

REFLECT ON:	Mark 5:21–34.
PRAISE GOD:	That his touch produces peace and freedom.
OFFER THANKS:	That faith is a gift that increases with use.
CONFESS:	Any tendency to play it so safe you actually begin to suffocate the faith you have.
ASK GOD:	To bring this woman's story to mind the next time you are faced with an opportunity to exercise real faith.

Lift Your Heart

Trying to live the Christian life without faith is like trying to eat a steak with a straw, or kissing someone without using your lips, or propelling an airplane with foot pedals. It doesn't nourish you, never thrills you, and won't get you anywhere. If you feel the spark of faith fading, ask God to take the little you have and fan it to flame. Before you go to bed each night this week, remind yourself of your need by lighting a small candle at your bedside and praying this prayer:

Father, forgive my little faith
Make it big
Reduce my ego
Make it small
Give me a chance
To touch you and be touched
No matter how foolish
No matter how frightened

No matter how strange I feel
Fan my small spark into a brightness
Lighting the way ahead.
Amen.

Pray it like you mean it, and God will not fail to provide you with opportunities to exercise your faith. (Don't forget to blow out the candle before you close your eyes!)

Herodias

HER NAME, THE FEMALE FORM OF "HEROD," MEANS
"Heroic"

HER CHARACTER: A proud woman, she used her daughter to manipulate her husband into doing her will. She acted arrogantly, from beginning to end, in complete disregard for the laws of the land.

HER SHAME: To be rebuked by an upstart prophet for leaving her husband Philip in order to marry his half brother Herod Antipas.

HER TRIUMPH: That her scheme to murder her enemy, John the Baptist, worked.

KEY SCRIPTURES: Matthew 14:3–12; Mark 6:14–29; Luke 3:19–20; 9:7–9

Monday

HER STORY

Her grandfather, Herod the Great, had ruled Judea for thirty-four years. Herod had brought prosperity to a troubled region of the Roman Empire, building theaters, amphitheaters, and race courses, as well as a palace and a magnificent temple in Jerusalem. In addition to such ambitious endeavors, he had even contrived to lower taxes on two occasions.

But Herod's reign contained shadows that darkened as the years went on. Herodias knew the stories well—how her grandfather had slaughtered a passel of Jewish brats in Bethlehem, how he had murdered his favorite wife (her own grandmother) and three of his sons for real or imagined intrigues. Advancing age and illness did nothing to improve his character. Herod was determined, in fact, that his own death would produce a time of universal mourning rather than celebration. So, in a final, malevolent act, he commanded all the leading Jews to gather in Jericho. Then he imprisoned them in a stadium and ordered them to be executed at the moment of his death. But the king was cheated of his last wish: His prisoners were set free as soon as he died in the spring of 4 BC.

Not a nice man, her grandfather

Herodias's husband and his half brother Antipas had been lucky survivors of Herod the Great's bloody family, but Antipas had proved the luckier of the two. For while Philip and Herodias languished in Rome with no territory to rule, Antipas was appointed tetrarch of Galilee and Perea. She could sense the man's power the first time he visited them in Rome. And power, she mused, was her favorite aphrodisiac.

Though Herod Antipas was married to the daughter of King Aretas IV, ruler of Nabatea, to the east, he quickly divorced her in favor of Herodias. In one dicey move, Antipas had stolen his brother's wife, compromised his eastern border, and alienated his Jewish subjects, whose law forbade wife-swapping, especially among brothers. But with Herodias beside him, Herod Antipas must have thought himself powerful enough to manage the consequences.

But neither Herod Antipas nor Herodias had expected their transgression to become a matter of public agitation. After all, who was there to agitate, except the usual ragtag band of upstarts? A real prophet had not troubled Israel for more than four hundred years.

But trouble was edging toward them in the form of a new Elijah, whom God had been nurturing with locusts and honey in the wilderness that bordered their realm. This prophet, John the Baptist, cared nothing for diplomacy. He could not be bought or bullied, and was preaching a message of repentance to all who would listen: "A voice of one calling in the desert, 'Prepare the way for the Lord, make straight paths for him.'"

John the Baptist spared no one, not the ordinary people who flocked to him in the desert, not the self-righteous Pharisees or the privileged Sadducees, and certainly not Herod Antipas or Herodias, whom he chided for their unlawful marriage. Herodias wanted Antipas to kill John, yet even he had to step carefully, lest he ignite an uprising among John's ever-growing number of followers. That would be all the excuse his former father-in-law, Aretas, would need in order to attack Antipas's eastern flank. So, according to the Jewish historian Josephus, Antipas imprisoned John in Machaerus, a fortress just east of the Dead Sea.

On Herod Antipas's birthday a feast was held in his honor and attended by a "who's who" list of dignitaries. During the evening, Herodias's young daughter, Salome, performed a dance for Herod Antipas and his guests, which so pleased him that he promised his stepdaughter anything she desired, up to half his kingdom.

Ever the good daughter, Salome hastened to her mother for advice. Should she request a splendid palace or a portion of the royal treasury? But Herodias had one thing only in mind. When Salome returned to the banquet hall, Salome surprised Antipas with a gruesome demand: "I want you to give me, right now, the head of John the Baptist on a platter."

Though Herod Antipas was distressed by her request, he was even more distressed at the prospect of breaking an oath he had so publicly made. Therefore, in complete disregard for Jewish law, which prohibited both execution without trial and decapitation as a form of execution, he immediately ordered John's death.

That night, Herodias must have savored her triumph over the man whom Jesus referred to as the greatest of those who had yet lived. John had been sent as the last of the prophets, a new Elijah, whose preaching was to prepare the way for Jesus. Had Herodias heeded John's call to repentance, her heart might have welcomed the gospel. Rather than being remembered as just one more member of a bloody dynasty, she could have become a true child of God. Instead of casting her lot with the great women of the Bible, however, she chose to model herself on one of the worst—Jezebel, her spiritual mother. By so doing, she sealed her heart against the truth and all the transforming possibilities of grace.

Tuesday

HER LIFE AND TIMES

THE HERODS

*B*oth husbands of Herodias were part of the Herodian family of rulers, as was Herodias herself. Her first husband, Herod Philip, as well as her second husband, Herod Antipas, were her uncles. The family of the Herods ruled in Judea and the surrounding areas for over 125 years. The first Herod, known as Herod the Great, was king of Judea from 37 to 4 BC. His reign was marked by division and domestic troubles, but also by prosperity. While in power, he built amphitheaters, palaces, fortresses, Gentile temples, and the temple of Herod in Jerusalem. This temple was his crowning achievement, noted by the historian Josephus as Herod's most noble work. The literature of the rabbis of that time states: "He who has not seen the Temple of Herod has never seen a beautiful building."

Herod the Great's five wives produced seven sons, most of whom went on to rule parts of the Near East for the Roman Empire. Philip, Herod's son by Mariamne of Simon, was Herodias's first husband. Herodias herself was the daughter of another of Herod's sons. That made her Herod's granddaughter as well as his daughter-in-law by marriage. Herodias wasn't the only one of Herod's children to form such relationships; Herod's great-granddaughter, Bernice, became the consort of her brother, Herod Agrippa II, also a great-grandchild of Herod.

The events at the birthday banquet described in Mark 6 are the culmination of years of corrupt living by a family who had power and knew how to use and misuse it. Herodias's actions, though horrifying, are not really surprising. Each step along the way to requesting John the Baptist's death was perhaps a small one, little noticed, but each step made its relentless way down a path to sin, until what would have been unconscionable years before now seemed acceptable and reasonable. Sin is like that. As your mother told you—and it's true—one small lie leads to another bigger lie that leads to another even bigger lie. The path of sin is strewn with small, seemingly insignificant decisions that lead nowhere but farther along the path away from truth and God.

Wednesday

HER LEGACY IN SCRIPTURE

Read Mark 6:14–29.

1. Note the different responses to John in verses 19–20. What do these responses tell you about Herod and Herodias?

2. How do you typically respond when confronted with a sin or failing? Do you get angry? Sulk? Listen to what the other person says, but without changing your behavior? Cry or feel hurt? Do whatever you can to please the other person? Face whatever is true in the other person's rebuke?

3. What are the signs in this story that power (control, getting her way) was important to Herodias?

4. When has getting your way seemed highly important to you? What did you do to get your way? What were the consequences?

5. What do you imagine it was like to be the daughter of Herodias?

Thursday

HER PROMISE

As negative as it sounds, the lesson or promise learned from Herodias can only be that sin will devour us. If sin always has its way in our lives, it will eventually consume us. There is only one way out: If we abandon our sin and repent, we will find forgiveness and a new life in Christ. He promises to forgive even the most horrific sins, the most depraved lifestyles, the most abandoned behaviors. We may still face the consequences of our sin, but we will no longer have to fear its judgment. With Christ as our mediator, we become as clean as if we had never sinned.

Promises in Scripture

I acknowledged my sin to you
*   and did not cover up my iniquity.*
I said, "I will confess
*   my transgressions to the LORD"—*
and you forgave
*   the guilt of my sin.*

—PSALM 32:5

He does not treat us as our sins deserve
*   or repay us according to our iniquities.*
For as high as the heavens are above the earth,
*   so great is his love for those who fear him;*
as far as the east is from the west,
*   so far has he removed our transgressions from us.*

—PSALM 103:10–12

Though your sins are like scarlet,
*   they shall be as white as snow;*
though they are red as crimson,
*   they shall be like wool.*

—ISAIAH 1:18

Friday

HER LEGACY OF PRAYER

For John had been saying to Herod, "It is not lawful for you to have your brother's wife." So Herodias nursed a grudge against John and wanted to kill him.

—Mark 6:18–19

REFLECT ON: Mark 6:14–29.

PRAISE GOD: That he gives us opportunities to repent and turn back to him.

OFFER THANKS: For the men and women in your own life who have had the courage to tell you the truth.

CONFESS: Any tendency to respond defensively to constructive criticism.

ASK GOD: For the grace to respond to correction with humility.

Lift Your Heart

*M*ost of us hate criticism. Part of our defensiveness stems from our inability to see the connection between brokenness and grace. How differently we would respond if we understood that repentance is like a garden hoe breaking up the soil to make it ready for the seed. If we want to cultivate the fruit of the Spirit in our lives—love, joy, peace, patience, kindness, goodness, faithfulness, gentleness, and self-control—we must cherish the truth, however it comes to us.

Being receptive to criticism doesn't mean we become women with low self-esteem. It simply means that we will be open about our sins and faults, believing in God's desire to forgive us and help us to change. This week, take some time for a little soul-searching. Is God trying to get your attention about something that is off-kilter in your own life? Is he raising up a prophet in your own family—a child or husband who is trying to tell you the truth? If so, listen, and then pray about what you hear. Resist the temptation to make the person pay for his or her words by sulking, holding a grudge, or criticizing him or her in turn. Instead, be the first to say you're sorry. A habit of repentance will make your heart fertile soil for God's grace.

Father, I know how deceitful the human heart can be. Please give me the courage to be honest and the faith to believe in your forgiveness. May my heart become a place of brokenness, where grace and truth can flourish.

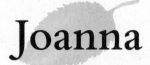

Joanna

HER NAME MEANS

"The Lord Gives Graciously"

HER CHARACTER: A woman of high rank in Herod's court, she experienced healing at Jesus' hands. She responded by giving herself totally, supporting his ministry, and following him wherever he went. The story of her healing may have been known to Herod himself.

HER JOY: To find the tomb empty except for the angels who proclaimed Jesus alive.

KEY SCRIPTURES: Luke 8:1–3; 24:10 (and Matthew 14:1–12 and Luke 23:7–12 for background on Herod and his court)

Monday

HER STORY

*J*oanna was a wealthy woman, accustomed to an atmosphere of worldliness. One didn't live in Herod Antipas's courts without learning to navigate the powerful currents of intrigue that swirled continuously around his throne. But nothing had so troubled and sickened her as the death of the prophet John. A holy man murdered for speaking the plain truth, his head was carried to Herodias on a platter, like a tantalizing dish to satisfy her appetite for revenge. How sad she had been as she watched Jesus grieving his cousin's murder.

Joanna's own life had been so altered by Christ that she may have hoped to influence Herod on his behalf. Married to Cuza, the manager of Herod's vast estates, she was well-positioned for the task. How intently Herod would have listened as she recounted the details of her miraculous healing. But after John's death, Joanna must have wondered what would become of Jesus should he ever have the misfortune of falling into Herod's hands. And what, for that matter, would become of his followers?

Though Joanna would have realized the escalating risks that faith required, there is not the slightest evidence she flinched from them. Unlike Nicodemus, she made no effort to hide her admiration for Jesus. Along with other women, she provided for his needs from her own purse. Perhaps her gifts made it just a little easier on this teacher who had no place to lay his head (Matthew 8:20).

All we really know of Joanna, in addition to her status as Cuza's wife, is that Jesus cured her of some spiritual or physical malady, that she was among a group of women who traveled with Jesus and his disciples, that she supported his ministry out of her own means, and that she was present at Jesus' resurrection along with Mary Magdalene and Mary, the mother of James. Whether her faith cost her dearly or little in either her marriage or at court is a matter for speculation.

Joanna was probably among the women present at the crucifixion. And like the others who went to the tomb to anoint Jesus' body, she must have fallen on her face in awe of the angels who greeted her with astonishing news: "Why do you look for the living among the dead? He is not here; he has risen! Remember how he told you, while he was still with you in Galilee: 'The Son of Man must be delivered into the hands of sinful men, be crucified and on the third day be raised again.'"

She would have run with the others to tell the disciples of the incredible discovery. Though Peter and the other disciples discounted the story as the ravings of hysterical women, Joanna would hardly have doubted herself. For she was a woman who lived in an atmosphere of power, and she had just witnessed a far greater power than Herod's. She would have recognized it as the same power that had healed her.

It didn't matter that her husband served a man opposed to Christ; Joanna knew where her allegiance belonged. A woman of high rank, she became part of the intimate circle of Christ's followers, casting her lot with fishermen and poor people rather than with the rich and the powerful. God honored her by making her one of the first witnesses of the resurrection.

Tuesday

HER LIFE AND TIMES

HEALING

For most minor illnesses, ancient people depended on family members or neighbors who had some skill in the healing arts. A more severe illness would be treated by a priest who also acted as a physician. Since most disease was thought to be caused by spirits or demons, priest-physicians were appropriate healers, though there was also an established medical profession, such as "Luke, the doctor" (Colossians 4:14). Medical practice focused heavily on spiritual remedies. Most Near Eastern people thought disease-causing spirits entered through the openings in the head. Some Egyptian physicians went so far as to drill holes in the patient's head in order to give the demons a means of escape.

The information in Scripture on disease has more to do with its prevention than its cure. When a patient recovered from a disease, regardless of the treatment that brought about healing, God was given credit. For instance, God is credited with the disappearance of Hezekiah's boil after it was treated with a poultice of figs (2 Kings 20:1–7).

One of Jesus' early healings was of a man suffering from the skin disease known as leprosy (Mark 1:40–42). People dreaded leprosy not only because of its destruction of skin and extremities but because it was thought to be contagious. Anyone with the disease was an outcast, unclean, separated from friends, family, and all that was familiar, with little or no hope for a cure. But then Jesus stepped into the picture. With only two words, "Be clean!" Jesus did what all the others had failed to do, and the man went away healed.

Joanna is listed with several other women whom Jesus had "cured of evil spirits and diseases." Scripture doesn't say what her particular ailment was, but it must have been something significant, something from which she had been unable to find relief through conventional methods. She and the other healed women now followed Jesus and supported him and his disciples.

No disease or deformity was beyond Jesus' healing power. He removed paralysis (Mark 2:3–12). He stopped bleeding (Mark 5:25–29). Those who were mute and blind could speak and see (Matthew 9:27–33; 20:29–34; Mark 8:22–26). Fevers left bodies at his touch (Mark 1:30–31). He restored shriveled limbs (Mark 3:1–5; Luke 13:11–13). Those possessed by evil spirits of one sort or another found relief and deliverance at Jesus' hands (Matthew 12:22; Mark 1:23–26; 9:17–29).

That same Jesus still heals today. Sometimes through the remarkable ability and knowledge of modern medicine and doctors. Sometimes without any human intervention. Sometimes by bringing the sick one home to heaven. Always divine, if not miraculous. And always with his loving, all-pervasive touch.

Wednesday

Read Luke 8:1–3.

1. What does it say about Jesus that women traveled with him and his disciples, and that the women were paying the bills?

2. What does it say about Joanna that she was doing this?

Read Luke 23:55–24:12.

3. Jesus' male disciples were hiding for fear that they, too, would be arrested. Why do you suppose Joanna and the other women risked being associated with a man who had been executed for treason?

4. What do you think surprised and frightened Joanna and the other women at the tomb (Luke 24:5)?

5. What do you admire about Joanna? How would you like to be like her?

Thursday

HER PROMISE

*J*oy comes in the morning. Joanna discovered this in a miraculous way on Jesus' resurrection day. She went to his tomb expecting to minister to his dead body and to grieve. Instead, her sorrow turned to tremendous joy. Our joy may not come this morning or tomorrow morning or even the morning after that. We face too many hardships, too many difficult situations, too much sorrow here on earth to think joy will arrive with each morning. But it will come. He has promised. At the end of the day, at the end of this life, there will be a joyful morning for all who trust in him.

Promises in Scripture

Weeping may remain for a night,
but rejoicing comes in the morning.

—PSALM 30:5

Where morning dawns and evening fades
you call forth songs of joy.

—PSALM 65:8

Satisfy us in the morning with your unfailing love,
that we may sing for joy and be glad all our days.

—PSALM 90:14

You who dwell in the dust,
wake up and shout for joy.

—ISAIAH 26:19

Friday

HER LEGACY OF PRAYER

*Remember how he told you, while he was still with you in Galilee:
"The Son of Man must be delivered into the hands of sinful men, be
crucified and on the third day be raised again."*

—LUKE 24:6–7

REFLECT ON: Luke 24:1–12.

PRAISE GOD: For the truth the psalmist proclaims: "The wicked
plot against the righteous and gnash their teeth at
them; but the LORD laughs at the wicked, for he
knows their day is coming" (Psalm 37:12–13).

OFFER THANKS: That the ultimate victory is God's—and ours!

CONFESS: Any tendency to believe God is well-intentioned but
weak.

ASK GOD: For a greater sense of his majesty.

Lift Your Heart

*H*andel's *Messiah*, a traditional Christmas favorite, is worth
listening to all year round. Handel wrote his masterpiece in
just twenty-four days, while on the verge of being thrown into debt-
ors' prison. When he finished the movement that became known as
the "Hallelujah Chorus," he turned to his servant with tears stream-
ing down his face and exclaimed, "I did think I did see all heaven
before me, and the great God himself." This week, consider purchasing a recording of the *Messiah*. As you listen to the lyrics and the
music, ask for the grace to "see all heaven before you, and the great
God himself."

*Lord, you laugh at the rulers and powers of this world who oppose
you. Help me to realize that no evil, regardless of how terrible or
prolonged it might be, can ever stand against you. Give me a greater
sense of your resurrection power and majesty.*

The Syrophoenician Woman

HER CHARACTER: Though a Gentile, she addressed Jesus as "Lord, Son of David." Her great faith resulted in her daughter's deliverance.

HER SORROW: That her child was possessed by an evil spirit.

HER JOY: That Jesus freed her daughter from spiritual bondage.

KEY SCRIPTURES: Matthew 15:21–28; Mark 7:24–30

Monday

HER STORY

*H*er body jerked and twisted, arms thrashing the air. Wide-eyed, the little girl spoke to ghosts her mother could not see, her face changing as rapidly as clouds in a sudden storm. Fear, surprise, and then a crazy kind of laughter, as though someone had stolen her soul. Dark hair stuck in gummy strands against her cheeks.

Her mother wondered what had become of the sweet child who had followed her like a puppy wherever she went. How she missed those soft kisses and the button nose that had nuzzled her cheek. She had hardly slept these last few nights for fear of what her daughter might do to herself. Neither of them, she thought, could stand much more.

Just that morning she had caught wind of a Jewish healer who, friends said, had come to Tyre hoping for relief from the crowds that mobbed him in Galilee. It didn't matter that Jews seldom mingled with Gentiles. She would go to him, beg his help, throw a fit herself if necessary. She would do whatever it took to get him to listen. It didn't take long to find him.

She approached Jesus, pleading, "Lord, Son of David, have mercy on me! My daughter is suffering terribly from demon-possession."

But Jesus ignored the woman, making no reply.

Finally, his disciples said to Jesus, "Send her away, for she keeps crying out after us."

But Jesus knew it would not be that easy to get rid of her. The only way, in fact, would be to answer her prayer. He told them, "I was sent only to the lost sheep of Israel."

Hearing him, the woman fell at his feet again, imploring, "Lord, help me!"

Then Jesus turned and said, "It is not right to take the children's bread and toss it to their dogs."

But the woman would not give up. "Yes, Lord," she said, "but even the dogs eat the crumbs that fall from their masters' table."

"Woman, you have great faith! Your request is granted," Jesus said.

So the Syrophoenician woman returned to her daughter, who was delivered from the evil spirit the very same hour that Jesus had spoken.

Scripture doesn't describe the little girl of this story in any detail; it says only that she was possessed by a demon. But judging from similar incidents, such as that of the Gerasene demoniac, whose story is told in Luke 8, or the little boy in Matthew 17, who kept throwing himself in the fire, the signs of demonic possession were probably both obvious and frightening.

But why did Jesus seem so rude to the poor woman, ignoring her request and then referring to her and her child as dogs?

His response may sound a little less harsh when you realize that the word he used for "dogs" was not the derisive one Jews ordinarily reserved for Gentiles. Instead, it was the term used for little dogs kept as pets. Jesus was also making it clear that his primary mission was to the Israelites. Had Jesus performed many healings and miracles in Tyre and Sidon, he would have risked the same kind of mob scenes he had just left behind in Galilee, thus inaugurating a ministry to the Gentiles in advance of his Father's timing.

The woman couldn't have known the reason for his silence, however, and it must have tested her faith. But rather than give up or take offense, she exercised her quick wit, revealing both a deep humility and a tenacious faith. It was a combination Jesus seemed unable to resist—fertile soil in which to grow a miracle. The Syrophoenician woman must have rejoiced that day to see the daughter she loved safe and sane, grateful for the life-giving bread that had fallen from the Master's table.

Tuesday

HER LIFE AND TIMES

DEMON-POSSESSION

The New Testament teems with stories of people possessed by demons. Demons are fallen angels, emissaries of Satan sent to earth to oppress human beings and lead them astray. Under Satan's control, their only goal is to further his purposes. They have supernatural powers here on earth: supernatural intelligence — they know and try to hide the truth (1 John 4:1–3), and they recognize Jesus as God's Son (Mark 5:7); and supernatural strength — a man possessed by demons could break away even when chained (Luke 8:29).

Though supernatural in their strength, demons are not more powerful than God or his Son. Whenever demons came face-to-face with Christ or his disciples in the New Testament, they trembled and did their bidding.

What the New Testament describes as demon-possessed people we might today depict as having an illness of some sort, physical or mental. How much distinction can be made between the two is uncertain. After Jesus cast a demon out of one man, he was described as "sitting there, dressed and in his right mind" (Mark 5:15). The man's demon-possession could easily have been extreme mental illness. At times, demon-possession caused muteness or blindness or convulsions (Matthew 9:32; 12:22; Mark 9:20). We can only speculate whether today we would view these illnesses as purely physical.

It is interesting to note that demons are mentioned only twice in the Old Testament (Deuteronomy 32:17; Psalm 106:37), yet over seventy times in the New Testament — all but a few of those in the Gospels. Perhaps Jesus' ministry to the sick exposed demonic activity as never before. Or perhaps Satan focused an extraordinary amount of his strength and power over the land of Israel while Jesus walked and healed there.

When Jesus left this earth, he sent the Holy Spirit to indwell his people. The life of Christ within us, as believers, is our defense against the forces of evil. We may suffer from physical, emotional, or mental illnesses that seem like demons within us, and God often uses the power of medical treatment to heal us of those illnesses — but let's not discount the power we possess within ourselves as children of God. That power forms a hedge of protection around and within us as we maintain a close relationship with God the Father, Christ his Son, and the Holy Spirit, our strength and comfort.

Wednesday

HER LEGACY IN SCRIPTURE

Read Matthew 15:21–28.

1. Why do you suppose Jesus ignored this woman at first?

2. Why do you think she didn't give up, despite apparent rejection?

3. Why did Jesus make an exception to his policy of focusing his ministry on Jews?

4. Do you tend to give up easily or persist? What does your current situation call for?

5. When a needy person approaches you, how do you typically respond? What if the person is *emotionally* needy—continually sticking close to you, interrupting your conversations with others, asking questions you can't answer, and generally wanting more than you wish to give?

Thursday

HER PROMISE

What possible promise can be found in a pagan woman whose little girl was possessed by an evil spirit? The Syrophoenician woman wouldn't have known what to do about her daughter had she not heard about Jesus. Somehow, she was given the faith to believe that he was capable of saving her child.

Evil spirits, unfortunately, are not creatures of a former age. We, too, must fight the evil powers in own lives. The difference now is that Jesus has won the ultimate victory on the cross. As believers, we share in his victory. He has given us authority over the evil forces that threaten us. We may still be fighting the battle, but, strange as it might sound, the victory is already won!

Promises in Scripture

Finally, be strong in the Lord and in his mighty power.

— EPHESIANS 6:10

Every spirit that acknowledges that Jesus Christ has come in the flesh is from God, but every spirit that does not acknowledge Jesus is not from God.

— 1 JOHN 4:2–3

The one who is in you is greater than the one who is in the world.

— 1 JOHN 4:4

Friday

HER LEGACY OF PRAYER

Then Jesus answered, "Woman, you have great faith! Your request is granted."
— MATTHEW 15:28

REFLECT ON: Matthew 15:21–28.

PRAISE GOD: For his power to deliver us from every form of evil.

OFFER THANKS: For the deliverance you have already experienced.

CONFESS: Any hopelessness about your children or others you love.

ASK GOD: To give you the same "terrier-like" faith that the Syro-phoenician woman had, so that you will never give up praying for the salvation of your loved ones.

Lift Your Heart

Though most of our children will never suffer from actual demonic possession, all of them are engaged, as we are, in a spiritual battle. As a mother, your prayers and your life play a role in the spiritual protection of your children. This week, pray Psalm 46 or Psalm 91 for the spiritual protection of your family. Or take a few moments to pray these verses from Psalm 125:1–2:

> Those who trust in the LORD are like Mount Zion,
>   which cannot be shaken but endures forever.
> As the mountains surround Jerusalem,
>   so the LORD surrounds his people
>   both now and forevermore.

Imagine that every member of your family is surrounded by God, just as mountains surround the city of Jerusalem. Offer each one to him, placing them in his care. When you are worried about a particular family member, pray a quick prayer asking God to surround him or her with his protection.

Lord, surround my children like the mountains surrounding Jerusalem. Encircle our family with your power and peace. Deliver us from evil now and forever. Amen.

Martha

HER NAME, THE FEMININE FORM OF "LORD," MEANS
"Lady"

HER CHARACTER: Active and pragmatic, she seemed never at a loss for words. Though Jesus chastened her for allowing herself to become worried and upset by small things, she remained his close friend and follower.

HER SORROW: To have waited, seemingly in vain, for Jesus to return in time to heal her brother, Lazarus.

HER JOY: To watch as Jesus restored her brother to life.

KEY SCRIPTURES: Luke 10:38–42; John 11:1–12:3

Monday

HER STORY

artha, Mary, and their brother, Lazarus, lived together in Bethany, a village just two miles from Jerusalem, on the eastern slope of the Mount of Olives. All three were intimate friends of Jesus.

During one of his frequent stays in their home, Martha became annoyed with Mary, her indignation spilling over like water from a boiling pot. Instead of helping with the considerable chore of feeding and housing Jesus and his retinue of disciples, Mary had been spending her time sitting happily at his feet. Feeling ignored and unappreciated, Martha marched over to Jesus and demanded: "Lord, don't you care that my sister has left me to do the work by myself? Tell her to help me!"

But Jesus wouldn't oblige. Instead, he chided her, "Martha, Martha, you are worried and upset about many things, but only one thing is needed. Mary has chosen what is better, and it will not be taken from her."

Jesus' tender rebuke must have embarrassed and startled her, calculated as it was to break the grip of her self-pity and reveal what was really taking place under her own roof and in her own heart. Perhaps this competent woman realized for the first time just how much she had been missing. Distracted by the need to serve Jesus, she had not taken time to enjoy him, to listen and learn from him. Her anger at Mary may have stemmed more from envy than from any concern about being overworked, for her sister had made her way into the circle of men to sit at the feet of the Teacher and learn from him.

Martha's story, of course, points to what is really important in life. She seemed confused and distracted, conned into believing her ceaseless activity would produce something of lasting importance. But Martha does more than simply instruct through her mistakes. She shows what it is like to have a relationship with Jesus so solid and close that no posturing or hiding is necessary. Martha seemed free to be herself in his presence. Where else should she have taken her frustration and anger, after all, but to Jesus?

Martha seems to have worked out her faith directly and actively, questioning, challenging, asking Jesus to rectify whatever had gone wrong. Her spirituality was like that of Jacob, who wrestled all night with an angel, or Job, who questioned God in the midst of his suffering, or Peter, who stumbled brashly forward into faith despite his mistakes.

In a later scene, after her brother died, we see Martha running to meet Jesus as soon as she heard he was near. Her greeting to Jesus was tinged with complaint: "Lord, if you had been here, my brother would not have died." But faith, too, was present: "I know that even now God will give you whatever you ask."

"Your brother will rise again," Jesus assured her.

"I know he will rise again in the resurrection at the last day," Martha replied.

"I am the resurrection and the life," Jesus said. "Anyone who believes in me will live, even though they die; and whoever lives and believes in me will never die. Do you believe this?"

"Yes, Lord," she told him. "I believe that you are the Christ, the Son of God, who was to come into the world."

But right after her tremendous expression of faith, Martha's practical side reasserted itself. When Jesus asked for the stone to be removed from Lazarus's tomb, she objected, raising the concern on everyone's mind: "But, Lord, there will be a terrible stink. Lazarus has been there four days!" How amazed she must have been when instead of the stench of death, Lazarus himself emerged from the tomb.

The more we delve into Martha's story, the more familiar it seems—as familiar as the face gazing at us in the bathroom mirror. A woman who placed too much importance on her own activity and not enough on sitting quietly before Jesus, she pleaded for fairness without realizing that her version of fairness was itself unfair. Her commonsensical approach to life made faith difficult. But she also loved Jesus and was confident of his love for her. How else could she have found the courage to keep pressing him for answers to her many questions? Martha offers a warmly human portrait of what it means to have Jesus as a friend, allowing him to stretch her faith, rebuke her small vision of the world, and show her what the power of God can do.

Tuesday

HER LIFE AND TIMES

WOMEN'S WORK

The work expected of a woman in Bible times was much more clearly defined than it is in our culture. There were things the women did and things the men did; things the female children did and things the male children did.

Martha was just doing what she thought was expected of her. She had been raised to take care of her guests, to care for the people in her household. Mary was the one who stepped outside of the cultural expectations of her time, sitting at the feet of Jesus with the men rather than working with Martha in the kitchen. When Martha complained, Jesus responded with characteristic boldness, ignoring the dictates of his time and urging Martha to stop and consider the choice Mary had made.

Women of that time kept busy from morning to evening with a daunting array of household tasks:

- Grinding grain for bread, then mixing, kneading, and baking the bread for the day
- Purchasing meat at a market or preparing an animal from the household's flock for meat to eat, then cooking that meat
- Carding, spinning, and weaving threads of various kinds to make cloth for clothing, bedding, and other household uses
- Sewing clothing for household members
- Drawing the water for each day's requirements
- Cleaning the house
- Washing the utensils and dishes used in meal preparation and eating
- Washing the family's clothing
- Teaching, disciplining, and loving the children in the household

The list could go on and on, and it is not so different from the lists many women today could make of their responsibilities as wives and mothers. The tasks may be overwhelming. They may seem tedious and exhausting. But they are never unimportant.

Jesus' words to Martha should not be construed to mean that "women's work" should be ignored and left undone. That would be unrealistic. However, such work should never take the place of daily and intimate contact with the members of our families and the Lord of our lives.

Wednesday

HER LEGACY IN SCRIPTURE

Read Luke 10:38–42.

1. What do you think would have happened if Martha had sat at Jesus' feet along with Mary?

2. What were Martha's positive qualities?

3. Martha was pretty frank with Jesus. If you were honest with Jesus, more honest than you've ever been before, what would you tell him?

4. What was Jesus trying to tell Martha?

Read John 11:17–27.

5. What does this passage tell you about Martha's qualities?

6. Are you more like Martha or like Mary? How? Which do you need more of in your life right now?

Thursday

HER PROMISE

*M*artha meets Jesus again in John 11 after the death of her brother, Lazarus. With characteristic forthrightness, she tells Jesus that if he had come earlier, Lazarus would not have died. Her statements open the way for Jesus to declare for all to hear—including us today—that he alone is the resurrection and the life. If we believe in him, even if we die, we live. What a promise! What a comfort! Through Jesus, death no longer has any power over us.

Promises in Scripture

Jesus said to her, "I am the resurrection and the life. Anyone who believes in me will live, even though they die; and whoever lives and believes in me will never die."

—JOHN 11:25–26

The saying that is written will come true: "Death has been swallowed up in victory."

"Where, O death, is your victory?
   Where, O death, is your sting?"

The sting of death is sin, and the power of sin is the law. But thanks be to God! He gives us the victory through our Lord Jesus Christ.

— 1 CORINTHIANS 15:54–57

Praise be to the God and Father of our Lord Jesus Christ! In his great mercy he has given us new birth into a living hope through the resurrection of Jesus Christ from the dead.

— 1 PETER 1:3

Friday

HER LEGACY OF PRAYER

Lord, don't you care that my sister has left me to do the work by myself? Tell her to help me!

—LUKE 10:40

REFLECT ON: Luke 10:38–41.

PRAISE GOD: For his patience.

OFFER THANKS: That God meets us where we are, rather than where we "should be."

CONFESS: Any tendency to resent other women in your life.

ASK GOD: For the grace to be completely honest with him.

Lift Your Heart

Martha took her complaint about her sister directly to Jesus. Is someone in your life causing you trouble—your daughter, mother, coworker, sister in faith, even a rival? Rather than expressing your grievance to anyone who will listen, take your complaint directly to God. Tell him everything that's bothering you. Ask him to give you understanding about how to respond to this person, even if it means that you, not she, are the one who needs to change.

Father, you know how difficult it is for me to relate to _____ _____. Please help me to know what you think of our difficulties. I ask you for the grace to let go of my own sense of hurt and grievance. If you want me to do anything at all to try to improve the situation, please make it clear to me. Help me to be sensitive and obedient to your guidance, I pray.

Mary of Bethany

HER NAME MAY MEAN
"Bitterness"

HER CHARACTER: Mary appears to have been a single woman, totally devoted to Jesus. The gospel portrays her, by way of contrast with her sister, Martha, as a woman of few words. As Jesus neared the time of his triumphal entry into Jerusalem prior to Passover, she performed a gesture of great prophetic significance, one that offended Judas Iscariot, the disciple who betrayed Jesus.

HER SORROW: She wept at the tomb of her brother, Lazarus, and must have experienced great sorrow at the death of Jesus.

HER JOY: To have done something beautiful for Christ.

KEY SCRIPTURES: Matthew 26:6–13; Mark 14:3–9; Luke 10:38–42; John 11:1–12:11

Monday

HER STORY

*J*erusalem was swollen with a hundred thousand worshipers, pilgrims who had come to celebrate the annual Passover feast. Every one of them, it seemed, had heard tales of the rabbi Jesus.

"I wouldn't have believed it myself if I hadn't been there," one man exclaimed. "I tell you, Lazarus drew his last breath a full four days before the Nazarene ever arrived."

"My cousin saw the whole thing," said another. "According to her, Jesus simply shouted his name and Lazarus came out of the tomb, still bound in his grave clothes."

"I hear the rabbi is coming to Jerusalem to be crowned king during Passover," said the first man.

"Better if he stayed home," said another. "The chief priests say the whole story is nonsense, that Jesus is a rabble-rouser who'll soon have the Romans up in arms against us all."

The rumors spread quickly, like floodwater spilling over a riverbank. The curious kept chasing after Mary, inquiring about her brother. Had he really been dead four days? Didn't he smell when he came stumbling out of the tomb? What was it like to live in the same house with a ghost? Did he eat and sleep? Could you see straight through him? Did he simply float through the air wherever he went?

She could hardly blame them for their crazy questions. Why shouldn't they be curious about the amazing event that had taken place in Bethany just weeks earlier? How could they know that Lazarus was as normal as any other living man? After all, raising people from the dead wasn't your everyday kind of miracle. These days she felt a rush of joy run through her, like wine overflowing a cup, whenever she looked at Lazarus. Her own flesh and blood had been called out of darkness by a man who was filled with light. How she longed to see Jesus again!

But shadows framed the edges of her happiness. No amount of celebrating could erase the memory of Jesus as he wept that day outside her brother's tomb. Even as others were celebrating the most spectacular miracle imaginable, he seemed strangely quiet. *What was he thinking as he gazed at them?* she wondered. She wished he would tell her, that she could plumb the secrets of his heart.

When Jesus finally returned to Bethany before the Passover, Martha served a feast in his honor. As Jesus was reclining at table with the other guests, Mary entered the room and anointed his head with a pint of expensive perfume. Its fragrance filled the whole house.

The disciple Judas Iscariot, failing to appreciate her gesture, objected strenuously: "Why wasn't this perfume sold and the money given to the poor? It was worth a year's wages." Though he cared nothing for the destitute, Judas was the keeper of the common purse, a man always looking for a chance to fatten his own pockets.

But rather than scolding Mary for her extravagance, Jesus praised her, saying: "Why are you bothering this woman? She has done a beautiful thing to me. The poor you will always have with you, but you will not always have me. When she poured this perfume on my body, she did it to prepare me for burial. I tell you the truth, whenever this gospel is preached throughout the world, what she has done will also be told in memory of her."

From her first encounter with Christ, Mary seems to have pursued one thing above all—the deepest possible relationship with him. She soaked up his teaching, took his promises to heart, listened for every change of inflection that would yield more clues about him. Love gave her insights that others missed. Somehow, she must have understood that Jesus would not enter Jerusalem to lasting acclaim but to death and dishonor. For a time, the light itself would appear to be smothered by the darkness. While everyone else was busy celebrating Jesus' triumph in raising Lazarus, Mary stood quietly beside him, sharing his grief.

Christ found Mary's extravagant act of adoration a beautiful thing, assuring everyone that she would be remembered forever for the way she lavished herself upon him. Mary of Bethany was a woman unafraid of expressing her love, determined to seek the heart of God—a prophetess whose gesture speaks eloquently even from a distance of two thousand years.

Tuesday

HER LIFE AND TIMES

THE PASSOVER

*A*ll able-bodied and ceremonially clean Jewish men, usually accompanied by their families, were required to attend Passover in Jerusalem as well as two other major religious feasts, Pentecost and Tabernacles (Exodus 23:17), throughout the year. By New Testament times, with Jews living all around the known world, most devout men attended these feasts when possible, but that was only occasionally.

The Feast of Passover took place in Nisan, the first month of the ancient Jewish year, our April. The most significant feast celebrated by the Jews, Passover commemorated their deliverance from slavery in Egypt. At that time, Moses had commanded each family to kill an unblemished one-year-old male lamb. He had instructed them to take the blood from the lamb and, using a brush made of hyssop branches, spread the blood on the sides and top of the door frame of each household. When the tenth and last plague came to Egypt, the angel of death entered only those houses without blood on the doorpost and killed the firstborn son in each family. Any home with blood on the doorway was "passed over."

Jewish families ate the meat of the lamb for their Passover supper, sharing with neighbors if the family was too small to finish the lamb alone. The meal also included a salad of bitter herbs as well as unleavened bread (bread made without yeast and hence unrisen). Before Passover, the house was thoroughly searched and cleaned to be sure no yeast was in the house to spoil the unleavened bread. This bread reminded the Jews of the haste with which they had to eat their last meal in Egypt before leaving slavery there. Psalms 113–118, known as the "Egyptian Hallel" (or Praise) psalms, were sung before and after the meal.

Often during their history, the Jews neglected to celebrate the Passover, as well as many of the other religious feasts God had instituted. The times when the Passover was reinstated are mentioned specifically in the Old Testament, and the ignorance of the people regarding the sacred nature of the feast is apparent. Most often, the restoration of the feast came about because of a religious revival (2 Kings 23:21–23; 2 Chronicles 30:1; 35:1–19; Ezra 6:19–22).

The Last Supper Jesus ate with his disciples, on the night that he was betrayed, was the annual Passover meal. Jesus gave specific instructions to several of his disciples for preparing this important meal. While he and his disciples reclined at the table, Jesus revealed that one of his twelve disciples would betray him and that he would be crucified. With the words, "This is my body" and "This is my blood," he gave new meaning and significance to the Passover lamb. When he was crucified the next day, he himself became the Passover Lamb, the Lamb of God who died in the place of sinners condemned to death.

Wednesday

HER LEGACY IN SCRIPTURE

Read John 11:28–44.

1. Do you hear verse 32 as an accusation, a statement of fact, or what? Why?

2. Put yourself in Mary's place. Your brother, who lives with you and supports you, has died. Then Jesus raises him. How do you react?

Read John 11:45–12:8.

3. Why do you think Mary made such an extravagant gesture, using perfume worth a year's wages?

4. Could Mary or anybody else at this dinner have predicted that Jesus might be arrested in less than a week? What makes you say that?

5. How can you express your love for Jesus? Where does money fit in, if at all?

Thursday

HER PROMISE

The Old Testament Passover lamb was only a shadow of what was to come. As our Passover Lamb, Jesus has completely and thoroughly accomplished our redemption from sin. Just as the little lamb died so that the firstborn in the Hebrew families would not die and would go free from Egypt, so Jesus, our Passover Lamb, has died so that we can be freed from our slavery to sin.

Promises in Scripture

John saw Jesus coming toward him and said, "Look, the Lamb of God, who takes away the sin of the world!"

—JOHN 1:29

But thanks be to God that, though you used to be slaves to sin ... you have been set free from sin and have become slaves to righteousness.

—ROMANS 6:17–18

Christ, our Passover lamb, has been sacrificed. Therefore let us keep the Festival, not with the old yeast, the yeast of malice and wickedness, but with bread without yeast, the bread of sincerity and truth.

—1 CORINTHIANS 5:7–8

Friday

HER LEGACY OF PRAYER

Why are you bothering this woman? She has done a beautiful thing to me.

—MATTHEW 26:10

REFLECT ON: Matthew 26:6–13.

PRAISE GOD: For giving us the ability to please him.

OFFER THANKS: For all the beautiful things God has done for you.

CONFESS: Any unwillingness to embrace the difficult parts of
                 the gospel as well as the joyful parts.

ASK GOD: To give you a greater hunger to live in his presence
                 and to seek his face.

Lift Your Heart

*L*overs like nothing better than to please their beloved. Mother Teresa of Calcutta was a woman who loved God extravagantly. Famous for her work with the poorest of the poor in India and throughout the world, she was always looking for a chance to do "something beautiful for God." How easy it is for us to neglect our Divine Lover by always asking him to do beautiful things for us rather than by developing our own capacity to please and delight him.

You don't have to travel to the other side of the world to find opportunities to do something for God. Look for him in the poorest of the poor in your own community—those who are emotionally impoverished, isolated, ill. Find a way to bring the light of God's love into their darkness. Spend time simply praising God for who he is and how he has revealed himself to you. Honor him by giving him something precious in your own life. Even the smallest gesture can become a beautiful gift for God.

Lord, you have done so many beautiful things for me, pursuing me when I cared nothing for you, restoring my hope, giving me a future worth living for. I want to offer myself generously—not as a miser doling out her favors in hope of a return, but as a woman completely in love with her Maker. Make my life a sweet-smelling fragrance to please you.

Salome
Mother of the Zebedees

HER NAME MEANS
"Peace"

HER CHARACTER: A devoted follower of Jesus, whose husband ran a fishing business, she shared the common misconception that the Messiah would drive out the Romans and establish a literal kingdom in Palestine. Her name was probably Salome.

HER SORROW: To have stood with other women at the cross, witnessing the death of Jesus of Nazareth.

HER JOY: To have seen an angel at Christ's tomb, who proclaimed the resurrection.

KEY SCRIPTURES: Matthew 20:20–24; 27:56; Mark 15:40–41; 16:1–2

Monday

HER STORY

*S*alome loved Jesus nearly as much as she loved her own two sons, James and John. She would never forget the day they left their father and their fishing nets to follow him. Lately, she, too. had come to believe that Jesus was the Messiah of God.

She had smiled when she heard Jesus had nicknamed her boys "the Sons of Thunder." Surely he had recognized the seeds of greatness in the two feisty brothers from Capernaum. Why else would he have invited them into his inner circle, along with Simon Peter? She had heard how Jesus had led the three up a high mountain. When they came down, her garrulous sons could hardly speak. But then the story came out.

"Jesus' face was blindingly bright like the sun....

"Moses and Elijah appeared and spoke with him....

"Suddenly a cloud surrounded us and a voice from heaven said, 'This is my Son, whom I love; with him I am well pleased. Listen to him!'"

Salome had listened. She had seen the glory and the power that radiated from the man. Though she had heard ominous rumors that Jerusalem's men of power hated Jesus, she also knew that the great King David had faced his own share of enemies before establishing his kingdom. And hadn't Jesus promised his disciples that they would sit on twelve thrones in his kingdom? "Everyone who has left houses or brothers or sisters or father or mother or children or fields for my sake," he had said, "will receive a hundred times as much and will inherit eternal life." How could she doubt him? Even with faith as small as a mustard seed, mountains could be moved.

Salome had left behind her comfortable home on the northwest shore of Galilee to join her sons. Now, as they journeyed up to Jerusalem, she remembered other words Jesus had spoken: "Ask and it will be given to you; seek and you will find; knock and the door will be opened to you." She would no longer deny herself the one favor her heart desired. Prostrating herself before him, she begged, "Grant that one of these two sons of mine may sit at your right and the other at your left in your kingdom."

But instead of replying to her, Jesus turned to James and John and said, "You don't know what you are asking. Can you drink the cup I am going to drink?"

"We can," they answered.

Jesus said to them, "You will indeed drink from my cup, but to sit at my right or left is not for me to grant. These places belong to those for whom they have been prepared by my Father."

Jesus, who knew Zebedee's sons better than anyone, realized that Salome was only voicing their rising ambitions. Like any loving mother, she had simply asked for what she thought would make her children happy. But as Jesus' reply and subsequent events proved, this mother didn't begin to comprehend what she was asking. Soon, the man she had approached as a king would himself die on a cross, and she would be one of the women witnessing his death.

After it was over, Salome may have remembered the anguished faces of the men who had been crucified with Jesus, one on his right hand and the other on his left — an ironic reminder of her request on the way up to Jerusalem. Such a memory would only have increased her terror for what might now happen to her sons.

Along with other faithful women at the cross, Salome was present on the morning of Jesus' resurrection. Surely the angel's words — "He has risen! He is not here!" — would have comforted her later in life when her son James became the first martyred apostle, dying at the hands of Herod Agrippa.

Instead of asking Jesus what he wanted for her sons, Salome acted as though she knew exactly what he needed to do on their behalf. She must have forgotten that Jesus had exhorted his followers to leave behind not only houses, brothers and sisters, fathers and mothers for his sake, but also children. In Salome's case, it didn't mean turning her back on her children but surrendering them to God. It meant putting Jesus above everything and everyone, loving him better than her own sons. Only then would she understand the meaning of what they would suffer as followers of Christ. Only then would she really know how to pray.

Tuesday

HER LIFE AND TIMES

MOTHERING

*I*n biblical times, when a man married, he gained another possession. Every wife was under her husband's absolute authority. When a man decided "to marry a wife," the meaning of the phrase was closer to "become the master of a wife." But even though a woman's position in the household was one of subservience to her husband, she was still in a higher position than anyone else in the household.

A woman's principal duty was to produce a family, preferably sons, who could ensure the family's physical and financial future. Mothers generally nursed their youngsters until they were about three years old. During that time, husbands and wives did not usually engage in sexual intercourse, a natural form of birth control that gave the mother time to devote herself to her youngest child.

Mothers had total care of their children, both sons and daughters, until they were about six years old. The children helped their mother with household tasks, and she taught them basic lessons on living in their culture. After six years of age, most boys became the family shepherd or began to spend the day with their father, learning the family business. David, as the youngest son, took care of his family's sheep and goats (1 Samuel 16:11), and Jesus probably spent time with his father, Joseph, learning his carpentry trade (Mark 6:3). Daughters stayed with their mothers throughout their growing-up years. Mothers taught them spinning and weaving and cooking, as well as how to behave and what to expect in their future roles as wives and mothers.

Gradually the role of mothers came to include activities like those described in Proverbs 31. Throughout Scripture, the role of mothering is given dignity and significance, so much so that God describes his love for us in terms of mothering. "As a mother comforts her child, so will I [the LORD] comfort you" (Isaiah 66:13). Paul describes his care for the Thessalonians as the care of a mother for her children: "We were gentle among you, like a mother caring for her little children" (1 Thessalonians 2:7).

When you find yourself lost in the chaos and clutter of caring for young children, remember the important part you play in keeping their world safe and happy. When you find yourself buried in the mess and muddle of raising elementary school children, remember how much they rely on you for their security. When you find yourself struggling with the disaster and disarray of raising teenagers, remember how much you love them and how much they need you to believe in them. Never forget: If you have children, they are one of your greatest legacies.

Wednesday

HER LEGACY IN SCRIPTURE

Read Matthew 20:20–27.

1. In asking from Jesus what she did (verses 20–21), what do you think Salome wanted for herself?

2. What "cup" (verse 22) was Jesus talking about?

3. What did Salome fail to understand about Jesus and his kingdom?

4. What, if anything, do you do to seek status or recognition for yourself? For your children?

5. Where do you think Jesus would draw the line in our ambitions for ourselves or our children?

Thursday

HER PROMISE

*T*hough the typical woman in biblical times was in a subservient role, her position as a mother is exalted by Scripture. God the Father recognized from the very beginning the important role a mother would play in her children's lives, and he promised to bless her. Those same promises apply to you today.

Promises in Scripture

God also said to Abraham, "As for Sarai your wife, you are no longer to call her Sarai; her name will be Sarah. I will bless her and will surely give you a son by her. I will bless her so that she will be the mother of nations; kings of peoples will come from her."

—GENESIS 17:15–16

He settles the barren woman in her home
as a happy mother of children.

—PSALM 113:9

Her children arise and call her blessed;
her husband also, and he praises her:
"Many women do noble things,
but you surpass them all."

—PROVERBS 31:28–29

Can a mother forget the baby at her breast
and have no compassion on the child she has borne?

—ISAIAH 49:15

Friday

HER LEGACY OF PRAYER

Grant that one of these two sons of mine may sit at your right and the other at your left in your kingdom.

—MATTHEW 20:21

REFLECT ON: Matthew 20:20–28.

PRAISE GOD: That his Son has shown us the true meaning of greatness.

OFFER THANKS: For all the ways, large and small, that God has served you.

CONFESS: Any pride and misguided ambition.

ASK GOD: For the grace to make the connection that the way down leads to the way up, that it is the humble woman who will be considered great in the kingdom.

Lift Your Heart

Many women have heard the message of servanthood and internalized it in unhealthy ways. Instead of realizing their inherent dignity as women, they have defined their worth primarily in terms of others. But both men and women are called to model themselves on Christ, who was not a person who suffered from low self-esteem. His humility wasn't a cover for a sense of unworthiness.

If you have made the mistake of living your life through your husband or your children, ask God for the grace to change. Admit you are a human being who needs care, consideration, and replenishment. Ask God to restore balance in your life. But as you go through the process of finding balance, don't eliminate the word *humility* from your vocabulary by embracing a life of selfishness. This week, ask each day for eyes to see another's need. Then ask for grace to serve in a way that truly models the humility of Jesus.

Lord, forgive me for any pride that has crowded you out of my heart. Whenever I am tempted to think or act with selfish ambition, place a check in my spirit. Give me, instead, the courage to be a servant. Make more room in my heart for your love. In Jesus' name I pray. Amen.

The Widow with the Two Coins

HER CHARACTER: Though extremely poor, she is one of the most great-hearted people in the Bible. Just after warning his disciples to watch out for the teachers of the law, who devour widows' houses, Jesus caught sight of her in the temple. He may have called attention to her as a case in point.

HER SORROW: To be alone, without a husband to provide for her.

HER JOY: To surrender herself to God completely, trusting him to act on her behalf.

KEY SCRIPTURES: Mark 12:41–44; Luke 21:1–4

Monday

HER STORY

With Passover approaching, the temple was packed with worshipers from all over Israel. The previous Sunday, Jesus had created a sensation as he rode down the Mount of Olives and into Jerusalem, mounted on a donkey. A large crowd had gathered, carpeting the road with palm branches and shouting: "Hosanna to the Son of David! Blessed is he who comes in the name of the Lord! Hosanna in the highest."

Some of the Pharisees, scandalized that Jesus was being hailed as Messiah, demanded, "Teacher, rebuke your disciples!"

"I tell you," he replied, "if they keep quiet, the stones will cry out."

Stung by his words, the teachers of the law began to plot how they could break the law by murdering him at their first opportunity.

Days later, after warning his disciples to watch out for the teachers of the law who preyed on widows for their money, Jesus sat opposite the temple treasury, in the Court of the Women. The place was crowded with people dropping their offerings in one of the thirteen trumpet-shaped receptacles that hung on the walls. But Jesus had eyes for only one of them. He watched as a widow deposited two small copper coins, less than a day's wages.

Quickly, he called to his disciples, "I tell you the truth, this poor widow has put more into the treasury than all the others. They all gave out of their wealth; but she, out of her poverty, put in everything—all she had to live on."

No one else would have noticed the woman. But Jesus, with eyes that penetrated both her circumstances and her heart, recognized the astonishing nature of her gift. Her gesture was a sign of complete abandonment to God.

Without faith, she wouldn't have offered her last penny, believing God would care for her better than she could care for herself. But there is yet another, more subtle aspect to her story. How easy it would have been for her to conclude that her gift was simply too meager to offer. What need had God for two copper coins anyway? Surely they meant more to her than they would to him. Somehow she must have had the grace to believe in the value of her small offering.

Maybe God, in a manner of speaking, did need what she had to offer. Perhaps her gesture consoled Jesus a short time before his passion and death. She had given everything she had to live on; soon, he would give his life.

The story of the widow and her two copper coins reminds us that God's kingdom works on entirely different principles than the kingdom of this world. In the divine economy, the size of the gift is of no consequence; what matters is the size of the giver's heart.

Tuesday

HER LIFE AND TIMES

MONEY

*T*wo tiny coins. Mark identifies them as two Greek lepta, tiny copper coins worth less than a penny.

Roman coins (denarius), Greek coins (drachma, farthing), and Jewish coins (mite, pound, shekel, and talent) are all mentioned in the New Testament. The Israelites typically used the coinage of the nation that ruled over them, but they also developed their own local system of coinage.

Coins didn't come into use in Israel until after the people returned from exile between 500 and 400 BC. Before that time people bartered, exchanging produce, animals, and precious metals for goods and services. A woman might barter a flask of oil for a new robe or the wool from a lamb for a new lamp.

The Israelites probably carried Persian and Babylonian coins back to Israel with them when they returned from exile there. These coins were rather crudely made. Each was individually punched from gold or silver or some other metal, then a design was hammered onto each side. Greek coins most often had images of nature or animals or gods stamped onto them. Later, Roman coins carried the image of the emperor of that time as well as his name. Coins have been found with the images of all twelve Roman emperors.

By Jesus' day, a large variety of coins had come into use in Palestine. New Testament Jews used coins from Rome and Greece as well as their own Jewish form of coinage. The temple tax had to be paid in Jewish currency—in shekels. Money changers set up their businesses in order to change other coinage into shekels for temple worshipers, then, adding insult to injury, cheating their customers. Jesus was not opposed to the operation of such businesses, but to their dishonesty and to their operation within the temple itself. He furiously scattered them, declaring that his Father's house was a house of prayer, not a business site (Matthew 21:12–13).

While money is necessary for life in most cultures, the Bible warns against placing more importance on it than it should rightfully have. The widow who gave all she had furnishes us with the best example of recognizing the need for money—she had money, although very little—but also the need to hold it lightly—she willingly and lovingly gave it away. Peter warns us not to be "greedy for money" (1 Peter 5:2), and the writer to the Hebrews admonishes us to keep our "lives free from the love of money and be content with what [we] have" (Hebrews 13:5). When writing to Timothy, Paul penned those famous, and often misquoted, words about money: "For the love of money is a root of all kinds of evil. Some people, eager for money, have wandered from the faith and pierced themselves with many griefs" (1 Timothy 6:10).

The pervasive lure of money and what it can provide—the need to have more and do more and get more—is probably more prevalent in our culture than in any other in history. Christians are just as susceptible to its enticements as anyone else. Money drives an effective and forceful wedge between our Savior and us. Jesus knew that and pointedly reminded us with these words: "No servant can serve two masters. Either he will hate the one and love the other, or he will be devoted to the one and despise the other. You cannot serve both God and Money" (Luke 16:13).

Wednesday

HER LEGACY IN SCRIPTURE

Read Mark 12:41–44.

1. Why would Jesus watch people putting money into the offering?

2. Why do you think he pointed out the widow to his disciples? What did he want them to understand about her and about the teachers of the law who preyed on women like her?

3. Why would someone give everything she had to live on?

4. Does giving your last dime seem to you like faith or folly? Why?

5. Describe your relationship with money. To what extent are you a spender, a saver, a giver, or a craver of money?

Thursday

HER PROMISE

*G*od's promise of provision is nowhere more evident than in this story of the widow who gave all she had. She had no one else to rely on—only God. That's true of us as well, isn't it? Regardless of our financial situation, whether we are financially well off or constantly skimming the bottom, we have no one else to rely on. Our true security is not in our belongings or our bank accounts, but in God alone. And he has promised to provide.

Promises in Scripture

The LORD himself goes before you and will be with you; he will never leave you nor forsake you. Do not be afraid; do not be discouraged.

—DEUTERONOMY 31:8

Those who know your name will trust in you,
*   for you, LORD, have never forsaken those who seek you.*

—PSALM 9:10

Some trust in chariots and some in horses,
*   but we trust in the name of the LORD our God.*

—PSALM 20:7

Therefore I tell you, do not worry about your life, what you will eat or drink; or about your body, what you will wear. Is not life more important than food, and the body more important than clothes? Look at the birds of the air; they do not sow or reap or store away in barns, and yet your heavenly Father feeds them. Are you not much more valuable than they?

—MATTHEW 6:25–26

Friday

HER LEGACY OF PRAYER

Jesus said, "I tell you the truth, this poor widow has put more into the treasury than all the others. They all gave out of their wealth; but she, out of her poverty, put in everything—all she had to live on."

—MARK 12:43

REFLECT ON: Mark 12:41–44.

PRAISE GOD: For judging not by outward appearances but as one who sees the heart.

OFFER THANKS: For blessings of money, time, energy, and emotional resources.

CONFESS: Any tendency to act as though your security depends more on you than it does on God.

ASK GOD: To make you a generous woman with the faith to believe that even small gifts are worth giving.

Lift Your Heart

This week, think of an area of your life that feels particularly empty or impoverished. You may be lonely, financially stretched, or worried about the future. Whatever it is, pray about it. Listen for the voice of the Holy Spirit. Is God inviting you to do something to express your trust? What kind of offering would be the most pleasing to him? Once you hear his voice, go ahead and give him what his heart desires.

Father, you are the source of every blessing. This week, help me to give, not only out of my wealth, but out of my poverty. Remind me that I belong to you, body and soul, heart and mind, past, present, and future.

Mary Magdalene

HER NAME MAY MEAN
"Bitterness"

HER CHARACTER: Though mistakenly characterized as a prostitute in many popular writings, the Bible says only that Mary was possessed by seven demons. She probably suffered a serious mental or physical illness from which Jesus delivered her. She is a beautiful example of a woman whose life was poured out in response to God's extravagant grace.

HER SORROW: To watch Jesus' agony at Calvary.

HER JOY: To have been the first witness to Jesus' resurrection.

KEY SCRIPTURES: Matthew 27:56, 61; 28:1; Mark 15:40, 47; 16:1–19; Luke 8:2; 24:10; John 19:25; 20:1–18

Monday

HER STORY

She made her way through the shadows to the garden tomb, grateful for the darkness that shrouded her tears. *How,* she wondered, *could the world go on as though nothing at all had happened?* How could the mountains keep from crashing down, the sky resist falling? Had everyone but her lost their minds? Had no one noticed that the world had collapsed two days ago?

For the past three years she had followed the rabbi across Galilee and Judea, providing for him out of her own small purse. She had loved his hearty laughter and the smile that flashed across his face whenever he saw her. Wherever they went, she felt privileged to tell her story, grateful to be among his growing band of followers.

She had grown up in Magdala, a prosperous town on the west bank of the Sea of Galilee. But she had not prospered. How could a woman thrive when she was filled with demons who controlled her mind? Though she had begged for mercy, no mercy had been given. Instead, her delusions locked her in a nightmare world, isolating her even from small pleasures and simple kindnesses.

But then Jesus had come. Like no rabbi she had ever encountered, he seemed neither afraid nor repulsed by her illness. "Mary," he had called to her, as though he had known her all her life. Despite the heat, she shivered as he drew near, her stomach suddenly queasy. Though she backed away, she could feel a great light advancing toward her, forcing the darkness away. Suddenly her familiar companions were themselves begging mercy, but no mercy was given.

Mary Magdalene, a woman possessed by seven demons, was restored to her right mind, her bondage a thing of the past. Eyes that had once been holes swallowing the light now shone like pools reflecting the sun.

Since then, everyone in Magdala had marveled at the change in her. How could Mary not love such a man? How could she not want to do everything for him? She thought she was living in heaven—to be close to Jesus; to witness healing after healing; to be stirred, surprised, and refreshed by his teaching. This, indeed, was joy to a woman unaccustomed to joy.

But Jesus had his share of enemies, she knew. Religious leaders in Jerusalem had been stung by his truth-telling, offended by his galling lack of diplomacy. Still, every trap they laid for him had failed ... until now.

How suddenly they had struck, even though Jerusalem was crowded with pilgrims for Passover. The temple guard had arrested him at night and then turned him over to Roman authorities, who mocked and whipped him nearly to death. The rabbi from Galilee, who had promised the poor in spirit they would surely inherit the kingdom of heaven, was now in chains. His hunger and thirst for righteousness had left him not full, but empty and broken. Unblessed, he had become a curse, his body hanging naked on a Roman cross.

Mary had done her best to fight off the shadows that crowded near again as she waited through the awful hours of his agony, unable to look at the spectacle before her, yet unable to turn away. Whatever his suffering, she needed to be near him.

When it was over, she had watched Nicodemus and Joseph of Arimathea unfasten his body from the cross. Gently they had wrapped him in myrrh and aloe, enough for a king's burial. Finally, as the stone rolled across the tomb, sealing it shut, she had turned away.

After the Sabbath was over, on the next day, Mary purchased yet more spices. Before the sun came up on Sunday, she approached the tomb. How on earth, she wondered, could she roll away the massive stone? But, to her surprise, the mouth of tomb lay wide open. Strips of linen were lying on the floor and the burial cloth that had been wrapped around Jesus' head was folded up by itself. *What had they done with his body?* she wondered. To be cheated of this last chance of touching him and caring for him was more than she could bear.

She stood outside the tomb weeping. Then, bending over, she looked inside. Two creatures in white sat on the stony shelf where the body had been laid. "Woman, why are you crying?" they asked.

"They have taken my Lord away," she said, "and I don't know where they have put him." Then she turned and saw a man studying her.

"Woman," he said, "why are you crying? Who is it you are looking for?"

Mistaking him for the gardener, she pleaded, "Sir, if you have carried him away, tell me where you have put him, and I will get him."

"Mary," he said.

Startled, she cried out, "Rabboni" (meaning Teacher).

By now the sun had risen. With it fled the darkness that had pursued her ever since she had heard the news of his arrest. Jesus, the one who had raised her from a living death, had himself risen from the dead.

Mary fell to the ground in awe, remembering the words of the prophet Isaiah: "The people walking in darkness have seen a great light; on those living in the land of the shadow of death a light has dawned." The garden that had so recently been a place of shadows and gloom now seemed green and bright, as though paradise itself had broken through.

The risen Jesus had appeared, not to rulers and kings, nor even first of all to his male disciples, but to a woman whose love had held her at the cross and led her to the grave. Mary Magdalene, a person who had been afflicted by demons, whose testimony would not have held up in court because she was a woman, was the first witness of the resurrection. Once again, God had revealed himself to the lowly, and it would only be the humble whose hearing was sharp enough to perceive the message of his love.

Tuesday

HER LIFE AND TIMES

WOMEN IN JESUS' LIFE AND MINISTRY

*C*ooking, caring for family members, spinning, weaving, sewing, baking bread, cleaning—all of these were common tasks for
women in New Testament times. Most women spent the majority
of their time and energy within their homes, caring for their families. But several women stepped outside the cultural expectations of
their time to play a significant role in the ministry of Jesus. Only
the twelve disciples are mentioned more often than certain women,
Mary Magdalene being one of them.

Mark tells us that a number of women "followed him [Jesus] and
cared for his needs" (Mark 15:41). During the years of Jesus' ministry,
when he and his disciples weren't earning an income, several women
stepped in to care for them. They used their own financial resources
to support Jesus and his disciples (Luke 8:3). While Jesus was teaching
and healing, these women probably spent their time purchasing food,
preparing it, and serving it. Perhaps they also found homes for Jesus
and his disciples to stay in while on their travels. These particular
women probably either didn't have children or had children who
were grown, so their responsibilities at home were decreased, and
they could instead provide for the needs of Jesus and his disciples.

Two women in Bethany, Mary and Martha, always generously
opened their home to Jesus when he was in their town, providing meals and a place to rest (Luke 10:38). Jesus was close enough
to these women and their brother, Lazarus, that he called them his
friends (John 11:11).

The most significant woman in Jesus' life was, of course, Mary, his
mother. She remained in the background during his years of public
ministry. Jesus' gentle care of her when he was hanging on the cross
reveals a son's true love for his mother.

Women watched Jesus suffer on the cross, remaining there until
he had breathed his last and was buried. Women were the first to

go to the tomb on Sunday morning and the first to witness his resurrection.

Luke's gospel in particular portrays Jesus as someone who both understood and respected women, conferring on them a stature that most of them had not previously enjoyed. Jesus' dealings with women throughout the Gospels gives all of us, men and women alike, a model to follow as we consider the status and treatment of the women with whom we come into contact every day.

Wednesday

HER LEGACY IN SCRIPTURE

Read Mark 15:33–41.

1. What do you think Mary Magdalene thought and felt as she heard Jesus cry out to God (verse 34)?

2. How might she have reacted when she saw him dead?

3. Why do you think she went to the cross to watch him die? Why not spare herself that?

Read John 20:1–16.

4. Why do you suppose Mary didn't recognize Jesus until he spoke her name?

5. How sure are you that Jesus knows your name (Isaiah 43:1)?

6. How would you compare your love for Jesus to Mary's? What feeds or dampens your love for him?

Thursday

HER PROMISE

*J*esus not only knew Mary's name, he knew everything about her. He remembered the day he had cast the demons out of her. He remembered her many practical kindnesses. He saw how she suffered with him as she watched him die on the cross.

Just as Jesus knew the intimate details of Mary's life, he knows about you. When you are tempted to lose hope, when life seems too empty to go on, when grief overwhelms you—Jesus cares. When those you love have let you down, when you think you can't go on for another minute, when your problems crush you—Jesus cares. He calls your name, just as he called Mary's. And you, too, can go on like the women who went from the tomb, perhaps still a bit afraid yet "filled with joy" (Matthew 28:8).

Promises in Scripture

Fear not, for I have redeemed you;
I have summoned you by name; you are mine.

—ISAIAH 43:1

Are not two sparrows sold for a penny? Yet not one of them will fall to the ground apart from the will of your Father. And even the very hairs of your head are all numbered. So don't be afraid; you are worth more than many sparrows.

—MATTHEW 10:29–31

[Nothing] will be able to separate us from the love of God that is in Christ Jesus our Lord.

—ROMANS 8:39

Cast all your anxiety on him because he cares for you.

—1 PETER 5:7

Friday

HER LEGACY OF PRAYER

Jesus said to her, "Mary."
She turned toward him and cried out in Aramaic, "Rabboni!" (which
means Teacher).

—JOHN 20:16

REFLECT ON: John 20:1–18.

PRAISE GOD: That the Father has revealed his love so powerfully
                 in Jesus.

OFFER THANKS: For the death and resurrection of Jesus, his Son and
                 our Savior.

CONFESS: Your doubts about God's power or willingness to
                 deliver you from some evil in your life.

ASK GOD: For the grace of deliverance.

Lift Your Heart

One day this week set your alarm clock so that you wake up a
half hour before dawn. Find a spot where you can watch the
sunrise. In the early morning shadows, tell God about some area of
darkness in your own life or in the life of someone you love. Perhaps it's an illness, a persistent sin, loneliness, a troubled marriage, an
addiction, or a wayward child. Whatever it is, surrender it by imagin-
ing yourself placing it in the garden tomb next to the body of Jesus.
As the sun rises, meditate on that first Easter morning and remember
that when Jesus walked out of the tomb, you walked out with him.
Ask God for the faith to wait and watch for his delivering power.

Lord, make me a woman like Mary Magdalene, who follows you not
because of a legalistic understanding of her faith, but because of an
overwhelming sense of gratitude and love for your own extravagant
grace. Help me surrender my darkness to you and flood me with the
light of your presence.

Dorcas

HER NAME MEANS
"Gazelle"; "Tabitha" Is Its Hebrew Equivalent

HER CHARACTER: An inhabitant of Joppa, a town on the Mediterranean coast, thirty-five miles northwest of Jerusalem, she belonged to one of the earliest Christian congregations. She was a disciple known for her practical works of mercy.

HER SORROW: To have suffered a grave illness.

HER JOY: To serve Jesus by serving the poor.

KEY SCRIPTURE: Acts 9:36–43

Monday

HER STORY

The winds roared over the coast, piling water in noisy heaps along the rocky shoreline. But though she lay quietly in the upper room of her house near the sea, Dorcas did not hear them. Nor did she notice the waves of grief that spilled into the room from the heart of every woman present. For once she had nothing to offer, no word of comfort, no act of kindness to soften their suffering. Instead, she lay still as other women ministered to her, tenderly sponging her body clean to prepare it for burial.

As Peter approached the house, he could hear the noise of mourning, a sound more desolate than the tearing wind. Two men had summoned him from Lydda, where he had just healed a paralytic. They urged him to come quickly because one of the Lord's disciples in Joppa had died. He had come in haste, hoping to reach Dorcas before she had to be buried.

As soon as he entered the room where her body lay, the widows surrounded him with tangible evidence of the woman they had loved, weeping as they held up robes and other items Dorcas had sewn to clothe the poor. Quickly, Peter shooed them from the room, as though to clear the atmosphere of despair. Then he knelt beside her body.

As Peter prayed, he remembered a promise Jesus had made: "I tell you the truth, anyone who has faith in me will do what I have been doing. He will do even greater things than these, because I am going to the Father." His faith rising like the wind outside, Peter addressed the dead woman, saying, "Tabitha, get up." Taking her by the hand, he actually helped her to her feet.

The next day, Dorcas stood alone on the roof of her house. The shore was littered with driftwood, trinkets from yesterday's storm. She breathed deeply, inhaling the sea's salty tang, soothed by the sound of waves lapping the rocks below. Strangely, the view looked somehow transparent, as though another world waited just behind the curtain of this one. Dorcas shaded her eyes with her hand, peering out at the sea. But she saw nothing other than the usual collection of fishing boats bobbing in the waves.

Sighing, she turned and went inside. She had things to do — clothes to sew, bread to bake, the poor to feed and clothe. But even in the midst of her busy preparations, her longing for that other world increased, like hunger pangs before a feast. She fed that longing with her many practical acts of love.

Though we don't know what went through Peter's mind as he knelt and prayed at Dorcas's bedside, we do know that God worked through him in an extraordinary way. And though Scripture doesn't tell us how Dorcas responded to her incredible experience, it doesn't take much to imagine her joy. The story of her miracle spread throughout Joppa, leading many to believe.

Tuesday

HER LIFE AND TIMES

DISCIPLES

*I*n Joppa there was a disciple named Tabitha (which, when translated into Greek, is Dorcas) (Acts 9:36). She is the only woman in Scripture to be honored with the designation of "disciple." The presence of women in groups of disciples is implied at times, but Dorcas is the only woman specifically called a disciple.

The word *disciple* in both Greek and English has its roots in verbs that mean "to learn." Those two verbs describe the activity or posture of the disciple of the New Testament. The word *disciple* is used 296 times in the English Bible. Two of those times occur in Isaiah, and all of the rest are found in the Gospels and in the book of Acts. The Scriptures use the word almost exclusively to name someone who is a follower of Jesus.

A disciple is first of all a learner, a pupil. The disciples of Jesus sat at his feet, and he taught them. They listened and soaked up the knowledge and wisdom of Christ as he talked to them and to the crowds that inevitably gathered around him. Jesus taught them many things, but all of his teaching can be summed up in his command to love God and love others (Mark 12:31). As disciples, they accepted what Jesus taught as truth, trusting him as their teacher and willingly putting into practice all of his teachings.

Second, a disciple is a follower. The disciples followed Jesus wherever he went. Jesus' first words to Peter and his brother Simon were, "Follow me." When Jesus called to James and John in their boat, they quickly left the boat and their father and followed Jesus (Matthew 4:18–22). The word *follow* here doesn't just mean being willing to walk along with the teacher, it means being willing to adopt the views and way of life of the teacher. The twelve disciples left their families and incomes and former lifestyles to follow Jesus.

A true disciple, Dorcas had learned of Jesus and had decided to follow him. She had adopted his views and lifestyle, lovingly living out his commands by ministering to the poor around her. There was no mistaking it, no quibbling, no uncertainty—anyone who knew Dorcas knew who she was and whom she followed. Her devotion is recorded for all the generations to follow with those simple, yet profound words: "In Joppa there was a disciple named ... Dorcas."

Wednesday

HER LEGACY IN SCRIPTURE

Read Acts 9:36–43.

1. What sorts of things do you think Dorcas was doing?

2. Describe what you think the scene was like when Peter brought Dorcas back to her friends and neighbors.

3. Dorcas was known for doing good and helping the poor. Where do these activities fit in your life?

4. Why do you suppose God chose to raise Dorcas but not any of the other disciples who presumably died in that year and the succeeding years?

5. God was definitely glorified through Dorcas's life, death, and resurrection. What if Dorcas had not been raised? Would God still have been glorified? How?

Thursday

HER PROMISE

*G*od is glorified in the story of Dorcas, not only in her being raised from the dead, but through her acts of kindness, her generosity, and her willingness to go out of her way to offer help to others. Don't think you must do great and noble and noticeable acts for your life to glorify God. He will be glorified through your simple acts of love and obedience, whatever they are, wherever you are.

Promises in Scripture

May the words of my mouth and the meditation of my heart
be pleasing in your sight,
O Lord, my Rock and my Redeemer.

—Psalm 19:14

Whoever oppresses the poor shows contempt for their Maker,
but whoever is kind to the needy honors God.

—Proverbs 14:31

"He defended the cause of the poor and needy, and so all went well.
Is that not what it means to know me?" declares the Lord.

—Jeremiah 22:16

When you give to the needy, do not let your left hand know what your right hand is doing, so that your giving may be in secret. Then your Father, who sees what is done in secret, will reward you.

—Matthew 6:3 – 4

Friday

HER LEGACY OF PRAYER

Peter went with them, and when he arrived he was taken upstairs to the room. All the widows stood around him, crying and showing him the robes and other clothing that Dorcas had made while she was still with them.

—ACTS 9:39

REFLECT ON: Acts 9:36–43.

PRAISE GOD: For his power over death.

OFFER THANKS: For answered prayers.

CONFESS: Any habit of limiting the power of prayer.

ASK GOD: To make you a woman whose love for God has practical ramifications for those around her.

Lift Your Heart

Is there a Dorcas in your life, a good woman or perhaps a good man? Maybe this person has been a great support in your own life. Resist the temptation to become depressed about what is happening to them and, instead, spend time this week praying in light of Dorcas's story. Let her miracle increase your faith and shape your prayers. If you have a photograph of the person, paste it to the dashboard of your car, your refrigerator, or your computer to remind you to pray. Ask God to bring light out of the darkness of their present circumstances.

Lord, show me how to pray with increasing faith, aware that your Spirit is no less powerful today than it was two thousand years ago. Act on behalf of your servant and glorify your name by what you do.

Lydia

HER NAME SIGNIFIES THAT
She Was a Woman of Lydia, a Region in Asia Minor

HER CHARACTER: A Gentile adherent of Judaism, she was a successful businesswoman who sold a type of cloth prized for its purple color. As head of her household, she may have been either widowed or single. So strong was her faith that her entire household followed her example and was baptized. She extended hospitality to Paul and his companions, even after their imprisonment.

HER SORROW: To see Paul and Silas beaten and thrown into prison for the sake of the gospel she had embraced.

HER JOY: That God's Spirit directed Paul and his companions to Macedonia, enabling her and others at Philippi to hear the gospel for the first time.

KEY SCRIPTURE: Acts 16:6–40

Monday

HER STORY

The wind rustled the branches overhead until they became a swaying canopy whose shadow danced across the circle of women bowed in prayer. It didn't matter that Philippi had too few Jews to support a synagogue; the river's edge had become their place of worship, a green sanctuary where they gathered each Sabbath to pray.

Lydia listened as a stranger from Tarsus invoked the familiar words of the Shema: "Hear, O Israel: The LORD our God, the LORD is one. Love the LORD your God with all your heart and with all your soul and with all your strength." Such prayers were like a gust of wind, fanning her longing. A Gentile who had come to Philippi from Asia Minor, Lydia was a prominent businesswoman who sold fine cloth to those who could afford it. Though not a Jew, she wanted to know this God powerful enough to part the sea yet tender enough to yearn for the love of his people.

Paul did not stop with the traditional Shema; instead, he spoke of a God whose Son, Jesus, had been murdered for love. This Jesus had risen from the grave after suffering the most agonizing death imaginable. He was Messiah, the merciful and holy One who had come to save God's people.

The women sat quietly as Paul told the story. Even the branches overhead had stopped their noisy rustling. But in the stillness Lydia felt a strong wind rushing through her. Tears rolled down her cheeks even though she felt like singing. Afterward, she and her household were baptized in the Gangites River, near Philippi. Lydia insisted that Paul and Silas (and probably Timothy and Luke) accept her hospitality. Her home may have become the very center of the church in Philippi.

Philippi seemed an unlikely place to plant the gospel. It had been named for Philip II, father of Alexander the Great, who had been attracted to the region by gold-bearing mountains to the north of the city. Now a prosperous Roman colony located on the main highway linking the eastern provinces to Rome, its citizens included large numbers of retired Roman soldiers. Despite its size, however, Philippi hadn't even enough Jews to provide the requisite quorum of ten reliable males to form a synagogue—and it had always been Paul's habit to preach first in the synagogue. Even so, Philippi did have its group of praying Jewish and Gentile women.

Interestingly, Paul had not planned to visit Philippi but had been on his way to Asia when he felt constrained by the Holy Spirit to turn aside. Soon afterward, he had a vision in which a man of Macedonia begged him, "Come over to Macedonia and help us." Days later, he found himself on the riverbank, preaching to the women who had gathered there for prayer.

Shortly after Lydia's conversion, she heard news that her house-guests, Paul and Silas, had been whipped and thrown into prison. Paul's crime had been to drive an evil spirit from a slave girl who had been harassing them. Upset at the loss of profits from her fortune-telling, the girl's owners dragged Paul and Silas before the city magistrates, claiming, "These men are Jews and are throwing our city into an uproar by advocating customs unlawful for us Romans to accept or practice."

That night, with their feet in stocks, Paul and Silas prayed and sang hymns to God while the other prisoners listened. About midnight an earthquake shook the foundations of the prison so violently that the doors flew open and the chains of the prisoners fell off. As a result, the jailer and his whole household were converted. After he was released, Paul returned to Lydia's home for a short while.

When Lydia said good-bye to the apostle and his companions as they continued on their missionary journey, she may have remembered the words of his accusers: "These men are throwing our city into an uproar." Indeed, God had thrown the entire region into an uproar from which it would never recover.

Lydia has the distinction of being Paul's first convert in Europe and the first member of the church at Philippi, a community that later became a source of great consolation to the apostle when he was imprisoned. Perhaps her prayers, joined with those of the other women gathered at the riverbank, helped prepare the way for the gospel to be planted in Europe.

Tuesday

HER LIFE AND TIMES

FABRICS AND DYES

*L*ydia's success as a businesswoman in the city of Philippi came from dealing in cloth that had been dyed a particular shade of purple. Originally from Thyatira, Lydia was probably privy to secret formulas for the dyes made there. Only those who belonged to the dyers guild were allowed to work as dyers. Made from the secretions of a shellfish found in the area, these special dyes colored the clothing of the well-to-do. The particular shades of purple ranged from a reddish scarlet to a deep purple tone.

Cloth dyed in various colors is mentioned as early as the exodus from Egypt, when the Lord instructed Moses to receive gifts from the people of Israel in order to make the tabernacle: "These are the offerings you are to receive from them: gold, silver and bronze; blue, purple and scarlet yarn and fine linen; goat hair; ram skins dyed red" (Exodus 25:3–5).

The best red or scarlet dyes were made from a grub that fed on oak as well as other plants. A less expensive form of red dye could be made from the root of the madder plant. The rind of the pomegranate formed the basis for dyes of blue shades. Yellow dyes were made from safflower and turmeric.

The most common garments in biblical times were made from wool, which came naturally in a variety of colors, from whites and yellows to tans and browns. Wool was also easily dyed other colors. Linen fabric was more difficult to dye but was found in early Egypt (Genesis 41:42) and was used in making the tabernacle curtains (Exodus 26). Leather for girdles, shields, sandals, purses, or pouches could also be dyed numerous colors.

Lydia's occupation, then, was an important commercial trade. She must have been at least moderately successful, for Scripture records the fact that she had her own house as well as servants. Her unique position as a woman in business gave her opportunity to travel, to learn of the Christ, and to offer her home and hospitality to Paul and his companions as ministers of the gospel.

Wednesday

HER LEGACY IN SCRIPTURE

Read Acts 16:11–40.

1. How do you think Lydia would describe her first meeting with Paul and his team by the river?

2. How do you suppose the events of verses 16–37 affected Lydia?

3. Why did Lydia and the other believers in Philippi need encouragement (verse 40) as Paul was leaving?

4. Think about the words, "The Lord opened her heart to respond" (verse 14). If this has happened to you, what were the circumstances, and what was your response?

5. Lydia responded to the Lord in a town profoundly hostile to the news of Christ. What response is the Lord currently asking of you, despite whatever obstacles you may be facing?

Thursday

HER PROMISE

*L*ydia's life reveals a God who longs for relationship with his people. Lydia's openness to the truths Paul preached was not her own doing; God saw her hunger for him, and he met her deepest need—her need for him. He is still touching hearts today. The longings you feel for intimacy with him, the emptiness you experience when you've tried everything else and still hunger, the burning need you have for wholeness—these can only be satisfied when you start with the Alpha and end with the Omega, Jesus Christ, your beginning and your end.

Promises in Scripture

Satisfy us in the morning with your unfailing love,
*   that we may sing for joy and be glad all our days.*

—PSALM 90:14

Why spend money on what is not bread,
*   and your labor on what does not satisfy?*
Listen, listen to me, and eat what is good,
*   and your soul will delight in the richest of fare....*
Seek the LORD while he may be found;
*   call on him while he is near.*

—ISAIAH 55:2, 6

But those who drink the water I give them will never thirst. Indeed, the water I give them will become in them a spring of water welling up to eternal life.

—JOHN 4:14

He said to me: "It is done. I am the Alpha and the Omega, the Beginning and the End. To the thirsty I will give to water without cost from the spring of the water of life."

—REVELATION 21:6

Friday

HER LEGACY OF PRAYER

On the Sabbath we went outside the city gate to the river, where we expected to find a place of prayer. We sat down and began to speak to the women who had gathered there.

—ACTS 16:13

REFLECT ON: Acts 16:6–14.

PRAISE GOD: For sending messengers of the gospel.

OFFER THANKS: That God enables us to believe by first opening our hearts to faith.

CONFESS: Any way you may have neglected prayer, especially in community with other believers.

ASK GOD: To help you make prayer a greater priority in your life.

Lift Your Heart

*I*t's interesting to note that the Holy Spirit directed Paul to Macedonia and, ultimately, to a group of women who had already gathered for prayer. It almost seems as though the women's faithfulness in prayer was a magnet that attracted God's Spirit. This week, invite a few friends to pray with you. Gather in your home or find your own "green sanctuary" outdoors. Sing hymns and ask God for a fresh outpouring of his Spirit in your churches, homes, neighborhoods, and nation. Pray for a greater opening for the gospel. Perhaps God will create an "uproar" in your city as a result of your prayers.

Lord, Scripture says that you inhabit the praises of your people. Come now and dwell with us as we seek your face. Let the fresh wind of your Holy Spirit fall on us. May our churches, homes, and neighborhoods become places of prayer, shaking the world around us in a way that brings you glory.

Priscilla

HER NAME, THE DIMINUTIVE OF "PRISCA," MEANS
"Worthy" or "Venerable"

HER CHARACTER: One of the first missionaries and a leader of the early church, along with her husband, Aquila, she risked her life for the apostle Paul. Priscilla was a woman whose spiritual maturity and understanding of the faith helped build up the early church.

HER SORROW: To experience opposition to the gospel from both Jews and Gentiles.

HER JOY: To spread the gospel and nurture the church.

KEY SCRIPTURES: Acts 18–19; Romans 16:3–4; 1 Corinthians 16:19; 2 Timothy 4:19

Monday

HER STORY

How good it is to have Paul back again, she thought. Ephesus was on fire with the gospel, their young church growing stronger each day. Paul's preaching and miracles had brought many to faith. Even the touch of his handkerchief had healed illnesses and delivered people from evil spirits.

Priscilla couldn't help laughing when she heard the story of Sceva's seven sons, Jewish exorcists who had tried to duplicate such wonders by driving out an evil spirit with a magic invocation: "In the name of Jesus, whom Paul preaches, I command you to come out."

But the spirit had merely mocked them, saying: "Jesus I know and I know about Paul, but who are you?" Then the man they were trying to deliver beat them so soundly they ran bleeding and naked from the house.

The Ephesians were so impressed by what had happened that a number of sorcerers held a public bonfire to destroy their scrolls. Their magical formulations and incantations seemed like useless trinkets in light of the greater power of Jesus.

But despite the progress of the gospel, Priscilla was aware of growing opposition. One day, she heard the sounds of a crowd forming in the streets. A silversmith was shouting to other crafts-men, all of whom made their living selling miniature images of the many-breasted goddess Artemis: "Men, you know we receive a good income from this business. And you see and hear how this fellow Paul has convinced and led astray large numbers of people here in Ephesus and in practically the whole province of Asia. He says that man-made gods are no gods at all. There is danger not only that our trade will lose its good name, but also that the temple of the great goddess Artemis will be discredited and the goddess herself, who is worshiped throughout the province of Asia and the world, will be robbed of her divine majesty."

The crowd erupted into a riot, seizing two of Paul's companions. Priscilla was distressed when Paul insisted on addressing the mob. She was certain such boldness could only end in worse violence. With her husband's help, she was able to restrain Paul until a city official calmed the crowd and it dispersed. Soon after, Paul set out to spread the gospel in Macedonia.

Though the book of Acts describes the riot in Ephesus, it does not tell us that either Priscilla or Aquila were actually present, only that some disciples prevented Paul from entering the fray, possibly saving his life in the process. Since Priscilla and her husband were leaders of the church in Ephesus, it is quite possible they were among those who intervened on Paul's behalf.

Priscilla's faith had been planted years earlier in an atmosphere of strife and controversy, first in Rome and later in Corinth. The lat-ter was a commercial center famous for its appetite for vice, hardly a place to nurture the faith of a new believer. Yet that was where

God transplanted her, along with her husband, Aquila, after Claudius expelled the Jews from Rome in AD 49, tired of their constant fighting about Chrestus (a probable reference to Christ).

Though various gods were worshiped in Corinth, none was more popular than Aphrodite, the Greek goddess of love, whose temple at one time boasted more than a thousand sacred prostitutes. Throughout the empire, the phrase "Corinthian girl" was just another name for "prostitute."

After the couple had been in Corinth for about a year, they met up with a man who would involve them in yet more controversy. Paul of Tarsus was a Jew who had ruthlessly persecuted Jesus' followers until his own dramatic conversion. Lately, he had been traveling in Asia Minor and Macedonia, preaching the gospel wherever he went. When he arrived in Corinth, he probably met the couple through their common trade as tentmakers. Priscilla and Aquila invited Paul to stay in their home and work with them.

As always, Paul preached the gospel first in the local synagogue and then to the Gentiles. And, as always, his preaching generated both faith and opposition. After eighteen months, leading Jews of Corinth hauled him before the proconsul to accuse him of spreading an illicit religion. After the charge was dismissed, Paul set sail for Ephesus, taking Priscilla and Aquila with him.

The three missionaries must have been eager to see a city that ranked in importance with Rome, Corinth, Antioch, and Alexandria. The capital of provincial Asia, Ephesus boasted a temple to Artemis (also known as Diana) so enormous that it was considered one of the seven wonders of the ancient world. After only a short while, Paul left for other ports, leaving the couple behind to lead the church that met in their home.

Before long another Jew arrived, preaching eloquently about Jesus to the Jews at Ephesus. But Apollos, a native of Alexandria, had grasped only a shadow of the gospel, one more in keeping with the message of John the Baptist than of Jesus. Rather than denouncing him for his inadequate presentation, Priscilla and Aquila merely took him aside and instructed him in the faith. They did their job so well, in fact, that believers in Ephesus eventually sent the gifted preacher to Corinth, where he advanced the work Paul had begun.

Priscilla must have been a spiritually mature woman, whose gifts equipped her for leadership. Her name actually precedes Aquila's four out of the six times they are mentioned in the New Testament, probably signifying her greater abilities as a leader or the fact that her family may have hailed from a higher social strata than his. Whatever the case, Priscilla's role in instructing Apollos and leading the early church is remarkable.

Along with Aquila, she was the best friend Paul could have had, helping him establish the church and risking her life for his sake. Paul mentions the couple's courage in one of his letters but doesn't elaborate on the circumstances.

Rather than withering in the soil of controversy, Priscilla's faith seemed to flourish. She helped establish the early church in an atmosphere of great hostility, risking her own life for the sake of the gospel she loved.

Tuesday

HER LIFE AND TIMES

TENTMAKING

*A*lthough tents themselves are often mentioned in the Bible, the skill of tentmaking is only mentioned once, here in Acts 18. Paul stayed with Aquila and Priscilla and worked with them in their tentmaking trade.

By New Testament times the Israelites had settled in towns and cities. They no longer lived a nomadic lifestyle, moving their tents from place to place. However, traders and travelers still used these tents, and some Near Eastern desert peoples still lived in them. Indeed, some desert peoples still live in tents today.

Tents of the time were made of strong cloth woven of goat hair. Lengths of the cloth were sewn together to form tents that were sometimes round and sloping, sometimes oblong. Poles held the tent up, along with ropes that were stretched to stakes, which were driven into the ground to hold the poles and the cloth firmly in place. Mats of papyrus or more goat hair formed side curtains and interior walls to divide the inhabitants from each other or from their animals.

Paul was originally from Tarsus, a major city of Cilicia, a province known for its production of superior cloth made of goat hair. Jewish parents took seriously the responsibility of teaching their sons a trade, and Paul's parents were no exception. Paul learned his trade and used it at times to support himself during his years of ministry.

As a tentmaker, Paul's skill may have been used in making things other than tents themselves. In the settled culture of his day, the market for tents was small. He may have instead produced leather products or clothing.

We usually think of Paul in terms of his great missionary adventures. Seldom do we think of him in terms of a trade that involved working not with his quick and able mind so much as with his hands. More than anything, Paul's work reveals to us the sacred nature of all work, whether esteemed or not by our culture. All work is valuable and worthwhile in God's sight, and all work is worth doing "with all your heart, as working for the Lord, not for human masters.... It is the Lord Christ you are serving" (Colossians 3:23–24).

Wednesday

HER LEGACY IN SCRIPTURE

Read Acts 18:1–28.

1. What does verse 2 tell you about what it was like to be a Jewish woman in the Roman Empire?

2. Make a list of everything this chapter says Priscilla did to advance the gospel.

3. What impression do you get of Priscilla as a person?

Read Romans 16:3–5.

4. What else do you learn here about Priscilla's service?

5. What role do you think God wants you to play in advancing the gospel?

Thursday

HER PROMISE

*S*cripture doesn't tell us exactly what role Priscilla played in the circumstances described in the New Testament. Was she active as a teacher? Or did she work in the background? But the very fact that her name appears along with her husband's every time does tell us something: She was a valued disciple, one who made a difference in Paul's life and in her world.

Whatever your role as a woman in your church, whether in the background or in a leadership position, you can be sure that what you are doing matters. Each task—no matter how small or large—is important to the spread of the gospel. You are an integral part of your church community, and God promises to use you.

Promises in Scripture

When Priscilla and Aquila heard him [Apollos], they invited him to their home and explained to him the way of God more adequately.

—ACTS 18:26

Greet Tryphena and Tryphosa, those women who work hard in the Lord. Greet my dear friend Persis, another woman who has worked very hard in the Lord. Greet Rufus, chosen in the Lord, and his mother, who has been a mother to me, too.

—ROMANS 16:12–13

Help these women [Euodia and Syntyche] who have contended at my side in the cause of the gospel.

—PHILIPPIANS 4:3

Friday

HER LEGACY OF PRAYER

Greet Priscilla and Aquila, my fellow workers in Christ Jesus. They risked their lives for me. Not only I but all the churches of the Gentiles are grateful to them.

—ROMANS 16:3–4

REFLECT ON: Acts 18:18–28.

PRAISE GOD: For making both women and men central to his plan of salvation.

OFFER THANKS: For women whose faith has nourished yours.

CONFESS: Any tendency to live out your own faith in a half-hearted manner, limiting the way God wants to use you.

ASK GOD: To make you unafraid of the controversy generated by a faithful life.

Lift Your Heart

It's a Wonderful Life is a movie that tells the heartwarming story of George Bailey's Christmas Eve visit with an angel, who cures his suicidal depression by showing him just how valuable his life has been. The truth is, most of us have affected others in far more positive ways than we might guess, especially if we belong to Christ. Though most of us won't encounter an angel who tells our life story from heaven's point of view, we can ask God for encouragement, remembering that any good we have done has been accomplished through his grace.

Here's a simple thing you can do to help you visualize the good effects of your faith. Consider that believers are like stones thrown into a pond—our lives are meant to have a rippling effect so others can feel the influence of our gifts and faith. This week, snatch a quiet moment on your knees or in your favorite chair and close your eyes. Imagine yourself as a stone in the hand of God. Watch him throw you out into the water. What kind of ripples do you see? Are they large or small? Perhaps your brother is a Christian because you shared your faith. Maybe a child has responded to God's forgiveness because she first experienced yours. Perhaps God has used you to bring justice to a situation of great injustice.

Thank God for all the ripples your life has already created, even if the circle of your influence still seems small. Unlike the ripples created by an ordinary stone, the ripple effect of faith need never stop as long as we live. Pray that God will make waves with your faith, even rocking a few boats along the way.

Father, I don't want to settle for the status quo, professing belief in you and then acting as though everything good in life comes from the world around me. Enable me to be like Priscilla, whose faith grew despite her surroundings. Let the ripple effect of my faith build up your church.

APPENDICES

ALL THE WOMEN IN THE BIBLE

Mother of the Zebedees
(Salome 2). . . .Mt 20:20–24; 27:56;
     Mk 15:40–41; 16:1–8
Mother 1 . . . . Mic 7:6
Mother 2 . . . . Eph 5:31; 6:1–3
Mother 3 . . . . .1Th 2:7
Mother-in-Law . . . . Mic 7:6
Mothers . . . . La 2:12
Mothers Who Ate
 Her Sons 2Ki 6:26–30
Naamah 1 . . . . .Ge 4:22
Naamah 2 . .1Ki 14:21, 31; 2Ch 12:13
Naaman's Wife 2Ki 5:2–3
Naarah 1Ch 4:5–6
Nahor's Daughters . . . . Ge 11:25
Naomi . . . . .Ru 1–4
Nehushta . . . . 2Ki 24:8; Jer 29:2
Nereus's Sister . . . . .Ro 16:15
Noadiah . . . . .Ne 6:14
Noah . . . . .Nu 26:33; 27:1–11;
     36:10–12; Jos 17:3
Noah's Wife/Noahs' Son's Wives. .Ge
 6:18; 7:1, 7, 13, 23; 8:16, 18; 9:10
Nympha . . . . Col 4:15
Oholah . . . . .Eze 23
Oholibah . . . . .Eze 23
Oholibamah . . . . Ge 36:2–25
Old Women. . . . . .Zec 8:4
Older and Younger Women . . 1Ti 5:2;
     2 Tit 2:3–5
One Wife . . . . .Tit 1:6
Oppressive Women . . . . Am 4:1
Orpah . . . . Ru 1:4–14
Paul's Sister . . . . Ac 23:16
Peleg's Daughters . . . . Ge 11:19
Peninnah 1Sa 1:2–7
Persis . . . . .Ro 16:12
Persistent Widow . . . . .Lk 18:1–8
Peter's Mother-in-Law . . Mt 8:14–15;
     Mk 1:29–31; Lk 4:38–39
Pharaoh's Daughter . . Ex 2:5–10; Ac
     7:21; Heb 11:24
Philistine Daughters. . . .2Sa 1:20; Eze
     16:27, 57

Phoebe . . . . Ro 16:1–2
Pilate's Wife. . . . . Mt 27:19
Potiphar's Wife . . . . Ge 39
Praying and Prophesying
 Women 1Co 11:5–15
A Pregnant Woman 1Th 5:3
Priests' Daughters . . . . Lev 21:9
Priscilla . . . . .Ac 18:2, 18–19, 26;
   Ro 16:3; 1Co 16:19; 2Ti 4:19
The Prostitute . . . . .Rev 17:1–18
Puah . . . . Ex 1:15–21
Putiel's Daughters . . . . Ex 6:25
Queen Mother. . . . . .Jer 29:2
Queen of Sheba . . 1Ki 10: 1–13; 2Ch
    9:1–12; Mt 12:42
Rachel. . . .Ge 29–31; 32:22; 33:1–2,
 7; 35:16–26; 46:19, 22, 25; 48:7; Ru
 4:11; 1Sa 10:2; Jer 31:15; Mt 2:18
Rahab . . . . .Jos 2:1–21; 6:17–25;
   Mt 1:5; Heb 11:31; Jas 2:25
Rebekah . . . . Ge 22:23; 24;
 25:20–28; 26:7–11, 35; 27; 28:5–7;
 29:12; 35:8; 49:31; Ro 9:10–13
Reu's Daughters. . . . . Ge 11:21
Reuel's Daughters . . . . . . Ex 2:16–22
Rhoda. . . . . Ac 12:12–19
Rizpah 2Sa 3:7; 21:8–12
Royal Bride. . . . . Ps 45:9–11
Rufus's Mother . . . . .Ro 16:13
Ruth . . . . Ru 1–4; Mt 1:5
Samson's Mother . . . . Jdg 13; 14:2–6
Samson's Wife . . . . . . .Jdg 14:1–15:6
Sapphira . . . . .Ac 5:1–11
Sarah (Sarai) . . . . Ge 11:29–31;
 12:5–13:1; 16:1–9; 17:15–21;
 18:1–15; 20:2–18; 21:1–12;
 23:1–19; 24:36, 67; 25:10, 12;
 49:31; Isa 51:2; Ro 4:19; 9:9; Gal
   4:21–31; Heb 11:11; 1Pe 3:6
Serah. .Ge 46:17; Nu 26:46; 1Ch 7:30
Serug's Daughters . . . . Ge 11:23
Servant Girl of Naaman's
 Wife 2Ki 5:2–4
Servant Girls at Peter's
 Denial. . . . . Mt 26:69–71;
   Mk 14:66–69; Lk 22:56–59;
     Jn 18:16–17

TIMELINE OF WOMEN OF THE BIBLE

B.C.	2000	1500	1000	500	1 A.D.	500

Eve
Noah's Wife

Sarah
Lot's Wife
Hagar
Rebekah
Leah
Rachel

Moses' Mothers
Miriam
Rahab
Deborah (1225)
Hannah
Samson's Mother
Delilah
Naomi
Ruth
Michal
Abigail
Bathsheba
Queen of Sheba
Jezebel
Widow of Zarephath
Athaliah
Woman of Shunem
Gomer
Vashti
Esther

Anna
Elizabeth
Mary
Mary Magdalene
Mary of Bethany
Martha
Woman at the Well
Adulterous Woman
Sapphira
Dorcas
Rhoda
Lydia
Priscilla
Lois
Eunice

WOMEN IN JESUS' FAMILY TREE

Abraham (Sarah)
Isaac (Rebekah)
Jacob (Leah)
Judah (Tamar)
Perez (unknown)
Hezron (unknown)
Ram (unknown)
Amminadab (unknown)
Nahshon (unknown)
Salmon (Rahab)
Boaz (Ruth)
Obed (unknown)
Jesse (unknown)
David (Bathsheba)
Solomon (Naamah)
Rehoboam (Maacah)
Abijah (unknown)
Asa (Azubah)
Jehoshaphat (unknown)
Jehoram (Athaliah)
Uzziah (Jerusha)
Jotham (unknown)
Ahaz (Abijah)
Hezekiah (Hephzibah)
Manasseh (unknown)
Amon (Jedidah)
Josiah (Zebidah)
Jehoiachin (unknown)
Shealtiel (unknown)
Zerubbabel (unknown)
Abiud (unknown)
Eliakim (unknown)
Azor (unknown)
Zadok (unknown)
Akim (unknown)
Eliud (unknown)
Eleazar (unknown)
Matthan (unknown)
Jacob (unknown)
Joseph (Mary)

JESUS

WOMEN IN JESUS' LIFE AND MINISTRY

Jesus Meets ...	What Happens	Scripture
Mary, his mother	She loves him as her son and Savior.	Mt 1–2; 12:46–50 Mk 3:31–35 Lk 1–2; 8:19–21 Jn 2:1–11; 19:25 Ac 1:14
Elizabeth	She gives birth to Jesus' forerunner.	Lk 1:5–80
Anna	She praises God for the baby Jesus.	Lk 2:36–38
Woman at the well	She believes Jesus is the Messiah.	Jn 4:1–42
Peter's mother-in-law	Jesus heals her.	Mt 8:14–15 Mk 1:29–31 Lk 4:38–39
Widow of Nain	Jesus raises her son from the dead.	Lk 7:11–17
Sinful woman at Simon's house	She washes Jesus' feet with her tears.	Lk 7:36–50
Joanna	She supports Jesus financially.	Lk 8:1–3; 23:55; 24:10
Susanna	She helps Jesus in his ministry.	Lk 8:1–3
Woman with the issue of blood	She is healed when she touches Jesus.	Mt 9:20–22 Mk 5:25–34 Lk 8:43–48
Jairus's daughter	Jesus raises her from death.	Mt 9:18–26 Mk 5:21–43 Lk 8:41–56
Syrophoenician woman	Jesus responds to her plea.	Mt 15:21–28 Mk 7:24–30
Woman caught in adultery	Jesus saves her and tells her to sin no more.	Jn 8:1–11
Mary of Bethany	She sits at Jesus' feet.	Lk 10:38–42 Jn 11; 12:1–8
Martha	Jesus sets her priorities straight.	Lk 10:38–42 Jn 11; 12:1–2
A woman in the crowd	She calls out a blessing on Jesus' mother.	Lk 11:27–28
Crippled woman	Jesus heals her.	Lk 13:10–13
Mother of James and John	She asks Jesus a favor, and he admonishes her.	Mt 20:20–28; 27:56 Mk 15:40–41; 16:1–2
Widow with two coins	She models a lesson on giving for the disciples.	Mk 12:41–44 Lk 21:1–4
Daughters of Jerusalem	They weep as Jesus walks to his death.	Lk 23:27–31
Women at Calvary	They mourn as Jesus dies.	Mt 27:55
Mary, the mother of James and Joses	She helps take care of Jesus.	Mt 27:56, 61; 28:1 Mk 15:40–41, 47; 16:1 Lk 24:10; Jn 19:25
Mary Magdalene	She faithfully follows Jesus.	Mt 27:56, 61; 28:1 Mk 15:40–47; 16:1–11 Lk 8:1–10; 24:10 Jn 19:25; 20:1–18

Praying the Names of God
A Daily Guide
Ann Spangler

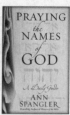

Praying the Names of Jesus
A Daily Guide
Ann Spangler

Names in the ancient world did more than simply distinguish one person from another; they often conveyed the essential nature and character of a person. This is especially true when it comes to the names of God recorded in the Bible. *Praying the Names of God* explores the primary names and titles of God in the Old Testament to reveal the deeper meanings behind them. *Praying the Names of Jesus* does the same thing for Jesus in the New Testament.

By understanding the biblical context in which these names and titles are revealed, readers gain a more intimate knowledge of Jesus and of his plan for their lives.

Praying the Names of God: Hardcover, Jacketed 0-310-25353-5
Praying the Names of Jesus: Hardcover, Jacketed 0-310-25345-4

Pick up a copy today at your favorite bookstore!

The Women's Devotional Guide to the Bible

Jean E. Syswerda

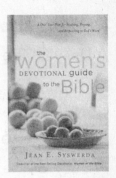

See the Bible through the eyes of the women who lived it!

With devotional studies that lead you from Genesis through the book of Revelation, *The Women's Devotional Guide to the Bible* offers more than just another plan to read through the Bible in a year. Many of the studies draw from the unique view point of the women in the texts — Eve's relationship to Adam and to God, Noah's wife's frustration and joy, Rachel's failure to trust God — while also acknowledging the spiritual needs and interests of all women: young and old, married and single.

This devotional guide is perfect for women who want:

- fresh insights and relevant truths from God's Word
- an easy-to-follow daily plan for an in-depth study of the Bible
- answers for how the entire Bible fits together to present overarching themes and purposes

The Women's Devotional Guide to the Bible is a fifty-two-week program based on the unique year-long guide to reading, study, and prayer found in the author's bestseller, *Women of the Bible*. Jean Syswerda's five-day approach allows for individual study, prayer, reflection, and small-group discussion each week — leading you to a more intimate relationship with God and his Word.

ISBN 10: 0-7852-1251-5
ISBN 13: 9780785212515

Pick up a copy today at your favorite bookstore!